THE BAPTISTS IN UPPER AND LOWER CANADA
BEFORE 1820

To the pioneer folk of Upper and Lower Canada—Loyalists, "late" Loyalists, and the hordes of land-seekers—living in what seemed like religious destitution, various American Baptist missionary associations in Massachusetts, Vermont, and New York State sent missionary preachers in the decade after 1800. Numerous small churches were established, but the War of 1812 disturbed these efforts, and much of the missionary activity itself had to be abandoned for an interval. This may well have stimulated the co-operation which had already appeared before the war between Canadian Baptist communities. Out of this co-operation were to develop conferences and associations of Canadian Baptist churches, until by 1820 all were members of Canadian groups. By 1818 travelling missionaries from the United States had almost ceased to visit; the Canadian churches had begun to raise up ministers from among their own members.

In this very complete investigation of early Baptist history in Canada, assembled from a wide variety of sources, every separate group has been recorded and its development traced, and all available information has been coordinated for the missionaries and ministers who served the groups. The book is a veritable encyclopaedia of early Baptist history and will be invaluable to future students of Baptist history or of Canadian religious history in general. This study of a developing cultural tradition strikingly parallels the struggle to master the physical features of a new land.

STUART IVISON has been minister of First Baptist Church, Ottawa, since 1932. He was born in Wheatley, Ontario, in 1906, and after his graduation from McMaster University was minister of First Baptist Church, Brockville, for two years. From 1941 till 1946 he served as a chaplain with the Canadian army. He has published widely on devotional and historical subjects during his career.

FRED ROSSER, Director of the Division of Administration of the National Research Council, was born in Denfield, Ontario, in 1902. He taught school before entering on his university career, and joined the National Research Council in 1937. He has published scientific and historical papers, as well as popular articles on the work of the National Research Council.

T0350047

BUTTONWOOD TREE NEAR CHATHAM

Water colour by Lt. Philip John Bainbrigge. Huge buttonwood trees were native in the Niagara Peninsula and throughout southwestern Ontario. Missionaries and itinerant preachers usually travelled along the forest trails on horseback as illustrated in the painting. (Bainbrigge Collection, Public Archives of Canada)

The Baptists

in Upper

and Lower Canada

before 1820

STUART IVISON

FRED ROSSER

UNIVERSITY OF TORONTO PRESS

PREFACE

IN 1859 the Rev. R. A. Fyfe, D.D., the acknowledged leader of the Baptists in Upper and Lower Canada at that time, deplored the lack of information about Baptist origins in these provinces. Urging his denomination to gather up and preserve its historical records, he declared, "Few things are more worthy of our attention than this."

Much material has been gathered since Fyfe's words were written. The Baptist Historical Collections at McMaster University, Hamilton, through the efforts of the University and the denominational Historical Committee, have been growing steadily. So far, however, very little published information on the development of the Baptist movement in this part of Canada has been available. How the earliest Baptist churches arose, and where, and who actually founded them, are questions that have been but vaguely answered up to the present. Yet the importance of church history, both local and general, for a proper understanding of Canada's total development is increasingly recognized. The moral and religious ideals of the people are as vital to a nation's growth as are the other factors so frequently stressed by historians.

Both authors of this study acknowledge their sense of obligation to the pioneers who formed the Baptist tradition in this country. Each of us had been following an independent interest in certain aspects of Canadian Baptist history for several years before our collaboration began. A letter from one in Ottawa to the other on the battlefields of Europe during World War II carried the suggestion that when the war ended we might work together to answer some of the questions often asked about the early Baptists of Ontario and Quebec. After ten years of joint inquiry the results of these efforts are now presented. At first it was planned to carry the story only as far as the War of 1812-14. We found, however, that 1820 marked the beginning of a new era: by this time most Canadian Baptist churches had severed their ties with American associations and had set up organizations of their own in Canada. The scope of this work, therefore, has been deliberately limited to the period between the American Revolution and the year 1820.

The research involved in this pleasant task has taken us to many interesting places and placed us under obligation to many people. Special thanks are due to the staff at the Public Archives of Canada, in Ottawa, where the studies began. (The petitions of pioneer settlers for grants of land have yielded a great deal of information about Baptist families.) Several visits were made to the Samuel Colgate Baptist Historical Collection at Rochester, N.Y., where great kindness was shown by those in charge. The librarians in the Department of Public Records and Archives of Ontario at Toronto, in the Buffalo Historical Society's library and museum, and in McMaster and other universities in both Canada and the United States have been most helpful. We are more than grateful to the many gracious people who so kindly made available to us valuable church records.

To our wives, who accompanied us on several of our trips and helped by transcribing records, we express our deepest gratitude. "Love suffereth long, and is kind!" The general secretary of the Baptist Convention of Ontario and Quebec and members of its executive committee have shown a deep interest and offered much encouragement.

Dr. Pauline Snure was good enough to read the text and give us the benefit of her criticism. The preparation of the manuscript was the work of Mrs. M. M. Hinchey, to whom we are deeply obligated. Much credit must be given to the experienced and friendly help of the staff of the University of Toronto Press, Mr. M. Jeanneret, Miss Eleanor Harman, and Miss Francess Halpenny. Finally, the financial assistance granted by the Canadian Social Science Research Council and the Publication Fund of the University of Toronto Press towards the cost of publishing a work of this kind is very much appreciated.

S. I.
F. R.

CONTENTS

ILLUSTRATIONS

THE BAPTISTS IN UPPER AND LOWER CANADA
BEFORE 1820

I

Background

THE HISTORY OF THE EARLY BAPTISTS OF UPPER CANADA begins with the appearance of settlements towards the close of the American War of Independence. The earliest settlements, made in the 1780's, were laid out for disbanded soldiers and refugee loyalists who had been forced out of the United States during the Revolution. As time went on, the original settlements were enlarged, and new areas were opened up to accommodate "later loyalists" who came to Canada after the war out of a desire to live under British rule. Many of these had actually been neutral during hostilities, and wanted simply to live a peaceful life under what they often described in their petitions for land as "the blessings of the British constitution." A third class of immigrants from the United States, attracted by the generous land policy of Canada, entered the province in increasing numbers towards the close of the eighteenth century and in the early years of the nineteenth.

The settlements of the 1780's were widely separated from each other. One of them straggled along the St. Lawrence River and Lake Ontario from the present boundary between the provinces of Ontario and Quebec to the Bay of Quinte. Another was situated on the Canadian side of the Niagara River. There was still another at Amherstburg, opposite Detroit, where a number of land grants had been made under the French régime.

Soon afterwards, in the 1790's, additional settlements grew up at intervening points. Townships were surveyed and land grants were made along the north shore of Lake Ontario from the Bay of Quinte to York, and in the area northeast of Kingston. Settlers located on the north shore of Lake Erie in the vicinity of Long Point, and also on the River Thames, in the region where Woodstock and Ingersoll now stand. Along Yonge Street, between York and Lake Simcoe, more new townships came into being.

In these pioneer communities there were Baptist settlers, and Baptist influence increased when, in another northward movement, Baptist associations in the new United States sent missionaries to Upper Canada. The connection of the early Baptist churches in Upper Canada, and in Lower Canada also, with the movement in the United

States is thus seen to be close, and description of the former makes necessary some account of the American background.

Our plan will be, therefore, to give first a section on the Baptist movement in the United States as it was when this new frontier of activity in the north was presented to it, and then to describe the Canadian settlements in which the Baptist influence was to find a field of service.

Baptists emerged as a distinct body within Protestant Christianity at the beginning of the seventeenth century, though in some respects their roots go back to much earlier times. Many of their beliefs had been advocated by pre-Reformation groups such as the Anabaptists of Europe. They appeared in Britain at the same time as the Congregationalists, with whom they shared the view that each local congregation should be self-governing, and a little later than the Presbyterians, by whom they were strongly influenced as to doctrine.

The Baptist movement of modern times, which now forms the largest "free church" (i.e., unconnected with the state) body of Christians in the world, began with John Smyth (d. 1612). Smyth was a clergyman of the established Church of England who adopted Puritan attitudes while at Cambridge University, where he was a Fellow of Christ's College. He was made chaplain of the city of Lincoln about 1600, but gradually came to share the views of the Separatists, which was the name given to those who at that time were leaving the Anglican Church because they felt it had not been reformed as completely as they desired after the break from Rome. By 1606 Smyth was pastor of a small Separatist congregation at Gainsborough, and was in close touch with John Robinson, another former clergyman of the Puritan party in the Anglican Church, who had become the leader of a Separatist group at Scrooby. Both congregations were driven by persecution to seek religious liberty in Holland, where they went in 1607 and 1608. Robinson's group went to Leyden, to become the founders of Congregationalism, and from there the first Pilgrim Fathers went to America, carrying Congregationalism to New England.

Smyth and his followers settled in Amsterdam, where in 1608 he formed the first Baptist church. At Gainsborough the requirement for membership in his Separatist church had been acceptance of a covenant, which bound members to follow certain rules "whatsoever it should cost them," but the basis for membership at Amsterdam was a declaration of personal Christian belief accompanied by the baptism of the professed believer. The adoption of baptism as a condition of membership gave rise to the use of the term "Baptist" to describe the people and churches that followed Smyth's teaching. This dramatic return to New Testament practice attracted wide attention and provoked much lively discussion. Even unfriendly Anglican critics pointed out to non-Baptist Separatists like Robinson that Smyth's action was at least logical, and that they ought to either return to the Anglican Church or go on to the Baptist position.[1]

A lay supporter of Smyth, Thomas Helwys of Basford, who had gone with him to Holland, decided in 1611 to return to England. With a dozen others he formed, towards the end of that year or very early in 1612, in Spitalfields, London, the first Baptist church on English soil. In a quaint book, *A Short Declaration of the Mistery of Iniquity,* dedicated to King James I, Helwys called for full religious liberty for all, including "heretics, Turks, Jews or whatsoever." This, so far as is known, was the first such claim to be made in England. He was imprisoned in Newgate, and there died. The permanent influence of Smyth and Helwys combined to give Baptists their two most important characteristics, evangelicalism and spiritual democracy, both of which they have carried to all parts of the world, especially to America.

The church established in Spitalfields by Helwys in 1611, and the five Baptist churches that were added during the next fifteen years, were of the doctrinal type known as "Arminian." That is, they accepted the view of the Dutch theologian, Jacobus Arminius (1560-1609) that the Atonement of Christ was of "general" (i.e., universal) scope, and that all men were free to accept its benefits. They rejected the Calvinist doctrine of predestination, placed little emphasis on creedal definitions, and were not greatly concerned about the fine points of either theology or church government. They stressed religious liberty and tolerance, preached Christianity as a force for moral transformation, and regarded the church as being made up of those who had been so transformed. Baptism was performed by pouring water on the forehead of the candidate. This belief in a "general" atonement led to their successors being known as General Baptists.

The force of Calvinistic ideas, however, was to be felt among Baptists as among other religious groups, so that by 1638 there were also congregations of "Particular" Baptists, who held that the Atonement was of "particular" application, i.e., for the sake of the elect only. Their formal confessions of faith, or doctrinal statements, strongly resembled the Westminster Confession of the Presbyterians. They adopted the practice of baptism by immersion. These groups soon became the main Baptist body in Britain, and it was their influence, rather than that of the General Baptists, which became dominant in America. The successors of the General Baptists on this continent were called "Free" Baptists, while the term "Regular" was often used, especially in the nineteenth century, to describe those who carried on the Particular Baptist tradition as it developed in the New World.

Baptist fortunes in Britain during the Puritan period (1640-60) varied with the attitudes of those who were in power at the time. Cromwell's New Model Army, by which he defeated Charles I, subdued Ireland and Scotland, and put down Charles's son, had many high-ranking officers who were Baptists. The zeal of these men is shown by the fact that wherever the Army went in England, Ireland, and Scotland, Baptist churches arose. William Allen, the adjutant general, Thomas Harrison, the deputy commander-in-chief (1650-51), Colonel Hutchison, General (afterwards Admiral) Richard Deane, Edmund Ludlow, commander-in-chief in Ireland, and Robert Lilburne, commander-in-chief in Scotland (1654), were all Baptists. John Milton, though never a member of a Baptist church, held Baptist views, and John Bunyan, author of *Pilgrim's Progress*, was a Baptist of the broader type, who went to prison for his principles during the reign of Charles II.

The Baptists of this period held firmly to their love of liberty even under stress of persecution, and engaged in personal missionary work wherever they had opportunity. They resisted the attempt of the Long Parliament to enforce Presbyterianism on the nation as the only authorized system of worship, and Milton was their spokesman in warning that "new presbyter is but old priest writ large." Another plea for liberty came from Roger Williams, a London lawyer who had emigrated to America in 1630 and joined the Baptists in 1639. Williams had been strongly influenced by the Baptist writer, John Murton, and had been persecuted in Massachusetts before being banished by the Puritan Congregationalists there in 1635. He was back in England in 1644, and took occasion to publish and present to Parliament his famous treatise, *The Bloudy Tenent of Persecution, for Causes of Conscience, Discussed*. English Baptists opposed Cromwell himself when, in his later years as Lord Protector, he adopted an attitude of hostility to their ideas of freedom. Throughout the seventeenth century they stressed their two cardinal principles of evangelism and liberty.

Like other religious bodies, Baptists of Britain were profoundly influenced in the eighteenth century by the Evangelical Revival of the Wesleys (its New England counterpart came to be known as the Great Awakening.) Though they did not respond to this revival as quickly as some other groups did, its effect on them was of a lasting nature. The new zeal engendered by it led to an increase in the vigour with which they proclaimed their message. Unlike some of the bodies that responded to the revival more quickly, Baptists in America were not greatly affected by the Unitarian reaction which followed it in New England, but maintained a strongly evangelical position, and were prepared to carry their gospel to the outlying settlements of the expanding frontiers when the opportunity came.

During the colonial period of American history, before the Declaration of Independence in 1776, the growth of the Baptists as a denomination was slow. The puritan Congregationalists of New England, advocates of theocracy as the desirable form of government, strongly opposed the Baptists for preaching the separation of church and state, as well as practising what they regarded as the heresy of believers' baptism. It was for holding such views that Roger Williams was banished from Massachusetts in 1635. He was not at that time a Baptist, and his later membership in the Baptist church was very brief; however, the new colony founded by him in Rhode Island openly recognized the principle of religious liberty, and there, in 1639, arose the first two Baptist churches on the North American continent, one at Providence and the other at Newport.

In Massachusetts a Baptist church was established at Swansea in 1663 and another at Boston in 1665, but stiff opposition was encountered for many years. The first president of Harvard University, Henry Dunster, was indicted by a grand jury for espousing Baptist principles, his chief offence being that he did not have his children baptized in infancy. After suffering the indignity of a public admonition, he was compelled to resign his post. Obadiah Holmes was whipped in Boston for having conducted a Baptist meeting in a private house in Lynn. In New Jersey, where greater freedom prevailed, a church was founded at Middletown in 1688. Baptist work began in New York City about 1669 and on Long Island around 1700, but opposition kept these causes weak for some years. In Connecticut a start was made at Groton in 1705, but again development was slow. The first English-speaking Baptist church in Pennsylvania was formed at Lower Dublin in 1688, and a branch of this church was organized in Philadelphia in 1689, assuming separate status as the First Baptist Church of that city in 1746. The earliest Baptist church in Vermont to maintain a continuous existence was that at Shaftsbury, organized in 1768; New Hampshire had no Baptist church at all until 1775, when one was organized at Newton.

Statistics for this early period are incomplete, but it has been estimated that, when the War of Independence began, the Baptists of the
American colonies numbered less than ten thousand, or one out of
every 264 persons in the population.[2] In New England itself, where
adherence was greatest, the entire strength of the denomination at the
close of the war is said to have been 151 churches with 4,783 members.[3]
This numerical proportion of Baptists to the total population helps to
explain why there were so few members of the denomination among
the loyalist refugees who came to Canada at the time of the war.[4]
Among the few thousand loyalists who entered Canada then the Baptists at best could only have made up a mere handful. Thus, although
many Baptists were undoubtedly sympathetic towards the Revolution,
it would be a mistake to attribute their small numbers among the
United Empire Loyalists to that fact alone.

With the cessation of hostilities in 1783, and the growth of religious
liberty in the United States, a period of rapid expansion and great
missionary activity began for the Baptists. The increasing popularity
of democratic ideas made their message acceptable where once it had
been suppressed. So rapidly did Baptists increase in numbers in the
United States during the last quarter of the eighteenth century, that
by 1800, instead of there being one Baptist among every 264 persons
in the country, the proportion had risen to one in 53; this trend continued in the early part of the nineteenth century until in 1850 the proportion stood at one in 29.[5] Churches were formed in rapid succession,
and grouped themselves into associations for the more efficient prosecution of their work. The letter circulated by the New York Baptist
Association to its member churches in the year 1793, only two years
after its organization, reflects the new atmosphere in which the Baptists now rejoiced to find themselves:

The spirit of persecution that has raged and spilt rivers of blood in other
nations is so stripped of its power in the United States of America that
every one of us may worship God according to what our conscience dic-
tates to us is agreeable to his word. . . . Undoubtedly the civil rights of
man are better understood than ever they were in any age of the world
before; the spirit both of civil and religious liberty has diffused itself far
and wide, and is making glorious progress among the nations. The bands
of slavery are bursting! We hope Babylon is falling![6]

In this atmosphere of enthusiasm individual church members began
to organize missionary and educational societies, and the associations
themselves often formed missionary committees to evangelize pioneer
communities beyond their own borders. Ministers took turns at going

"on tour" as missionaries, and their colleagues within the association would supply their pulpits while they were away. The society or committee sponsoring such a tour would usually raise a small fund to pay part, if not all, of the expenses incurred by the Missionary. Fired with the evangelistic spirit, these Baptist missionaries pressed north, west, and south with the expanding American frontier, and northwards into Canada, where their loyalist friends and relatives had gone during the Revolution, and continued to go for some years afterwards. In the opening years of the nineteenth century at least six Baptist missionary organizations in the United States were playing a part in evangelizing the pioneer settlements of Upper Canada. These were

1. The Shaftsbury Baptist Association, of Vermont, New York and Massachusetts;
2. The Massachusetts Baptist Missionary Society;
3. The Lake Baptist Missionary Society, renamed the Hamilton Baptist Missionary Society, which was later merged with the Baptist Missionary Convention of the State of New York;
4. The New York Missionary Society (joint Baptist and Presbyterian);
5. The New York Baptist Missionary Society;
6. The Black River Baptist Association.

Since the records of these societies cast a good deal of light upon the history of Baptist work in Ontario, a brief account of the part played by each of them will be useful at this point.

Shaftsbury Baptist Association

The oldest Baptist church in the territory which ultimately became the state of Vermont was founded at Shaftsbury in 1768 and the second oldest was established at Pownal in 1773. In the year 1780 these two churches, along with three others in nearby parts of Massachusetts and New York State, formed the Shaftsbury Baptist Association.[7] This body became a powerful centre of Baptist influence, and drew into its fellowship a great many churches. From its ranks were formed several other associations in the neighbouring parts of Vermont, New York, and New Hampshire, but its outreach to distant parts was such that in time it came to include five churches in Upper Canada. These were Charlotteville, Townsend, Clinton, Oxford, and Malahide. It numbered among its leaders men of great force of character and remarkable personal qualities, including the Rev. Caleb Blood, who was nine times elected to the office of moderator, and the Rev. Lemuel

Covell, an indefatigable evangelist who was chosen clerk in the year 1800.

In 1801, with Blood as moderator and Covell as clerk, the Shaftsbury Association undertook to raise a special sum of money to send missionaries out on tour, and the following year a missionary committee, composed after apostolic precedent of twelve members, six ministers and six laymen, was appointed to administer the fund that had been contributed. Caleb Blood himself volunteered to go on tour that year, and became the first of a considerable company of missionaries to represent the Association in the newly settled parts of western New York State and Upper Canada. Between the years 1802 and 1820 the Shaftsbury Association sent no fewer than fifteen different preachers into this province on various tours which lasted anywhere from a few weeks to several months each.

In 1877, the Association celebrated its ninety-seventh anniversary at Shaftsbury where it had been founded. To honour the occasion, the Association's official historian, Stephen Wright, composed a poem, which, though of doubtful literary merit, conveys something of the missionary zeal of those early days; it refers to the Canadian aspect of its work in the closing lines:

> Rich harvests were thus gathered beyond Niagara's roar
> And churches of believers were planted far and near;
> The tidings of salvation along Ontario's shore
> Were wafted on the breezes with right goodwill and cheer.[8]

Massachusetts Baptist Missionary Society

The Massachusetts Baptist Missionary Society was organized in 1802 in the city of Boston under distinguished auspices.[9] Prominent among its leaders was the Rev. Dr. Samuel Stillman, who, after a few years as assistant minister of the Second Baptist Church, Boston, had become pastor of the First Baptist Church in that city in 1765 and continued in this charge for forty-two years until his death in 1807. Another outstanding personality among the trustees of the Society was the Rev. Dr. Thomas Baldwin, pastor of the Second Baptist Church, Boston, from 1790 till 1825. Under the presidency of Dr. Baldwin, the Massachusetts Baptist Missionary Society was incorporated by an act of the legislature of Massachusetts in 1808.[10] Membership was open to any person subscribing one dollar or more each year to the funds of the Society, but it was provided in the by-laws that seven out of the twelve trustees, and all of the officers, must be members of a Baptist church.

The purpose of the Society at the beginning was the sending of missionaries into those parts where no regular ministry was available to the pioneer settlers. An appeal was made for volunteers to engage in this form of service and those who were selected for appointment were given detailed instructions by the trustees as to how they were to conduct themselves while on tour.[11] They were to concentrate their efforts on preaching the gospel, and were to avoid "allusions to those political topics which divide the opinions and too much irritate the passions of our fellow citizens." They were asked to keep an exact journal of their daily experiences and to submit detailed reports to the Society from time to time. Finally, they were furnished with a letter of commendation addressed to "Our Christian Brethren and Friends whose lot is cast in the Wilderness, remote from the stated ministry of the Word and ordinances."

Such credentials seemed essential to both sponsors and missionaries because of the many free-lance preachers who were then roaming the frontiers. The task of the genuine Christian missionary was often made very difficult because of the harm done by certain men who had gone before him, and made the people they encountered suspicious of all who came in the name of religion. The journals of Caleb Blood and Asahel Morse, missionaries of the Shaftsbury Association, both speak of the damage done by "impostors."[12] The phrase "ministry of the Word and ordinances" in the letter of introduction furnished by the Massachusetts Baptist Missionary Society to its missionaries is worth noting. It indicates that the men who initiated this work had definite ideas of sound churchmanship. They were not interested in promoting the highly emotional type of frontier revivalism that was so common among some sects, but aimed at establishing what they called "regular churches in proper gospel order" in as many communities as possible.

A few months after its establishment the Society started the *Massachusetts Baptist Missionary Magazine* which specialized in the publication of missionary news, both home and foreign. In its columns appeared reports submitted by the Society's representatives, and its early files are a treasure trove of information for the historian. The first number appeared in the month of September, 1803. Edited by Dr. Baldwin, the *Missionary Magazine* began as a semi-annual publication, running thirty-two pages to each issue. Soon it became a quarterly, appearing in March, May, September, and December, and by 1817 it was being issued every two months. Finally it was issued monthly, devoted chiefly to the cause of missionary work in foreign countries, and its title was changed to the simple one of *Missions*, by which it is still known.

In the years 1803, 1805, 1807, and 1808 the Society sponsored tours into Upper Canada. Joseph Cornell, Peter P. Roots, Jesse Hartwell, Valentine Rathbun, and Phinehas Pillsbury were the missionaries who came into this province on those occasions, and their work had lasting effects upon the Baptist movement here. Their journeys will be described more fully in a later chapter.

Lake (Hamilton) Baptist Missionary Society

At Pompey, Onondaga County, in the state of New York, at the home of the Rev. Nathan Baker, the Lake Baptist Missionary Society came into being on August 27, 1807.[13] The meeting adjourned without completing its business of organization, but on October 28 the new society met again at Hamilton, N.Y., and proceeded to elect its officers and directors. The Rev. Ashbel Hosmer was made president, Rev. Peter Roots vice-president, Elisha Payne, at whose home the meeting took place, secretary, and Jonathan Olmstead, treasurer. This, again, was an organization of individuals.

The Rev. Peter Roots, vice-president of this new body, had been active as a missionary for the Massachusetts Society from its beginning, and he did not relinquish his connection with the latter body when he assumed his new office. David Irish, who had been prominent in the Shaftsbury Association, was one of the original directors of the Lake Missionary Society. The first missionary to be employed was the Rev. Salmon Morton, who received an appointment for two months and was paid an allowance of four dollars per week. The field in which the new society was chiefly interested was western New York State, and it did no extensive missionary work in Upper Canada. One of its representatives, Elder Nathan Baker, visited Clinton in September 1815, and another, Timothy Sheppard, preached in the Bay of Quinte area in 1817.[14] Its main importance for this study is that many of its leading workers had at one time or another visited this province under other auspices, and it is due to the records kept by this society that we are able to gather information about their careers.[15]

The name of the Lake Baptist Missionary Society was changed to the Hamilton Baptist Missionary Society in 1808, one year after its formation. In 1814, under the influence of John Peck, the personal friend of Luther Rice of Burma, it extended its interest to missionary work abroad. That same year it followed the example of the Massachusetts Society and began publication of a magazine, called *The Vehicle*. In 1821, at the prompting of the Hudson River Association, the churches of New York State decided that they would no longer leave missionary work to private societies, but would enter that field directly themselves. As a result there was formed the Baptist Mission-ary Convention of the State of New York which was controlled by the churches and not by individuals. For a time there was a certain amount of tension between the new convention and the Hamilton Baptist Missionary Society, but the differences were gradually resolved and the Society was merged with the Convention in 1825.

New York Missionary Society
New York Baptist Missionary Society

In 1791 the First and Second Baptist Churches of New York City, along with four other churches belonging formerly to the Philadel-phia Association, formed the New York Baptist Association.[16] The first moderator of this new association was the Rev. Elkanah Holmes, whose name also appears on various occasions as the special preacher at its annual meetings.[17] A missionary interest also led in 1796 to a co-operative effort by the Baptists and Presbyterians of New York City in forming the New York Missionary Society.[18] This body was especi-ally concerned about work among the Indians and, in addition to efforts of this kind in various parts of the South, it established what was called its "North West Mission" among the Tuscarora Indians near Fort Niagara and the Senecas not far away at Buffalo Creek.[19] In the year 1800, Elkanah Holmes was appointed by the New York Missionary Society to its North West Mission. Recommended to the Society by the New York Baptist Association as one who "had formerly experience of a suitable service,"[20] he went first to Fort Niagara, but soon established his residence at Tuscarora Village near Fort Schlos-ser.

For a time all went well. Holmes gained the confidence of the Indians and in addition to serving them he preached to the white settlers along the Niagara River as far as Buffalo. Missionaries on their way to Upper Canada used his house as a stopping-off place, and occasionally he accompanied them over the border. He made the acquaintance of Joseph Brant and as early as February 1801, we find him transmitting a letter from Brant to the Society with regard to pro-posed work among Brant's people. In June of the same year he carried a reply from the secretary of the Society back to Brant, along with other literature setting forth the Society's purpose.[21]

In May 1806, however, a dispute arose between the Baptists and the

Presbyterians of the New York Missionary Society over what type of church should be organized among the Indians at Tuscarora. The Baptists withdrew their support from the Society and immediately formed a new body called the New York Baptist Missionary Society.[22] This placed Elkanah Holmes in a difficult position. In 1807 he tendered his resignation to the now wholly Presbyterian New York Missionary Society, and his support was undertaken jointly by the New York Baptist Missionary Society and the Massachusetts Baptist Missionary Society, to whom his work had long been known because of his many contacts with their missionaries.[23] In 1808 he withdrew from Tuscarora Village and settled in Queenston in Upper Canada, leaving the Presbyterians free to appoint their own missionary to the Indians on the American side of the river.[24]

The career of Elkanah Holmes, and his relationship to the work carried on by the New York Missionary Society, is a subject of importance to anyone studying the development of Baptist work in the Niagara district. The frequently mentioned "Elder" Holmes, sometimes called William, whose name has appeared in several accounts of the early history of the Beamsville church, was without doubt the Rev. Elkanah Holmes of the New York Missionary Society. The part played by him in the events that took place along the Niagara frontier and in the affairs of the churches at Queenston and Beamsville will be made clearer in later chapters, when we come to discuss the history of individual churches and the careers of the men who served them as ministers.

Black River Baptist Association

The Black River Association, which came into existence in 1808, included churches in Jefferson County of New York State as well as those in the adjacent territory along Lake Ontario and the St. Lawrence River.[25] The Rev. Emory Osgood, one of its leading ministers, was interested in Upper Canada, having collected funds for mission work there while he was connected with the Hamilton Missionary Society.[26] In 1817, within the Association, there was organized the Black River Missionary Society for Foreign and Domestic Missions. Specifically included in the objects of the new society was the raising of funds for home mission work in "the counties of Jefferson, St. Lawrence, Franklin, and the adjoining parts of Upper Canada."

According to the historian David Benedict, the work of the Black River Association in its early years was greatly assisted by both the

New York and Massachusetts Baptist Missionary Societies. The extent of the Association's work in Upper Canada, even after its own missionary society had been formed, is not clear, but it is quite definite that it had at least some contact with the churches of this province. The Rev. Peleg Card, who spent his later years in the Belleville district, and whose grave may be seen in the Fairview cemetery at Wicklow, Ontario, was one who came to Canada from the Black River Association, and remained in this country.

From this account it can be seen that the Baptists of the United States, with more than a century of development behind them, were well equipped with an organization that could carry their message to the new settlements in the north when immigration to Canada began. The missionary spirit that led the Baptist William Carey from Britain to India, making him the pioneer of a great movement that was to affect all denominations, prompted men less famous but just as fervent as he to follow the pioneer settlers to their new homes on the Canadian frontier.

The new churches which showed the success of the missionary effort reflected, as was natural, the principles and practices of their sponsors. Guided by this example, the Baptists of Upper and Lower Canada before 1820, for the most part, adopted a polity of the type which in later years came to be described as "regular." The main source of their churchmanship was the Philadelphia Confession of Faith, which had been adopted by the Philadelphia Association in 1742.[27] It was essentially a re-issue of a confession published by the Particular Baptists of Great Britain in 1677 and 1689, for though it contained additional articles dealing with the singing of psalms, and the imposition of hands upon the newly baptized church member, it did not alter the sections on the nature of the church. The confession of the Particular Baptists of Britain was, in turn, largely derived from the Westminster Confession of Faith of the Presbyterians, so that the doctrinal line of descent of the earliest Baptist churches in Ontario and Quebec led back to Calvin and Geneva. In Oxford County, however, the Arminian tendencies inherited from the General Baptists of Britain led to the formation of some Free Communion and Free Will Baptist churches, but this was at a slightly later period and there were only a few of them. Before 1820, only those churches holding to Calvinistic theology and "regular" church order had any hope of being received into the associations that had sponsored their establishment.

A careful watch was also kept on the later activities of the new churches by their sponsors. Characteristic expressions of the leaders of that day were the phrases, "proper gospel order," and "according to gospel rule." Any important step on the part of the local church must satisfy the conditions implied in these two formulas; if it did not, the action would be condemned by the association and the church might find itself excluded from membership in that body. In such ways the Baptist associations of New York and New England exercised a determining influence on Canadian Baptist polity.

II

First Settlements in Upper Canada

FOR A CLEARER UNDERSTANDING of the origin and growth of Baptist churches in the new Canadian setting, and of the activities of the missionaries from the American societies, a rather specific knowledge of the beginnings and development of the settlements themselves is necessary. In this chapter we propose, therefore, to trace the progress of settlement in Upper Canada during the earlier part of the period covered by this study, and to indicate briefly the places where Baptist sympathizers or congregations first appeared. In the following chapter will begin a more detailed description of the rise of the Baptist movement in what is now the province of Ontario.

St. Lawrence and Bay of Quinte Settlements

The first surveys along the St. Lawrence River, west of the land occupied by the French Canadians, were made in the summer and fall of 1783 at the instigation of General Haldimand, who had succeeded Sir Guy Carleton as governor in 1778.[1] (At this time there was no province of Upper Canada — the whole British territory as far west as Detroit was included in the province of Quebec.) On July 16, 1783, the King had approved instructions for a survey and grant of lands to the loyalists.[2] Single men were to receive 50 acres each, and heads of families 150 acres, plus 50 acres for each member of the family. From the year 1763 there had been a recognized scale of land grants to disbanded troops, and it was now decreed that discharged privates were to receive 100 acres and non-commissioned officers 200 acres, plus 50 acres for every member of the soldier's family.[3] On August 7 of the same year, new instructions were approved, authorizing grants of 1,000 acres to field officers, 700 acres to captains, and 500 acres to subalterns and warrant officers. Promises made to some units at the time of their enlistment caused variation in this plan and, as the scheme progressed, 200 acres came to be the standard grant for most claimants.[4]

Land was surveyed along the St. Lawrence in 1783 in parcels of thirty-six square miles each. These were at first deliberately left unnamed, and designated by number only — in the same fashion as the royal seigniories under the old French system. It was not long, however, before the English term "township" came into general use, and each township was given a name.

Thus Townships 1 to 8 along the St. Lawrence west of the French settlements (where Highway No. 2 now runs from Lancaster to Brockville) became known as Charlottenburg, Cornwall, Osnabruck, Williamsburg, Matilda, Edwardsburg, Augusta, and Elizabethtown. The "Lake Township," or Lancaster, occupying land at first regarded as too marshy for settlement, was subsequently added between Charlottenburg and the line of the present interprovincial boundary.[5] After a gap of forty miles west of Elizabethtown, came other townships, also surveyed in the year 1783, beginning at the old fur-trading post of Cataraqui. These, numbered 1 to 5 at first, were later named Kingston, Ernestown, Fredericksburg, Adolphustown and Marysburg, the last mentioned being situated on the east side of what is now Prince Edward County.

The surveys completed, General Haldimand was ready to begin settling the disbanded troops and unincorporated loyalists who had collected at such points as Montreal, St. Johns, and New Johnstown (Cornwall). These settlers came to the thirteen new royal townships in 1784. Supplies of food, clothing, equipment, and money were granted by the government. By the fall of the year, rations were being issued to more than five thousand people, many of whom, as refugees, had been receiving government assistance for two years already.[6] Only those who had actually suffered for their loyalty to the Crown were supposed to receive this aid.

It is not easy to follow the distribution of the various regiments in the thirteen townships. Elements of the King's Royal Regiment of New York (Sir John Johnson's), the King's Loyal Americans (Jessup's Rangers, also called Jessup's Corps) and the King's Rangers (Colonel James Rogers') went to the townships west of Cataraqui, but other elements of the same units, it is clear, settled along the St. Lawrence in the present counties of Stormont, Dundas, and Glengarry. In this latter region, the policy of placing Roman Catholics nearest to the French border was followed, with the result that the Catholic Highlanders of Sir John Johnson's first battalion were located next to the French, in what is now Glengarry. Among the Haldimand papers there is an interesting "general abstract of men, women and children settled on the New Townships on the River St. Lawrence, beginning at No. 1, Lake St. Francis, and running upwards."[7] This document makes it clear that the whole of the King's Royal Regiment of New York, and those attached, settled in Townships 1 to 5 on the St. Lawrence, and

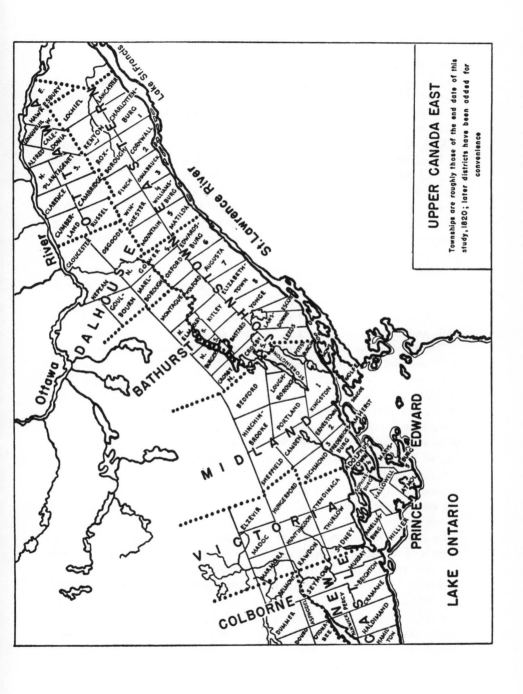

UPPER CANADA EAST

Townships are roughly those of the end date of this study, 1820; later districts have been added for convenience

that elements of the King's Loyal Americans (Major Jessup's Corps) and those attached settled in Townships 6, 7, and part of 8 in the same region. Along with the disbanded troops in these townships were loyalists and Germans from central New York State and from as far away as Pennsylvania.

Kingston (Township No. 1, Cataraqui) was first occupied by a party of loyalists led by Captain Michael Grass, who had assumed leadership of this group at the suggestion of Haldimand himself. Township No. 2 in this area (Ernestown) was taken up by the remaining elements of the King's Loyal Americans (Major Jessup) and those attached. Township No. 3 (Fredericksburg) was settled by the King's Rangers (Colonel Rogers), and by some of the second battalion of Sir John Johnson's unit, the King's Royal Regiment of New York. Township No. 4 (Adolphustown) was settled by the remainder of Sir John Johnson's second battalion and by a party of loyalists under Major Van Alstyne. To Township No. 5 (Marysburg) went several detachments of disbanded regular soldiers, led by Colonel MacDonnell, and a party of Hessians, headed by Baron Reitzenstein.[8]

Territory on the Bay of Quinte just west of the present site of Deseronto was set aside for some of the Mohawk Indians who had come from around Fort Hunter in the Mohawk valley of New York State. Haldimand's abstract states that a number of loyalists and Rangers of the Six Nation Indian Department settled with the Mohawks on their new location in this part of Canada. The rest of the Mohawk tribe who were driven from the United States found sanctuary on the Grand River, in western Ontario, where another reserve was set apart for their use. Their chief, Joseph Brant (Thayendanegea), took an interest in both reserves allotted to his people, and ultimately made his own home between the two where the town of Burlington now stands.

In June 1788, instructions were issued for surveying the forty-mile stretch of territory between Elizabethtown and Kingston.[9] As a result, the new townships of Yonge, Lansdowne, Leeds, and Pittsburg were laid out. The gore of Yonge ultimately became a separate township next to Lansdowne and was named Escott. At the same time the great "Twenty Mile Woods," east of Kingston, frequently mentioned by early travellers as a barrier to their progress, was penetrated by a road.[10] To the original township of Marysburg on the Prince Edward peninsula there were added five more, named Athol, Hallowell, Sophiasburg, Hillier and Ameliasburg.

Of special significance to this study is the township of Augusta, one of the original eight on the St. Lawrence; here a Baptist missionary

ENCAMPMENT OF THE LOYALISTS AT JOHNSTOWN

A new settlement on the banks of the River St. Lawrence in Canada. Water colour by James Peachey, June 6, 1784.
(Public Archives of Canada)

preached in 1807, and a church was formed in 1818. As surveys were pushed farther back from the river in the direction of the Rideau Lakes, the townships of Bastard and Kitley, north and west of Augusta, also became centres of Baptist activity, following the arrival of James Stark in 1789. The first Baptist work in the Bay of Quinte region was begun, under the leadership of Joseph Winn, a licensed Baptist preacher from New York State, in Hallowell, near West Lake, and in Ameliasburg, south of the Carrying Place.

The North Shore of Lake Ontario and Yonge Street

Along the north shore of Lake Ontario and in the area north of the Bay of Quinte, new settlements arose as immigrants continued to arrive during the last fifteen years of the eighteenth century. Tracts of land were purchased from the Indians to be divided into townships.[11] Thurlow was surveyed as early as 1787, and in 1791 Lord Dorchester instructed the Surveyor General and his deputy to lay out a row of townships along the lake front as far as York.[12] He stipulated the number of townships to be set up in this stretch, and supplied their names (in the end, the number proved to be fewer than he proposed, and not all of the names suggested by him were used). Some changes were made in the order of the townships in later years. Certain territory at the Carrying Place was transferred from Ameliasburg to Murray, and Brighton, which is situated between Murray and Cramahe, became a separate township in 1852. Those townships that became centres of Baptist activity before 1820, chiefly under the influence of Asa Turner and Reuben Crandall, were Thurlow, Sidney, Murray, Cramahe, and Haldimand along the waterfront, and Rawdon, Seymour, and Percy to the north of these.

Moving westward along the lake front towards York (Toronto), we need pause only to note that a group of Baptists from Pittsford, Vermont, led by Abel Stevens, considered establishing themselves as a Baptist colony in Scarborough Township in the 1790's, but decided against this and made their way eastward to Bastard and Kitley, where a Baptist witness was already established. In York itself, the Baptist cause took no root before 1820, though it is known that the Rev. Alexander Stewart, a Baptist minister from Scotland, went there in 1818 and taught in the common school for a period of two years after his arrival. The settlements along Yonge Street north of York, for a distance of at least thirty miles, were visited by Baptist preachers very early in the nineteenth century. The township of Markham, settled originally by German Lutherans under the famous land speculator

William Berczy,[13] had at least one organized Baptist congregation, with an ordained minister, Elijah Bentley, in charge, by the year 1805.

The Niagara Peninsula

The old landing place at the mouth of the Niagara River, and the fort not far away, were built on land belonging to the Seneca Indians. In 1764 Sir William Johnson on behalf of the King obtained from the Senecas a piece of land to include the fort and landing place and a strip one mile wide on each side of the river, extending upstream from the mouth a distance of fourteen miles.[14] British possession of the strip on the west bank depended on the goodwill of the Mississagas, who claimed ownership of the land on that side. Though Butler's Rangers had built log barracks on the Canadian side of the river in 1778, it was not until May 17, 1781, that a treaty with the Mississagas gave the British legal possession of a definite piece of land in that vicinity.[15]

In 1779, the year after Butler's Rangers had established their camp, General Haldimand suggested in a letter to the Secretary for War and the Colonies, Lord Germain, that some of the older Rangers might be encouraged to clear land and grow food for the garrison at Fort Niagara, thus easing the strain on the long supply line from Montreal. The commandant of the fort, Lieutenant Colonel Mason Bolton, thought, however, that they had better go slowly with any plans to occupy further land belonging to the Indians. "We must be cautious," he wrote, "how we encroach on the land of the Six Nations, as we have informed them that the Great King never deprived them of an acre since 1759, when he drove the French away." Further discussion followed and eventually Bolton agreed that some of the loyalist refugees might be encouraged to clear land and plant crops.

In 1780 Lord Germain approved the scheme, and that year, when the commanding officer of the Rangers, Lieutenant Colonel John Butler, visited Quebec, Haldimand discussed the matter with him. In July 1780, Haldimand wrote to Bolton setting forth the rules for establishing the settlement. Butler, who was experienced in farming, was to assist with the project. The land was to be leased on a yearly basis by the Crown, free of rent, to all settlers. Seed and implements would be supplied, and all produce was to be sold to the commandant of the fort for the use of the garrison. It was not to be sold to traders.

By the fall of 1781, some seven or eight Rangers had been joined at Niagara by their families, and in 1782 Butler announced his intention of discharging older men with large families so that they might settle on the land. This could only be done, however, as new reinforcements arrived for his battalion. On August 25, 1782, Butler reported that there were sixteen families, comprising a total of forty-eight persons, in his little community of settlers. The heads of families named in his report were Isaac Dolson, Peter Secord, James Secord, John Secord, George Stuart, George Fields, John Depue, Daniel Rowe, Elijah Phelps, Philip Bender, Samuel Lutz, Michael Showers, Hermanus House, Thomas McMicking, Adam Young, McGregor Van Every.[16]

In 1783, as has been noted, the King approved instructions for surveys and land grants to loyalists. When these regulations were published in July that year, several soldiers asked to be discharged in order to settle, but their requests were refused until the necessary arrangements could be made for their location. Meanwhile the settlement at Niagara had grown to include forty-six families, with forty-four houses and twenty barns already built. The total amount of land cleared by fall, 1783, was 713 acres, of which 123 acres were sown to fall wheat and 342 acres were ploughed ready for spring.[17]

Early in 1784 Joseph Brant asked for a grant of land on the Grand River for the loyalist Indians of the Mohawk tribe, some of whom were also being settled on the reserve set aside for them on the north shore of Lake Ontario near the Bay of Quinte. On March 23 of that year, Sir John Johnson was instructed to purchase the whole territory lying between Lakes Erie, Ontario, and Huron from the Mississagas, the intention being to grant to the Mohawks the tract requested by their chief, Joseph Brant, and to reserve the rest for loyalists, "or any future purpose."[18] It turned out that part of the vast territory in question was claimed by the Chippewas, with whom a separate agreement of purchase would be necessary, but the Mississagas agreed to sell nearly three million acres for the sum of £1180, 7s 4d. This included the whole of the Niagara Peninsula, and the land between Lake Erie and the River Thames as far west as Catfish Creek, at whose mouth Port Bruce now stands.[19]

With the conclusion of this purchase from the Indians, the way was open for townships to be surveyed and for settlers to apply for specific locations. On July 21, 1784, Colonel de Peyster, the new commandant at Fort Niagara, reported that surveys had not yet been started, and he submitted a list of 258 persons, including disbanded Rangers, Brant's volunteers, and loyalists, who had applied for land.[20] The Mohawks began to take up their grant almost immediately, and that same summer the Rev. John Stuart, Church of England clergyman from Kingston, who made a tour of Niagara and the Grand River reserve, preached to the Mohawks in what he described as "a decent, commodious church, erected by themselves."[21] Mr. Stuart was well acquainted with the Indians, having served as chaplain to the garrison at Fort Hunter in the Mohawk valley before the War of Independence. Later, in 1788, he again visited the Grand River settlement, bringing with him the beautiful silver communion service which had been given to the Mohawks at Fort Hunter by Queen Anne in the year 1712.[22]

It was not until June 1787, that Townships 1 and 2, later named Niagara and Stamford, were surveyed by a former subaltern in Butler's Rangers, Lieutenant Philip Rockwell Frey.[23] By this time a good deal of land had been occupied by squatters, who staked out claims in a rough and ready fashion, hoping that when the official surveys were made they would, without too much difficulty, obtain clear title to the properties on which they had settled. The problems created by this practice were clearly stated by the well-known land surveyor, Augustus Jones, in a letter to the acting Surveyor-General, D. W. Smith, in 1792, four years after he had surveyed the tract between Chippewa Creek and Fort Erie. "The Settlers," he explained, "after measuring off the customary Width of a Lot had fixed arbitrary Division Lines between each other, not considering how the side lines would intersect at right angles in order to make it agreeable to their Possessions or Clearings."[24]

During the summer of 1787, the borders of the Niagara community were extended as far as Fort Erie in one direction and Ten Mile Creek in the other.[25] In the next year, 1788, a good deal of progress was made in the surveying of the townships near the Niagara settlement. By October, Lieutenant Frey reported that he had surveyed all the settled communities from Fort Erie westwards along the Lake Erie shore as far as the Sugar Loaf hills, near the present site of Port Colborne.[26] "I have taken care," he wrote to John Collins, the deputy surveyor general, "to carry on my surveys only in such Parts of the country where I found the people were taking up lands and settling in a promiscuous manner, in order before they made any considerable improvements, to ascertain to each individual his exact boundaries without laying out a whole township for a few families and afterwards be at a loss from what fund to satisfy my chain and axe men." During the same year of 1788 Mr. Augustus Jones was also at work surveying in the townships of Bertie, Clinton, and Grimsby.[27]

The story of settlement in the Niagara district has been presented at some length because its rate of development has a particular bearing on the dating of the first establishment of Baptist interest there. The suggestion has sometimes been put forward that the earliest Baptist church in the peninsula, at Clinton, was established by 1782, or perhaps even as early as 1776. The facts connected with the progress of settlement in the Niagara Peninsula would seem to rule this out conclusively. Ownership of the whole peninsula by the Indians until 1784, and the policy followed by the British authorities of preventing settlers from invading Indian territory until it had been legally purchased by the Crown, make it extremely unlikely that there was any settled community on Thirty Mile Creek before 1784 at the earliest.

Evidence of Baptists in the peninsula may be sought in the various lists of claimants, settlers, and discharged soldiers compiled at the time. Butler's list of families in his community at Niagara in 1782, for example, contains no names recognizable among later lists of Baptist church members. In 1787 there arrived in Quebec province the Commissioners of Claims appointed by the British government to take evidence from loyalists who were seeking compensation for losses suffered during the war. Commissioners Colonel Thomas Dundas and Jeremy Pemberton had sat the previous year in the Maritime Provinces, and now moved to Montreal, where the claims of the Niagara loyalists were heard. A perusal of the list of claimants from this area is interesting for the student of Canadian Baptist history, since it includes only two family names, House and Kentner, which are known to have had a connection with the earliest Baptist church in the Niagara Peninsula, in Clinton.[28] Though it has been stated that there was a Mrs. Overholt among the claimants who went to Montreal, and it has been supposed that she was a member of the family of that name which later became prominent among the Baptists of Clinton Township, it is clear that this is not correct. The woman whose claim was put forward at Montreal in 1787 was Mrs. "Obenholt," not Overholt, and the evidence given at that time by her son, John Obenholt, shows that she was still in the United States.[29]

However, significant activity was to begin in Clinton following the arrival of two prominent families, the Overholts and the Beams. The account book of Augustus Jones for his surveying work, already mentioned, shows that one of the assistants employed by him for a period of twenty-three days between December 1788 and February 1789 was Jacob Overholt, son of Staats Overholt, a loyalist whose family did become prominent in Baptist church life. Jacob Beam, founder of Beamsville, came to Canada and settled on the Thirty Mile Creek in 1788.[30] As it is definitely known that the Beam family arrived from the United States in 1788, and the Overholts appear to have settled in Clinton about the same time, it is reasonable to conclude that Baptist work in the area began soon after the arrival of these two families, perhaps in 1789 or 1790. At first that work was undoubtedly in the nature of religious meetings held in their homes. More than ten years were

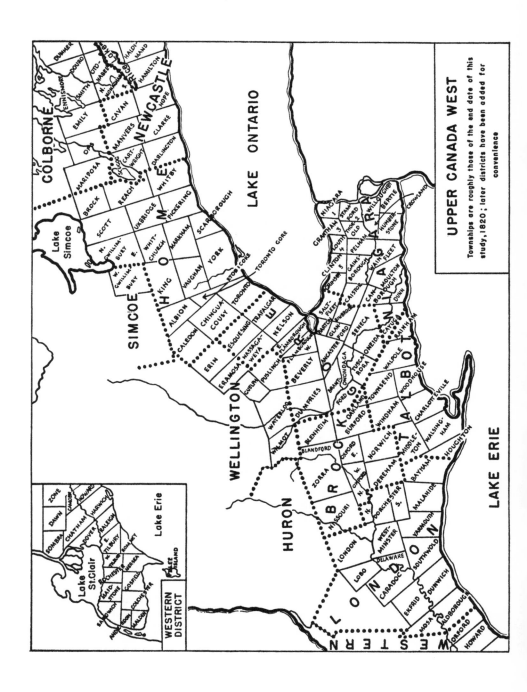

UPPER CANADA WEST

Townships are roughly those of the end date of this study, 1820; later districts have been added for convenience

LAKE ONTARIO

LAKE ERIE

COLBORNE

NEWCASTLE

SIMCOE

HOME

WELLINGTON

HURON

BROCK

NIAGARA

TALBOT

LONDON

WESTERN

Lake Simcoe

Lake St.Clair

Lake Erie

PELEE ISLAND

WESTERN DISTRICT

to elapse before any regularly ordained Baptist minister appeared on the scene, even for a brief visit, and still more years were to pass before there was any properly constituted church. (A more detailed analysis of developments at Clinton is to be found in chapter VI.) The organization of what is now known as the Beamsville Baptist Church took place in 1807.

Long Point, on Lake Erie

From the days of the earliest explorations made by white men through the waters of Lake Erie, the Long Point peninsula had attracted attention. Extending southward into the lake like a scimitar, it helped to form, along with Turkey Point to the east, a large bay where boats could find shelter. When, in 1788, Lord Dorchester divided western Quebec into four administrative districts, it was this prominent geographical feature that was chosen to mark the division between two of them, Nassau and Hesse.

The point itself, of course, was included in the purchase of territory from the Mississagas in 1784, and in 1790, by an additional purchase from the Indians, the Crown obtained legal control of all the land from Long Point to the channel Ecarté emptying into Lake St. Clair. Claims of previous ownership through individual purchase from the Indians were swept aside, but land grants made under the French régime around Amherstburg were respected.[31] In June 1790, deputy surveyor Patrick McNiff reported to the new land board of Hesse that, acting on instructions from the commandant at Detroit, he had made a coasting survey of the Lake Erie shore. Along much of it he had found the approach to the land very difficult because of the high banks. Between Rondeau and Long Point the only places of easy access were the River Tonty, or Kettle Creek, where Port Stanley now stands, and Rivière à la Barbue, or Catfish Creek. He found, however, to quote his own words, "on the back of Long Point, very good land, not so hilly as what I have passed, timber, Bass, Black Walnut and Hard Maple, but marshy in front for twenty or thirty chains."[32]

When John Graves Simcoe arrived at Quebec in 1791 as the newly appointed lieutenant-governor of Upper Canada, he was soon convinced from his study of such maps and preliminary surveys as were available that Long Point was destined to be of great strategic importance for settling his province in time of peace and defending it in time of war. His official correspondence during his term of office shows how thoroughly this place had conquered his imagination.[33] As a factor in the defence of Upper Canada he regarded it as being more important than Detroit or Niagara. These two places, he said, could be taken by assault quite easily by an enemy five thousand strong, even though the entire military resources of the province could be concentrated at either place for its defence, whereas Long Point could be held by an ordinary garrison. He therefore proposed to post some of the Queen's Rangers there, build a block house on the island opposite the bay, and perhaps spend the winter of 1793-94 there himself. At the same time, he planned to strengthen the defences of Toronto, and to establish his capital at a place to be called New London, at the navigable head of the La Tranche river, which he renamed the Thames.

Simcoe's enthusiasm for his plans in this area was almost boundless. He believed that naval craft could be constructed sixty miles up the Grand River during the winter and floated down to Lake Erie on the high water in the spring. Similar ships could be built, he thought, in winter time at Oxford on the Thames (Woodstock), and sent on the spring freshets to Lake St. Clair. He hoped that from the head of the Thames he might establish communication by water with Toronto, thus avoiding the necessity of going by way of Fort Erie, which lay so close to the American frontier. He felt that London, his capital, being well inland from the lakes along the border, could be defended against surprise attack. The key to the protection of this whole system, however, in his view, must be Long Point, which would hold off the invaders who might be expected to launch their assault from Presque Isle directly across the narrow part of the lake only thirty miles away.

In view of its importance for defence, Simcoe was anxious that no land grants should be made near Long Point until the garrison had been established there, though he thought the surrounding country to be ideal for settlement and vigorously denied the rumour that it was an unhealthy region in which to live. His plan was that only selected settlers of proven loyalty should be allowed to take up land in this locality. There was to be no settlement *en masse* for fear that American sympathizers would infiltrate the district. In 1794 he stated that he was sure no houses had been built there before his arrival in the province, except such as might have been erected contrary to government regulations.[34] As a matter of fact, a fair number of squatters had taken up land around Long Point before his arrival, as was shown by various petitions submitted to the land board later on. In 1794 it was found necessary to empower the Surveyor-General or his deputies to remove such squatters from their holdings if they could not produce evidence of their right to occupy them, or if their claims conflicted with those of settlers who had proper authority.[35]

Despite his great enthusiasm, Simcoe's plans for Long Point were never carried out. In the autumn of 1795 he visited the place, drew a plan for the location of a town to be called Charlotteville, and selected sites for barracks and a mill. Lord Dorchester, however, favoured Kingston over Long Point as a suitable place at which to build a harbour, and he rejected the idea of any more military establishments in view of the Jay Treaty, which had been concluded between the United States and Britain in November 1794. By this treaty (which takes its name from Chief Justice John Jay, United States ambassador to Britain), Britain had agreed to evacuate her forts along the American frontier, where garrisons had been maintained ever since the Revolution. The authorities in Britain, believing that the defence of Upper Canada was primarily a naval problem, felt that York, not New London, was the place to be developed at once.[36] In 1796, therefore, after Newark had served as a temporary capital for four years, the seat of government was moved to York, where it remained.

After his visit to Long Point in 1795, Simcoe instructed the acting Surveyor-General to grant lots of two hundred acres each to settlers in that area if they were properly recommended. By 1796 Townships 1, 2, and 3 (Walsingham, Charlotteville, and Woodhouse), had been surveyed and the Surveyor-General had a long list of applications for grants. Simcoe's town of Charlotteville, on Turkey Point, enjoyed but a brief history. Its court house, which for a time housed the Court of Quarter Sessions for the London District, was used by troops during the War of 1812 and was destroyed by fire in 1815. The court was then moved to Tisdale's Mills in Charlotteville Township, and Vittoria, the village which sprang up at this spot, replaced the forsaken town of Charlotteville as the district capital.

At Vittoria arose the Charlotteville Baptist Church, first of the denomination in the Long Point area, and bearing the name of the township in which it was established. In Townsend, sixteen miles away, there were also Baptist settlers who were eager to give expression to their distinctive witness, and there too a congregation of baptized believers was gathered. In Charlotteville and in Townsend two lay preachers were responsible for the commencement of Baptist work, and ultimately both these men were ordained to the ministry. Their names were Titus Finch and Peter Fairchild.

The Thames River Settlements

In 1791 Mr. Patrick McNiff began his survey of the Thames River valley, and two years later had pushed as far up the river as Delaware, much to Simcoe's satisfaction.[37] Details of McNiff's work, and that of other surveyors along the Thames, are found in their correspondence with the Surveyor-General and in the proceedings of the district and county land boards. In the same year a large parcel of land on the south side of the river east of the present village of Thamesville was granted to a group of Munsee Indians. Christianized by missionaries of the Moravian Brethren, these Indians had suffered terribly during the American Revolution, when their village in Ohio was all but wiped out by terrorists. When they were brought to Canada by their missionary, David Zeisberger, they built the town of Fairfield-on-the-Thames where their descendants are still found, though their settlement is now called Moraviantown.[38] News of this grant to the Moravian colony on the Thames led Abel Stevens and his associates in Vermont to hope that they might establish a Baptist colony along similar lines, but their hope was not fulfilled.

The Thames had provided an overland route from Niagara to Detroit for winter travellers for some time when Simcoe made the journey in 1793. Sleighs could be drawn on the ice of the river and of Lake St. Clair, and the so-called "Winter Express" made at least one round trip along this route each season. On his winter journey in 1793 Simcoe met the "Express" both going and coming; travelling with it, or close behind it on its way to Detroit, was the land surveyor, Augustus Jones.[39] Along this route, at strategic points on the river, Simcoe planned townsites at Oxford, London, and Chatham.

It was in West Oxford Township that Baptist work first gained a foothold, since this settlement could be visited by itinerant preachers to Charlotteville and Townsend. Early missionary reports refer to the regret felt by certain missionaries from Baptist bodies in the United States that they were unable to press nearer to Detroit than Oxford, owing to lack of time.[40] Although the Baptist witness does not appear to have been established in strength very far west of Oxford until after 1820, some adherents of this communion were probably in the Amherstburg area as early as 1811, for on February 16 of that year the Townsend church despatched a letter to "the brethren at New Maldin," which presumably refers to Baptists living in Malden Township where the Detroit River joins Lake Erie.[41]

The Talbot Settlement

Lieutenant Thomas Talbot was an Irishman who joined Simcoe's staff at Quebec as his confidential secretary in 1791. He accompanied the Lieutenant-Governor on many of his tours, including the journey from Newark to Detroit in February and March of 1793. He was impressed with the need for immigration to Upper Canada, and agreed with Simcoe that the great tract of land lying between the Thames River and Lake Erie was as fine as any in North America. Talbot received his majority in the 85th Foot Regiment in 1793 and in 1794 left for England to continue his army career. By 1795 he was in command of the 5th Foot with the rank of colonel and seemed well on the way to prominence as a soldier. Despite his rapid advance he forsook soldiering and returned to Upper Canada with the intention of placing settlers in the choice stretch of country north of Lake Erie and west of Long Point, which he had admired so much in his travels with Simcoe. He was determined that part of the stream of immigration flowing through the United States should be turned towards Upper Canada and thus strengthen the British position in North America. Simcoe was of the same opinion, and his proclamation on land grants in 1792 had been circulated to loyalists still residing in the United States with great effect.

Simcoe himself had left Canada before Talbot returned. From the standpoint of development through immigration and settlement, Upper Canada owed more to John Graves Simcoe than to any other person during these early years. Though his widely circulated invitation to settlers and his policy of land grants led to undesirable speculation, he must be given credit for initiating the great movement of people which swelled the population from ten thousand to thirty thousand during his five-year term of office between the years 1791 and 1796, and the system of roads planned by him for military purposes became the arteries through which flowed the life blood of this new corner of empire.

In May 1803, Talbot landed on the shore of Lake Erie at a point about midway between its eastern and western extremities, and sixty miles west of Long Point itself. He had already chosen the place for himself and had marked the occasion by proclaiming, "Here I will roost." In 1804 he obtained an initial grant of five thousand acres in the townships of Dunwich and Aldborough, and embarked upon a great scheme of colonization. Arbitrary and overbearing in his attitude, he ruled his domain somewhat like an ancient feudal lord, and for many years was able to ignore the provincial government, dealing directly with the Colonial Office in Britain. One of his achievements as a director of settlement was the great road which bears his name, much of which is now incorporated in the King's Highway No. 3. After the disturbances caused by the War of 1812 had subsided, his settlement grew very rapidly. Eastward from its centre at Port Talbot it reached as far as the townships of Malahide and Bayham, the former being named after his birthplace in Ireland. To the west it stretched to the very fringes of the old settlement around Amherstburg, taking in the townships of Sandwich, Romney, Mersea, Maidstone, and part of Gosfield. By 1822, according to his own boast, his empire had been extended to include some twenty-three townships with a population of twelve thousand souls.[42]

It was on the Talbot Road in Malahide in the year 1816 that Elder Reuben Crandall organized the Talbot Street Baptist Church, sometimes called the Malahide Church, and now bearing the name of Aylmer, in which town it is situated today.

Territorial Divisions of Upper Canada

For a better understanding of the geographical references in the narrative which follows, this account of the formation of the settlements in which Baptist churches first appeared in Upper Canada may well close with a brief explanation of how the province came to be divided into districts and counties with the increase in settlement and the subsequent need for more complex administration than that of the original townships. The system did not remain constant, and the main developments are here set forth in their chronological order.

1788. Lord Dorchester, the former Sir Guy Carleton, on his return to Canada as governor in 1786, divided the territory that was later to become Upper Canada into four districts for purposes of administration. These were named Lunenburg, Mecklenburg, Nassau and Hesse. Lunenburg took in the townships west of French Canada from Lancaster to Elizabethtown, and Mecklenburg extended from Elizabethtown to the mouth of the Trent River. Nassau stretched from the Trent River to a north-south line bisecting Long Point on Lake Erie, and therefore included the whole of the Niagara Peninsula. Hesse was made up of the rest of the province to its western limits. A judge and a sheriff were appointed for each district, and in 1789 land boards were set up in all four districts to deal with petitions from applicants for land grants.

1791. The old province of Quebec was divided into two provinces. The western part, consisting of the four districts named above, became Upper Canada and the eastern part was named Lower Canada.

1792. John Graves Simcoe divided the four districts into nineteen counties, which he named Glengarry, Stormont, Dundas, Grenville, Leeds, Frontenac, Ontario (including the islands of Amherst, Simcoe,

Wolfe, and Howe), Addington, Lennox, Prince Edward, Hastings, Northumberland, Durham, York, Lincoln, Norfolk, Suffolk, Essex, and Kent. The purpose of the county was to provide a basis for representation in Parliament, and from these nineteen counties sixteen members were chosen for the first parliament of Upper Canada which met at Newark. This body changed the names of the four districts to Eastern, Midland, Home, and Western.

1800. The number of the districts was increased to eight and the counties to twenty-three:

(1) EASTERN DISTRICT: Glengarry, Stormont, Dundas, Prescott, and Cornwall.
(2) JOHNSTOWN DISTRICT: Grenville, Leeds, and Carleton.
(3) MIDLAND DISTRICT: Frontenac, Lennox, Addington, Hastings, Prince Edward and everything north of these, including the islands in the Ottawa River.
(4) NEWCASTLE DISTRICT: Northumberland and Durham, with all the lands in their rear.
(5) HOME DISTRICT: east and west ridings of York.
(6) NIAGARA DISTRICT: the county of Haldimand and the east, west, north, and south ridings of Lincoln.
(7) LONDON DISTRICT: Norfolk, Oxford, and Middlesex.
(8) WESTERN DISTRICT: Essex and Kent.

1820-36. The number of districts was increased during this period to twelve with the addition of Ottawa, Bathurst, and Gore, and the elevation of Prince Edward County to district status. The new district called Gore was taken from parts of the Niagara, Home, and London districts.

1837. The districts of Brock, Talbot, Simcoe, and Victoria were created, bringing the number up to sixteen.

1838. Four more districts were added, named Dalhousie, Colborne, Wellington, and Huron.

In the year 1849 the districts were abolished and the county became the recognized unit for local government above the municipal level, for judicial purposes, and for parliamentary representation. County boundaries underwent many changes as more and more land was occupied. Township boundaries were much more stable, remaining mostly as they were laid out in the original surveys, but even these changed as the province grew. With the opening up of northern Ontario in more recent times the districts have been revived in areas where the population is too sparse for the successful working of the county system.[43]

III

Baptist Missionary Tours into Upper Canada
1801-1810

THE FIRST PROPERLY ACCREDITED Baptist missionary from the United States to visit Upper Canada, as far as we know, was Elkanah Holmes of the New York Missionary Society, who visited Joseph Brant on the Grand River early in 1801. His purpose was to establish work among the Mohawk Indians, and he seems to have made no contact with Baptists among the white settlers on that trip. It is known, however, that Caleb Blood was sent by the Shaftsbury Association in the fall of 1802, that Joseph Cornell came on behalf of the Massachusetts Baptist Missionary Society in January 1803, and that Lemuel Covell and Obed Warren, of the Shaftsbury Association, made a tour in the fall of 1803.

In a report of November 1803, Covell wrote: "Mr. Proudfit and Mr. Dunlap have each made a tour in that country, and have left evident traces of their usefulness."[1] The Rev. Alexander Proudfit and the Rev. John Dunlap were Presbyterian ministers connected with the Northern Missionary Society, an interdenominational body in which Presbyterian influence was stronger than any other. It had been organized at Lansingburgh, New York, in January 1797, and Proudfit and Dunlap, two of its officers, hoped to do missionary work among the Indians west of Detroit. What contact they had with Baptists on their way across Upper Canada is not known, but Covell's remark seems to indicate that they had some.

The date when Baptist work was officially begun in Upper Canada by a missionary to the white settlers seems to be fairly well decided by the Rev. Nathaniel Kendrick, who, giving an account of his own tour in 1808, said, "Mr. Blood was the first Baptist missionary that ever visited these parts, and wherever he went the people hold him in grateful remembrance."[2] Since Mr. Kendrick knew Elkanah Holmes intimately, and was thoroughly familiar with his career as a missionary, his statement that Caleb Blood was the first to work among the settlers in Upper Canada must be accepted as authoritative. With the

Rev. Caleb Blood, therefore, and his autumn journey of 1802, this account of the various missionary tours into Upper Canada begins. The journeys will be described in their chronological order, year by year, until we come to the end of the first decade of the nineteenth century, when all such tours seem to have ceased until after the War of 1812-14.

1802

Rev. Caleb Blood

At the annual meeting of the Shaftsbury Association in 1802, the Rev. Caleb Blood, the moderator and at that time also pastor of the Fourth Baptist Church in Shaftsbury, volunteered to go on tour among the outlying settlements for a few weeks in the fall. His journey began on August 24. Details of his tour are recorded in a letter written by him to a friend in Boston on January 10, 1804, and published in the May issue of the *Massachusetts Baptist Missionary Magazine* for that year.[3] After spending considerable time in the northwestern parts of New York State, including the Genesee River country and the great tract known as the Holland Purchase, which was controlled by the Holland Land Company, Mr. Blood followed the southern shore of Lake Erie down to the region of Buffalo. The Canadian part of his journey began at this point, and it can best be described in his own words:

When I had gotten through this wilderness, I struck Lake Erie, went down to its outlet, and crossed over into the westerly part of Upper Canada. Here I found large settlements of white people, who understood our language; but when I first entered the province, I travelled twenty-five miles before I found a house where people would willingly open their doors for preaching, and scarce any willing to converse on religious subjects. This route was down the Niagara River towards Lake Ontario.

When I came to Queen's Town, I was introduced to a Mr. Thomson, a Scotchman, who received me with great hospitality, and was anxious for preaching. With him I left my horse the next morning, and went on foot two miles down the river to the landing. I crossed into the wilderness on this side, and after climbing a precipice of rocks, found a kind of house made of rough logs. Here I found Elder Holmes, missionary to the Indians. . . .

While I was here, I had opportunity to make some appointments among the people of Upper Canada. On Thursday I went on my way up Lake Ontario. Here I found large settlements of white people, all destitute of preaching. In some settlements it was hard to get them willing to hear preaching. I was, in some cases, obliged to adopt measures I had been wholly unaccustomed to. I was forced to go into settlements and put up, and then go from house to house and beg of them to come and hear, and did not give out when one after another told me they did not choose to attend; and even when they said they would, and did not, I still tried them again. For when I could once get them to hear, they were as anxious to hear more as any people I ever saw. Then I made appointments on my return. Thus I went and preached in every settlement until I had gone some distance beyond the head of Lake Ontario. I imputed much of this backwardness in hearing to the people's having been so greatly imposed on by vicious characters who had been among them, in the profession of preachers. I must here mention a trying circumstance. Word came to me, with a request to go about fifty miles farther, to a place called Long Point Settlement, on Lake Erie, informing that there was a work of divine grace in that place; that there were thirty or forty persons stood ready for baptism, and no administrator whom they could obtain within two hundred miles of them; but I had my appointments back through the Province, and could not go to their relief. This tried my feelings beyond expression. I endeavoured to give the case up to God, and returned according to my appointments.

As I came back through the Province, the people attended meetings which were full and very solemn. Some hopeful symptoms of good appeared among them. I gave them encouragement that we should send a missionary among them next year and they were anxious that we should. I left them with reluctance, crossed the water at the outlet of Erie, and spent two weeks with the Seneca Nation of Indians. . . .

The kind Lord returned me in safety to my family and people, and I found all things well. I attempted in my poor way to preach about as many times as there were days in the three months of my absence; and if I suitably acknowledge divine goodness, I can say, that I think I never enjoyed so great a degree of the divine presence in preaching in any other three months in my life.

At the annual meeting of the Shaftsbury Association in 1803, the missionary committee reported that Mr. Blood had gone from Cayuga to the head of Lake Ontario. They had advanced him thirty dollars towards his expenses, of which he had spent $22.34. So gratified was the Association with the work he had done that a special resolution was passed authorizing him to keep the remaining $7.66 for his own use![4] It is significant that in his travels across the Niagara Peninsula from Fort Erie around to the regions beyond Hamilton and Dundas, Blood makes no mention of coming in contact with any organized Baptist church. His many preaching engagements were evidently carried out in private homes, like that of Mr. Thomson at Queenston. Of the existence of a Baptist church at Beamsville at that time he says nothing, in spite of the fact that he passed directly through the settlement both going and returning.

1803

Rev. Joseph Cornell, Rev. Lemuel Covell, & Rev. Obed Warren

On September 15, 1802, while Caleb Blood was preaching in the Niagara Peninsula of Upper Canada for the Shaftsbury Association, the newly organized Massachusetts Baptist Missionary Society met in Boston to appoint its first missionary. Elder John Leland having declined, the appointment was offered to Elder Joseph Cornell, of Galway, N.Y., who accepted.[5] In January 1803, amid the heavy snows of winter, he preached in the pioneer settlements of western New York State, and on the last day of the month found himself at the St. Lawrence River, opposite Kingston, with a letter in his hand urging him to pay a visit to the Canadian side. His own report to the Society,[6] written after his return home, on April 6 that spring, reads in part as follows:

January 31. I was at a loss about going to Canada, on account of the danger in crossing the river. Three horses were drowned in attempting to cross last week, and one man perished the week before. But I received a letter from there, and their requests are so urgent, that I ventured through the woods to the River St. Lawrence; and God directed my pilot and myself safe across into Cataraqua. In this neighbourhood, the people in general appear to be very loose in their morals.

From this, I rode north-east about twenty-four miles, where I found a people which manifested a great desire for preaching. They had laboured under great disadvantages, as they said, for want of some to teach them. I was the first missionary that ever visited this place. I found a goodly number here inquiring after truth, but many of them the most entangled with the doctrine of the pharisees that I ever saw. I preached as long as I dared to tarry, on account of the river's breaking up. Our assemblies were large, as they called them. The attention was wonderful!

Their hearts were so cemented together in Stephentown, that after passing an examination of their *faith* and *practice*, they formed themselves into a church, consisting of fourteen members. We met the Lord's day after, and it would have given pleasure to our churches in general to have seen the assembly meeting, when they had to come through water up to their sleigh boxes, and were all filled with animation. When I came to preach in the afternoon, from Col. ii, 2, the great Comforter was pleased to fill the hearts of his children; and when drawing to the close of the service, our hearts sobbed, our eyes flowed, our lips quivered, and our voices sounded in prayer to the great Head of the Church, that he would keep this little vine from the wild boar of the woods, and make its boughs like Joseph's branches.

The thought of parting excited the most tender and cutting feelings; for they feared they would be forgotten by their brethren. They send their earnest request for further help if their fathers and brethren can think them worthy to come under their roof. Brethren, I cannot paint to you this most affecting scene; for some, in this Province, have lived here fourteen

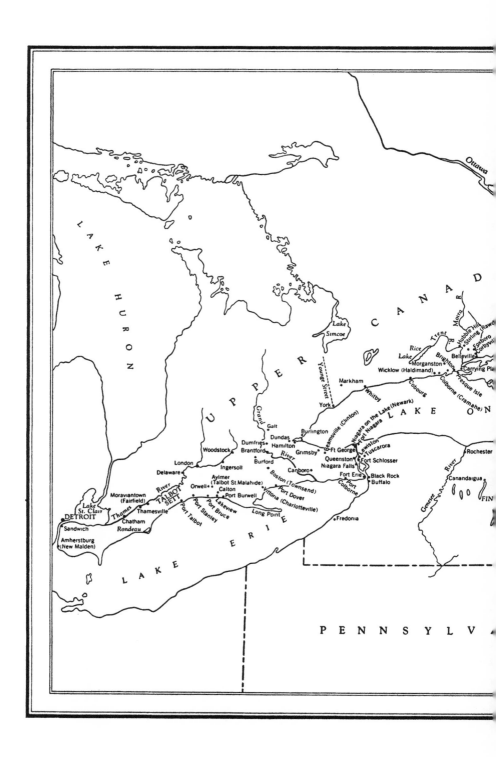

LAKE HURON

UPPER CANADA

Ottawa R

Moira R

Hubble Hill
Rawdon
Stirling
Foxboro
Forbyville
Belleville
Brighton
Carrying Place
Morganston
Colborne (Cramahe)
Presque Isle

Trent R

Rice Lake

Cobourg

Wicklow (Haldimand)

Lake Simcoe

Yonge Street

Markham

York

Whitby

LAKE ONT

Grand River

Galt

Dumfries
Dundas
Burlington
Hamilton
Brantford

Beamsville (Clinton)
Niagara on the Lake (Newark)
Ft Niagara
Ft George
Lewiston
Queenston
Tuscarora
Fort Schlosser

Rochester

Woodstock

London

Delaware

Ingersoll

Burford

River

Grimsby

Canboro

Niagara Falls

Genesee River

Canandaigua

FIN

TALBOT SETT

Orwell
Aylmer
(Talbot St.Malahide)
Calton
Lakeview
Port Burwell

Boston (Townsend)

Port Dover

Fort Erie
Black Rock
Buffalo

Port
Colborne

Moraviantown
(Fairfield)

Thames River

Thamesville

Port Talbot
Port Bruce
Port Stanley

Vitoria (Charlotteville)

Long Point

Fredonia

Lake St. Clair
DETROIT

Sandwich

Chatham

Rondeau

Amherstburg
(New Malden)

LAKE ERIE

PENNSYLV

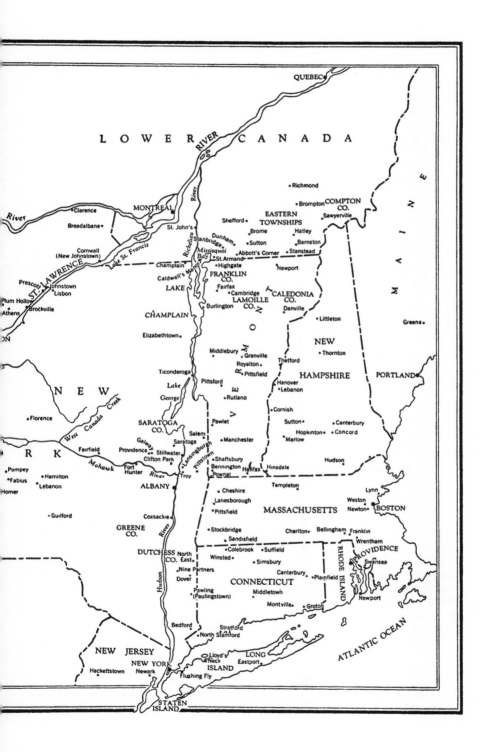

years, and they told me they had not heard one sermon, from any regular preacher, except the Methodists. Brother Darbesher now lives in the town of Young, and is a licensed Baptist preacher. It is proposed to have him ordained as soon as Providence opens a door for it to be done agreeably to gospel rule.

I have seen children in this Province, from nine to fourteen years of age, who did not know what a Bible was, before I shewed them one! . . .

I rode and preached about 200 miles in this Province, and I was never more satisfied that I was where my Master had work for me to do, than here; for every denomination have set open their doors for me to preach. And I think it must have moved our Christian friends, to hear them express their strong desires for hearing the gospel of Christ. For they long to have their neighbours brought from working *for* life, to believe in a change of heart, wrought by the divine power of God, and feel its effects, in bringing them to work for a holy principle *of life* in their soul.

After my visit here, I returned and crossed the Iroquois [St. Lawrence] by what is called the Thousand Isles, eleven miles on the ice. . . . My joy was so great with the visit I had had, that I almost forgot the trouble of passing through twenty miles of woods, crossing dangerous rivers, and ploughing through brooks and mud sloughs.

As Caleb Blood retraced his steps across the Niagara Peninsula towards the American border in the fall of 1802, he promised the settlers of that region, and sent word to those at Long Point on Lake Erie, that the Shaftsbury Association would send out more missionaries next season. At the annual meeting in the summer of 1803 he found his brethren in ready agreement, and Elders Lemuel Covell, of Pittstown, N.Y., and Obed Warren, of Salem, N.Y., were appointed to go on tour that fall, "bearing the word of life to those who sat in the region and shadow of death."[7] In the letter written by Caleb Blood to his Boston friend in 1804,[8] he described these events:

Agreeably to the encouragement I gave the people in Upper Canada, our Association sent two missionaries this year, viz., brother Covell [the original misprints Carell] and brother Warren. They have returned and had a very prosperous journey. Before they went, I sent on a letter to Upper Canada, to give information of their coming. When they came there the people were ready to receive them; their doors were open, and they had access to all their villages and settlements. The attention of the people seemed roused up, and encouraging symptoms attended their labours. They went to Long Point Settlement, and found it as I had been informed; they baptized thirty in that place, and assisted in gathering a church [Charlotte-ville, now Vittoria.] Here they found a young brother [Titus Finch], whom they baptized, and advised the church to improve and encourage him in preaching.

They then went about 60 miles farther, to a settlement on the River Retrench [Thames]. Here they found a people overjoyed to see them. Some appearance of the work of God was there and they baptized some. On their return through the province the people were ready to hear preaching either by night or by day. They sent forward a petition to the Shaftsbury Association for a permanent missionary or preacher of abilities to be steadily with them, till they can get into some regulation, so as to support themselves. To this petition there are hundreds of names; and some of the first characters in those parts took great pains to set their names to the petition. Should such a thing be done, there is every reason to believe great good would attend it, but I see no way at present that it will be in our power to answer their request.

Our collections for this business are small. I did not receive, when I went, near enough expenses for the journey. We were able to do better by our brethren who went this year. How it will be in the future, I cannot say. But this is not all; as circumstances are in that country at present, we must send a man of good abilities, experience, and piety, or we had better send none; and I do not know of one to be obtained if we were able to send him. The way we have done to obtain these we have sent, is, by supplying their pulpits while they are gone.

Lemuel Covell's own journal records that he and Warren set out on August 23 and that he himself was away until December 31.[9] Warren, according to the Association minutes, was gone a month less than Covell.[10] They received fifty dollars each towards their expenses; this sum must have exhausted the funds of the missionary committee, which reported to the Association that total receipts for the year were $99.22. By September 21 the pair had arrived at Buffalo Creek where they met Elkanah Holmes. He had come there from Tuscarora to talk to the Seneca Indians about settling a missionary among them. The discussions lasted for several days, and Holmes was not able to accompany Covell and Warren into Canada when they crossed over to Fort Erie on Saturday, September 24.[11]

At Fort Erie, says Covell, "we put up at Dr. Chapin's, a gentleman from the State of New York who resides there. The Doctor and his lady treated us with the utmost friendship and hospitality." On Sunday, September 25, Covell preached about two miles out of Fort Erie. During the week, from Monday the 26th till Friday the 30th, they toured along the Canadian side of the Niagara River, calling on Archibald Thomson, of Stamford, and on Isaac Swayze, near Newark, where Warren preached. Thomson was a native of Hawick in Roxburghshire, Scotland, who had settled on the Delaware before the American Revolution, and had later come to the township of Stamford, Upper Canada. He was a Presbyterian, and very hospitable to missionaries.[12] Isaac Swayze, a loyalist from New Jersey, served as a member of the Upper Canada legislature from 1792 to 1796 and again from 1800 to 1808.[13]

Covell crossed to the American side on Saturday, October 1, and spent Sunday with Elkanah Holmes at Tuscarora, while his companion stayed on the Canadian side and preached at Stamford. On Monday, October 3, Covell rejoined Warren at Thomson's, and the two of them, in company with "an old Baptist brother named Sloot," who travelled with them for a week, set out westward towards the Long Point and Thames River settlements, holding services along the way wherever they could. Covell wrote:

From Queenston goes the main country road to the head of Lake Ontario which is upwards of 50 miles, and thence, one way, round the head of said Lake to York . . ., and the other way, to Grand River, where it takes various directions, and leads the traveller through an excellent country of vast extent, and many settlements formed and rapidly increasing.

In their whole week's travel between Queenston and Long Point, where they arrived on Saturday, October 8, they had not found a single Baptist church. On this point Covell is explicit, and his words are worth quoting:

We found no church of the Baptist order, though there were a number of brethren in several places. There had, a few years since, been a Baptist church at the Thirty Mile Creek, near 30 miles from Queenston, but they have pretty much lost their visibility, although a number of members still reside there.

At Long Point itself, much preparatory work had already been done by the two lay preachers in that locality, Titus Finch and Peter Fairchild. The coming of Covell and Warren resulted in the establishment of a strong church in the township of Charlotteville. The reception accorded the missionaries and the events of the next nine days are described by Mr. Covell:

At this place we found a number of Christian brethren, who had lived a number of years without the privileges connected with Gospel ordinances for want of an administrator. They had frequently sent the most pressing requests to one and another, but had always been unsuccessful. . . . We spent nine days in the place, every one of which was taken up in preaching and other religious exercises. The people laid aside all worldly business, except works of necessity, and attended meetings in crowds every day during our stay. In these nine days we preached 17 times and heard brother Finch once, baptized 30 persons, gave them fellowship as a church, assisted them in doing some business in church matters, and administered to them the Lord's Supper.

The statement of Caleb Blood, already quoted, that the missionaries had "found a young brother, whom they baptized, and advised the church to improve and encourage him in preaching," is clarified beyond all doubt by Covell's diary, in which, on October 17, 1803, as he was leaving Long Point, he wrote:

There are two brethren who improve in public[14] in that country, by the names of Finch and Fairchild. Brother Fairchild resides at some distance from the body of brethren, but visits them at times. Brother Finch lives among them and labours with them steadily; but neither of them are ordained, and when we arrived there, brother Finch had never been baptized.

Their Long Point visit at an end, Covell and Warren went on Monday, October 17, to Burford, accompanied by Finch and Fairchild. The next day Covell turned back towards Queenston, while Warren and the other two went to the Mohawk settlement on the Grand River and to the "River Retrench" (Thames). Arriving at Archibald Thomson's on Friday, October 21, Covell spent the next nine days between the Indians on the American side and the settlers around Queenston and Newark. On Sunday, October 23, he preached at Tuscarora, and on Monday the 24th at Newark, staying overnight at the home of Isaac Swayze. The rest of that week he spent with Elkanah Holmes and the Indians, remaining to preach to them on Sunday morning, October 30, but that evening he went back to Archibald Thomson's for a service and there found Mr. Warren who had returned from his visit to Oxford on the Thames.

On October 31 Warren went to Newark, while Covell went across the Niagara River and fetched Holmes back with him to Rose's place, where they stayed that night. On November 1 Covell and Holmes held a service at Thomson's, Holmes doing the preaching, and after service Warren arrived back from Newark. All three preachers stayed with the Thomson family that night, and next morning Covell and Warren said farewell to Holmes and their host, made their way to Fort Erie, and were in Buffalo by nightfall. Their Canadian visit for that year was over, and they travelled home across New York State, preaching as they went.

Covell's home-coming to Pittstown on the last day of the year was greeted with acclaim. He preached to a great congregation about his experiences, and the highlight of the occasion was his singing of a hymn, written by himself, and entitled, "Triumphs of Grace in the Wilderness."[15]

In June 1804, the missionary committee of the Shaftsbury Association reported to the annual meeting held at Clifton Park:

. . . during the year they had received ninety-nine dollars and twenty-two cents, including the surplus in our fund at the last session — that they had employed Brother Warren of Salem and Brother Covell, of Pittstown, in a mission through the western country from Cayuga to Long Point, on the north side of Lake Erie, in the Province of Upper Canada — that Brother Warren had spent upwards of three, and Brother Covell upwards of four months in their employ on said mission, for which they had voted them fifty dollars each, towards their expenses — that Brother Covell had made a particular and circumstantial report of their travels and labours, and the prospects of success attending our efforts in those parts; and in particular, that in the town of Charlotte-Ville, at Long Point in Upper Canada, they had baptized thirty persons, and gave them fellowship as a church in sister relation, and that the said church had sent a letter by them to the Association, desiring to be received into their connection, and to be visited by their ministers as often as possible, and that Missionary labours may be continued in that Province; and, likewise, that a very large number of the inhabitants of that Province had sent, by them, a written request that a permanent mission might be established in those parts.

The Association then unanimously approved the action of its missionary committee, voted to receive the church at Long Point into its fellowship, and designated it officially in its records as the "Baptist Church of Christ at Charlotte-Ville." A letter was then addressed to the new Charlotteville church and to the people of Upper Canada in general.

1804

Rev. Joseph Cornell, Rev. Peter P. Roots, & Rev. Hezekiah Gorton

In the fall of 1803 Joseph Cornell, of Galway, N.Y., again took the road on behalf of the Massachusetts Baptist Missionary Society, arranging his trip so as to reach the St. Lawrence River after the ice was strong enough to bear his weight. Before reaching the St. Lawrence, he heard that the Rev. Peter P. Roots was also on his way to this country and hastened to overtake him. Cornell followed Roots over the river at Kingston, where the latter had crossed on February 3, 1804, and travelling westward along Lake Ontario, caught up with him at Haldimand. Here he found Roots in conference with three Canadian ministers, Joseph Winn, of Ameliasburg, Asa Turner, of Thurlow, and Reuben Crandall, of the Cramahe and Haldimand church. These three churches had formed the Thurlow Baptist Association in 1802, first such body in the province. On February 16 and 17, 1804, it held its third annual session.[16] The two visiting missionaries were welcomed to the councils of the tiny organization. Cornell was honoured by appointment to the moderatorial chair, and Roots was elected clerk. In their suddenly assumed official capacities, they found themselves being directed by the Association to send a letter to the Massachusetts Baptist Missionary Society thanking the members for having sent them to the province, and asking that they might be sent again soon!

Up to this point, Roots had apparently been travelling on his own initiative, without the support of any organization, but from now on he and Cornell joined forces for the rest of their tour, and in his report to the Society later Roots wrote of his companion, "I can truly say, the longer I was with him, the more I loved him." Both men wrote full accounts of their trip for publication in the *Massachusetts Baptist Missionary Magazine.*[17]

Having completed their work with the Thurlow Association, they turned back towards Kingston again. Cornell followed the lake shore, while Roots went through the settlements farther north, and obtained several preaching engagements through the courtesy of the Rev. Robert McDowell, the doughty Presbyterian minister who had come to Canada as a missionary of the Dutch Reformed Church in the United States. At Ernestown the two friends met again and preached to audiences that were composed chiefly of Presbyterians and Episcopalians. In Kingston they had difficulty gathering a crowd, but by going about the streets all afternoon and inviting everyone they met, they managed to fill a large room at the home of a shoemaker, and Cornell said "the attention was much greater than we expected."

Leaving Kingston, they went to Bastard Township, and visited Steventown, where Cornell had planted a "little vine" the year before. Here they expected to officiate at the ordination of Daniel Derbyshire, but found that an additional candidate had appeared in the person of Abel Stevens, the founder of the settlement, the validity of whose former ordination in the United States was in question. After suitable examination of these two aspirants to the pastoral office, the ordination took place during the first week in March, amid scenes of great enthusiasm. The number of ordained Baptist ministers in the eastern part of Upper Canada was thus increased to five, though Derbyshire and Stevens, being separated from Winn, Turner, and Crandall by more than one hundred miles, had not yet made their acquaintance. Cornell had attended more than twenty ordinations in his lifetime, but he considered the one at Steventown "the most solemn and impressive" his "poor unworthy soul" had ever experienced.

Leaving Steventown, the two missionaries tramped through deep snow back to the St. Lawrence, and with Abel Stevens as their guide, crossed over to the New York side on March 7. Three days later they parted company, and made their separate ways back to their homes, Cornell to Galway and Roots to Eastport. "Farewell to Canada for the present," Roots had said in his diary of March 6, "I hope, however, to see it again next winter if the Lord will," and see it he did, though he traversed another part of the province on that occasion.

During the fall of 1804, the western part of the province received a visit from a missionary of the Shaftsbury Association. His name was the Rev. Hezekiah Gorton, and he was connected with the Shaftsbury organization from 1798 to 1805, after which he went into central New York State.[18] No journal of his trip through the Niagara Peninsula has been found, but among the minutes of the Association for the following year there is a concise review of his achievements, in the report of the Association's missionary committee:

The missionary work had been prospered during the year, through the labours of Elder Gorton, who spent three months on a tour through the western country as far as Long Point, or Charlotteville, in Upper Canada, and who reported as follows: "That he found the people in general much engaged to hear preaching; that in some places in the Province of Upper Canada they were so anxious to hear the gospel that they would encounter difficulties insurmountable and dangers indescribable to get to meetings for preaching; and there appeared a general solicitude to have us send them missionaries; that he found the church at Charlotteville in trials, but left them in more comfortable circumstances; that there was some revival of religion in that place, and seven persons baptized while he was there; that he also presented a written request from the church and society in that place, and another from a number of inhabitants in other parts of the province earnestly requesting us to send missionaries to visit them as often as possible; and above all, to settle a permanent missionary in that country . . ., manifesting at the same time their willingness to do all in their power to help him with such things as they have to bestow for the comfort of his family."[19]

1805

Rev. Peter P. Roots & Rev. Lemuel Covell

Faithful to the resolution he had made early in the year, Elder Roots left home on December 13, 1804, with a view to paying another visit to Canada, but this time he entered at a different point and covered much more ground.[20] On January 5, 1805, he crossed the Niagara River to Fort Erie, and went on to Queenston, where the hospitality of Archibald Thomson was extended to him as it had been to others before him. He was unable to visit Elkanah Holmes at Tuscarora because of the ice in the river at the crossing point, so he set out for

Charlotteville by way of the head of Lake Ontario. On his return from Long Point he stayed overnight at Burlington with Joseph Brant, who invited him to visit the Mohawks on the Grand River, but he declined because he had just come from that direction. In the area he had covered up till then he had not found any ordained Baptist minister at all, and only a few of other denominations, for some of whom he had not a very high regard, as he says they were "given to wine, card playing, etc."

From Burlington he started around the north side of Lake Ontario, travelling east until he came to a settlement on the Humber River, where he stopped to preach. The next day, January 30, he went on to York, where, he said, there were about one hundred dwelling houses, the first having been built in 1793. In York people were still discussing the dramatic disappearance of the ship *Speedy* in Lake Ontario off Newcastle, and Roots was deeply impressed with the story of this famous tragedy. He wrote in his journal:

On Lord's day the sixth of October last, a number of persons, among whom were some of the principal characters in this country, went on board a vessel at York, bound to Newcastle in another county, to attend court there; but the vessel with all whom it contained (I think twenty-seven persons) was undoubtedly buried in the bottom of the Lake; but nobody knows where. O how sudden the change! Instead of attending an earthly court, they were summoned to the bar of God!

Form York Mr. Roots went north for about thirty miles along Yonge Street, which he found thickly populated, and he attended public worship in several places. He then set out for Kingston, preaching as he went at places where he had made appointments in advance. Owing to a miscalculation in dates, he missed the fourth annual meeting of the Thurlow Baptist Association, which was held at Thurlow on the second Friday in February, but he saw some of their leaders and noted their desire for help from the United States. He was impressed not only with the hunger of the people for spiritual food, but with their need for books and education as well. He paid tribute to the work done by Methodists, but thought the people deserved something more solid in their religious diet than the Arminian doctrines they were being offered. "If the people had sound, evangelical ministers," he said, "many pious people, who are called Methodists, would soon find that their experience differs widely from the Arminian creed." On the first day of March he crossed from Kingston back to New York State, evidently without visiting Steventown where he and his friend Cornell had experienced such refreshing times the year before.

On August 30, 1805, Lemuel Covell left Pittstown on a tour that kept him away for six months, and it was not until March of the following year that he saw his home again. As far as Buffalo, which he reached on October 8, he was accompanied by his friend, the Rev. David Irish, of Aurelius, N.Y., but Mr. Irish turned homeward on October 10 and Covell went on alone. This time he did not cross from Buffalo to Fort Erie, as he had done in 1803, but went down the Niagara River on the American side until he met Elkanah Holmes at Tuscarora Village, and was pleased to find both Mr. and Mrs. Holmes in good health.

On Saturday, October 19, he crossed into Canada, for a stay of two months. He baptized twenty persons, assisted at the organization of the church in Townsend where Peter Fairchild was the lay preacher (a fuller description of this event is given on pages 102-104), and presided over the ordination of Titus Finch, pastor at Charlotteville, whom he had baptized two years before.[21] He was deeply moved by the need for more ministers in Upper Canada, and had several invitations to settle permanently in the province, but his family affairs prevented his doing so. On December 18 he was back at Tuscarora with Mr. and Mrs. Holmes, and from there retraced his steps to Pittstown through the state of New York. At the annual meeting of the Shaftsbury Association in June 1806, held at Troy, N.Y., he presented letters from the churches at Charlotteville and Townsend, and the latter was admitted to membership in the Association. For his six months' work as a missionary Covell received one hundred dollars, but, as we shall see later, his expenses had been so heavy, and the financial return so small, that he was deeply in debt.

1806

Rev. Lemuel Covell & Rev. David Irish

At the Shaftsbury Association meeting in June 1806, Covell volunteered to go on tour again that fall, though he was to move from Pittstown to Cheshire in the meantime. In August he set out, and arrived at the familiar rendezvous in Tuscarora Village on Monday, September 22, where he found David Irish of the Massachusetts Baptist Missionary Society waiting for him. Covell had become ill during his journey, and was so unwell when he reached Tuscarora that Holmes and Mr. Irish kept him there and "treated him in the best manner we were able," as Irish expressed it in his diary.[22] After a day's rest he seemed better, and on Tuesday, September 30, the two men crossed over to

Queenston. The plan was that Holmes should join them later, and that their many appointments should include a visit by Covell and Holmes to the Mohawk settlement on the Grand River. After several engagements near the frontier they proceeded to Clinton on Wednesday, October 1, but Covell was so ill by this time that he had to remain at the home of Jacob Beam and allow Irish to go on by himself next day.

Pursuing his course westward, Irish preached at the head of Lake Ontario, and reached Townsend on Saturday, October 4. Here there was great activity. Services were held several times a day until the following Tuesday, and a number of converts offered themselves for baptism. On Monday, October 6, the church held a business meeting, at which the ordination of Peter Fairchild was proposed and agreed to "without a dissenting voice." Then followed visits to Charlotteville and the Great Bay on Lake Erie where more baptisms took place. On Tuesday, October 21, Mr. Irish was back in Townsend for Fairchild's ordination, a council having been summoned for that purpose. At this meeting, or at the baptismal service which followed it, Irish learned that Covell's illness had become dangerous, and the following day he resolved to leave for Clinton to see for himself how matters stood. When he was twenty miles from Jacob Beam's he learned that Covell had died on October 19, and on his arrival at Clinton, Thursday, October 23, he found that his friend had been buried, and that Elkanah Holmes was at that very moment holding a memorial service, having come from Tuscarora for the purpose.[23]

Though shocked at being left alone, and somewhat depressed in his spirit, Mr. Irish returned almost at once to his work among the people who were clamouring for his services. "Oh how my poor heart felt!" he wrote, "I was left among strangers almost 300 miles from home, and one of the most dear and intimate friends I ever had, taken away in such an unexpected time! But the Judge of all the earth will do right." The church at Townsend received the news of Covell's death with expressions of profound sorrow, and the emotional forces released by this event added power to the spiritual revival that was taking place. So crowded were the days that in order to accommodate the last candidate desiring baptism before Mr. Irish left, they "repaired to the water after nightfall, like Paul and the jailor." Another weekend was spent in Charlotteville, and then visits were made to Oxford on the Thames and to settlements on the Grand River, where more baptisms took place, the first that had ever been witnessed in that community.

Turning back towards Niagara, Mr. Irish passed through Clinton,

Grantham, and Niagara-on-the-Lake, and finally got across the river to Tuscarora. Thither he was pursued by a delegation from Upper Canada, who implored him for one more week of his time, to which he at length consented. The week was spent around Queenston, Grantham, and Niagara, where private dwellings were opened for religious services and several more people were baptized. Writing his report of these events in the month of December, Irish said, "Had I not thought that duty to my family called me home, I would not have left them yet." As it was, he felt that he had done all that could reasonably have been expected of him, and left the province when the week was finished. His tour, which this time had been spent chiefly in Upper Canada, had lasted 72 days, during which he had travelled 800 miles, preached 70 times, and baptized 33 people. For a distance of one hundred miles from Queenston westward he had found much work to be done, with Finch and Fairchild the only Baptist ministers in all that area, and very few ministers of any other denomination. He hoped that the following year he might be able to spend at least six months in Upper Canada.

1807

Rev. Phinehas Pillsbury, Rev. Jesse Hartwell, Rev. Valentine Rathbun & Rev. Asahel Morse

After a short tour in Lower Canada in the month of March 1807, the Rev. Phinehas Pillsbury, employed by the Massachusetts Baptist Missionary Society, followed the south shore of the St. Lawrence across New York State until he came to Lisbon, where he crossed into Upper Canada. Four miles up the river from his crossing point was the village of Johnstown, where he preached. He then rode to Augusta, and there preached a number of times and baptized a young woman. As there was yet no Baptist church in Augusta with which she could unite, he was able only to give her a certificate of her baptism. His next call was Steventown, in the township of Bastard, where he found the Rev. Daniel Derbyshire in charge. While there Mr. Pillsbury baptized a man and his wife. The church, he said, was "somewhat low, but not altogether discouraged." Finding the road through the Twenty Mile Woods in bad condition, he did not go to Kingston, and after visiting several places between the Woods and Johnstown, he returned across the St. Lawrence into New York State on May 28, by way of Oswegatchie, where Prescott now stands.[24]

In the month of August 1807, the Rev. Jesse Hartwell and the Rev.

Valentine Rathbun spent three weeks in Upper Canada on behalf of the Massachusetts Baptist Missionary Society. Few details of their journey are given, but Hartwell stated that he "tarried in the Province twenty-two days, preached thirty-three times, and baptized six persons." From the minutes of the Townsend church we learn that the two men were there from August 27 to 29. Hartwell baptized Rebeckah Perry on the 27th, and Rathbun conducted a "covenant meeting" on the 29th, "when a very agreeable interview took place." On August 30 Mr. Hartwell preached at the home of Jacob Beam, where Covell had died, and such a large crowd assembled that the meeting had to be held out of doors. The pair left Canada on September 7, and while they were spending a few days with Elkanah Holmes at Tuscarora, a missionary from the Shaftsbury Association, the Rev. Asahel Morse, passed through on his way to Upper Canada.[25]

This Baptist missionary to Canada was a very business-like gentleman.[26] A Calvinist in doctrine and strict in his views of church polity, he did his best to "set in order" the affairs of the churches he visited. He was appointed by the Shaftsbury Association at their June meeting to undertake this tour, and he arrived at Clinton on September 24. There he preached in the home of Jacob Beam, now commonly referred to by the missionaries as "the house where brother Covell died." As for the owner of the house, his position in the community is indicated by Mr. Morse's references to him in his journal as "Father Beam," and "Old Father Beam."

The first task which he set himself was to straighten out the affairs of the congregation at Clinton, which he found was not a "regular church in gospel order," since it lacked a proper covenant and possessed no written articles of faith and practice. Unable to stay with its members for very long just then, he proposed to visit them on his return, advising them in the meantime to call a council of church members from Charlotteville and Townsend to consider their case. He then passed on over the usual route by way of the head of Lake Ontario to the Grand River, Townsend, and Charlotteville. These two churches he found to be making satisfactory progress under their pastors, Peter Fairchild and Titus Finch. He next visited Oxford on the Thames, where he held joint meetings with the Methodists, despite his poor opinion of their Arminian theology. Here he baptized a Mr. Burtch; and Captain Sweat and Mr. Haskins offered their homes for services. When he judged the audience unable to follow a doctrinal discourse, he resorted to what he called "sentimental sermons," but hoped they might do some good nevertheless! His last appointment in the Thames River settlements was in the township of Blenheim. On October 16 Mr. Morse was back at Clinton, and met with the council that assembled there that day to organize the church according to proper "gospel order." The members of the church having agreed to accept the doctrinal statements of the Otsego and Shaftsbury Associations as their basis of uniting together, they were constituted a church of the Baptist order and Morse extended to them the right hand of fellowship.

Soon afterwards Mr. Morse left for home, and arrived on November 28. According to his report he was "absent 105 days, travelled almost 1600 miles, attended 115 meetings, preached 101 sermons and heard four." In June 1808, the missionary committee of the Association reported that during the past year "We have employed Brother Asahel Morse three and a half months, for which we have paid him $70.00 . . . ; Brother Morse has made a report to this committee of his mission through the western settlements of New York, into Upper Canada, as far as Long Point."

Elder Morse also submitted a report for publication in the *Massachusetts Baptist Missionary Magazine,* which he concluded by saying, "This was the first tour I ever undertook in a new country, among people of different characters and habits; but can say, the pleasure and satisfaction it has afforded me were greater than I expected." Several years later he penned another account[27] of what he saw on his tour of Upper Canada:

In A.D. 1807, I accepted an invitation to go on a Missionary tour into Upper Canada, given me by the Shaftsbury Baptist Association. I left home the 15th. August, and passed through the Genesee country to Niagara. . . . After visiting in the vicinity and attending several meetings, I went over the Niagara River into Canada, and commenced my labor in that dismal region of moral darkness and the shadow of death.

The face of the country is very level, smooth and easily tilled. The soil is exceedingly rich, and timber, grass, wheat and Indian corn and other vegetables are of the most luxurious growth. A great part of the country lying between Niagara on the east and the River Thames (Letrench) on the west; and the Lakes Ontario and Erie, were covered with white pine, intermixed with some other timber of various kinds. The pines especially towards Grand River where I passed, were far more lofty than any timber in New England. I was informed by a number of respectable men who had cut and measured them, that some of them were more than 250 feet in length.

The body of the people were grossly ignorant. There were but few schools and the most of them of the lowest kind. Many families had no books, not even a Bible. A great part of the inhabitants were the tories, who left the States in the war of the revolution; it is not a great wonder that they were in a wretched condition. Many better inhabitants have taken residence there since.

I was in the province two and thirty days, attended 54 meetings and preached 51 sermons, baptized four persons and gave fellowship to a church in Clinton at Thirty Mile Creek. I viewed the great falls and whirl, so-called, 4 miles below, on both sides of the river. I presume there is not one fourth part of the running water between Boston and the western shore of New York State as there is in that river which pours its mighty flood over the tremendous cataract. I left Canada and returned to Tuscarora, and tarried with father Holmes and in the vicinity near a week; then I set my face homeward.

A sketch of Elder Morse's career and an appraisal of his character will be included in a later chapter, dealing with biographical accounts of missionaries.

1808

Rev. Peter P. Roots, Rev. Clark Kendrick & Rev. Nathaniel Kendrick

The Rev. Peter Roots was employed during the whole of the year 1808 by the Massachusetts Baptist Missionary Society, but he seems to have spent only half of one day in Canada. This brief trip across the border was described by him in a letter to the trustees of the Society on August 13 of that year:

BELOVED FATHERS AND BRETHREN,

I have received your appointment for six months, and, if God permit, I hope to fulfil the same. The following is a brief account of my travels and missionary labours since the commencement of the year A.D. 1808.

The first Lord's day in Jan. I preached near Fort Erie in Canada. Some of the British soldiers attended with the inhabitants, and the whole assembly behaved with propriety, and gave attention to the word. After meeting I crossed Niagara river and preached at Buffaloe in the evening. . . .[28]

No further reference to any Canadian tour appears in Mr. Roots' reports for 1808, so we must conclude that this one flying visit was his only contact with the province that year.

In the autumn of 1808, the Rev. Nathaniel Kendrick, accompanied by his cousin, the Rev. Clark Kendrick, visited Upper Canada, the former being sent by the Shaftsbury Association, and the latter by the Massachusetts Baptist Missionary Society. Clark Kendrick's report contains no details of the places visited, and in it he expresses doubt about the wisdom of attempting work among the Indians. He pays tribute, however, to the people of the province who desired more missionaries to settle among them, and gave it as his opinion that two good men should be sent as soon as possible. They should, he thought, be of outstanding qualities.[29]

Nathaniel, however, wrote not only to the Shaftsbury Association but also to the editor of the *Massachusetts Baptist Missionary Magazine,* and his letters are full of interesting information. From the Niagara River he travelled westward to Townsend, his cousin accompanying him, and a letter from the Townsend church to the Shaftsbury Association, dated September 26, 1808, states, "Our beloved Elders Clark and Nathaniel Kendrick are with us at this time."[30] From the minutes of the Townsend church we learn also that Nathaniel Kendrick preached on September 18 and presided over a business meeting of the church. On September 24 he met with some Baptists at Oxford to consider the formation of a church, but, their numbers being small, they decided to become a branch of the Townsend church (see also page 115).[31]

After this Clark Kendrick returned to the United States, while Nathaniel went around the head of Lake Ontario to York, and visited the Thurlow Association which was in session about seventeen miles from there, probably in Markham (see page 101). He then returned to Niagara and met Elkanah Holmes, who had by this time severed his connection with the Indian work at Tuscarora and was preparing to move his family to Queenston, where a church had been gathered. Formal organization of this congregation into a church took place while Kendrick was there during the third and fourth weeks of October. Holmes at this time was also giving some assistance to the church at Clinton, which Kendrick described as "small and destitute." There was no other Baptist minister within eighty miles of Queenston. Of his tour as a whole, which included a large area of New York State, as well as Upper Canada, Kendrick reported, "I was absent from home eighty-five days, and rode 1280 miles, preached 62 sermons, attended and heard 11 sermons preached by other ministers, attended two church meetings, twice administered the Lord's Supper, baptized two persons, attended several conferences and met with two Associations."[32]

1809

Rev. Nathaniel Kendrick

As far as we know, Nathaniel Kendrick was the only Baptist missionary to come to Upper Canada in 1809. In April of that year the church in Clinton addressed a letter to him suggesting that he visit them during the course of the summer, and, if possible, settle with them as their pastor.[33] "This," said his biographer, "was gratifying

REV. NATHANIEL KENDRICK, D.D.

First President of Colgate University and a prominent missionary to Upper Canada in 1808 and 1809. (From an engraving in *The First Half Century of Madison University, 1819-1869; or, The Jubilee Volume,* 1872)

REV. DANIEL HASCALL, A.M.

A prominent missionary to Upper Canada sent by the Shaftsbury Baptist Association. (From an engraving in *The First Half Century of Madison University, 1819-1869; or, The Jubilee Volume,* 1872)

evidence that his labors in that region, although brief, were highly appreciated."[34] In the fall of 1809 he came to Queenston and Clinton, the latter church appointing a committee "to confer with Elder Kendrick concerning the letter we wrote to him last spring."[35] Nothing came of their proposal, however, and he returned home on November 10.

1810

Rev. Daniel Hascall & Rev. George Witherell

With the year 1810, Baptist missionary tours into Upper Canada ceased until after the War of 1812-14. The Shaftsbury Association minutes for 1811 record that in the previous season the missionary committee had employed "Elder George Witherell as a missionary to the destitute settlements in the western part of the State of New York and the Province of Upper Canada for the term of three months for which we paid him $60 — that we have likewise employed Bro. Daniel Hascall to travel and preach on the same route with Bro. Witherell for 3 mos. for which we paid him $60." The minutes also record that the two missionaries had made an acceptable report of their missions to the committee, but no details of their tour are given.[36] The minute book of the Townsend church contains an entry dated October 21, 1810, which reads, "Sermon by Eld. George Witherill a missionary from the States." It therefore seems reasonable to conclude that these two followed the usual route from the Niagara frontier to Townsend, Charlotteville, and return. In the minute book of the Clinton church it is recorded on November 24, 1810, that "Samuel and Elizabeth Kitchen, baptized of late by Elder Witherill do now present themselves to the church." It would appear that the Kitchens had been baptized by Mr. Witherell at some place other than Clinton, for when they presented themselves to the church for membership they were asked for letters of transfer. Having none, they were admitted on the basis of their "experience."

IV

Baptist Missionary Tours into Upper Canada
1815-1817

THE FOUNDATIONS of Baptist work in Upper Canada were severely shaken by the War of 1812-14. In the eastern part of the province the ranks of the ministers had already been depleted by the removal of Asa Turner, the pioneer of Thurlow, to Scipio, in New York State. Daniel Derbyshire of Steventown had died, and Abel Stevens was now an old man, whose place was not too well filled by his son, Abel Stevens Junior. Reuben Crandall left the Bay of Quinte area to become an itinerant preacher around Townsend and the Talbot settlement, leaving Joseph Winn, of Ameliasburg, whose service dated back to the 1790's, as the only remaining minister in that region.

In the Niagara Peninsula, Elkanah Holmes, who had been strongly anti-British from his youth, welcomed the invading Americans to his home at Queenston, and was in turn obliged to flee the country with them when they were later driven back over the border. In Markham Township the Rev. Elijah Bentley, who had founded the Baptist church there in 1803, gave expression to pro-American sentiments in a sermon preached in May 1813, and was charged with sedition. He was found guilty by a jury at the June Assizes that year, and in addition to being sentenced to jail for six months, he was bound over to keep the peace for five years.

These disturbances greatly weakened the churches where they occurred. The depletion of ministerial ranks by the defection of Holmes and Bentley, the death of Derbyshire, and the removal of Turner to the United States put the main burden of maintaining the Baptist cause in Upper Canada during the war years upon the shoulders of the three original loyalist pioneers. Finch at Charlotteville, Fairchild at Townsend, and Joseph Winn at the Bay of Quinte remained staunchly at their posts. Reuben Crandall was engaged in itinerant work during this period, and other help was given by a number of licensed preachers not yet ordained, but the lack of leadership was all but disastrous in many places.

On the American side of the border, also, there were divided loyalties. That the war was exceedingly unpopular in Maine and New Eng-

land is well known. Christian people in the United States felt deeply
the breaking of ties with their brethren in this country, and regretted
that war cut off communication with them. Of the Baptist churches
in Canada, David Benedict, the historian, had to say regretfully:
"What is their state since this Canadian war commenced, I have not
learnt."[1] The circular letter of the Shaftsbury Association for the year
1812 was written by Obed Warren, who saw in the war a sign of God's
displeasure with his country, and the logical result of the discord between neighbours, the covetousness, extortion, and love of luxury
which had accompanied the increase of wealth in the United States.[2]
The letter went on to say:

> We have been visited with the judgments of war and pestilence with
> which God was pleased in ancient times to chastise sinful and idolatrous
> nations; and it may be truly said as it was of Israel, "yet have ye not
> returned unto me, saith the Lord," . . . .
> It is not our business, as messengers of the churches, or ministers of the
> gospel, to enquire into the political causes which involved our nation in a
> war, but it is our duty . . . to search for and find out the moral causes which
> have procured this divine displeasure.
> As citizens of the United States, pray for the peace and prosperity of the
> nation, and act a rational and candid part in promoting its welfare, for in
> the peace of our country *we* may enjoy peace.

During the war years the *Massachusetts Baptist Missionary Magazine* continued to publish news of the work done by Baptists in Britain
as though the two nations were at peace. The progress of William
Carey's mission in India was fully reported, and the magazine included
long letters from Carey himself to friends in the United States. Correspondence from British Baptist leaders like Andrew Fuller appeared
regularly in its columns, and signs of progress in Britain were hailed
as providing an example to be followed in America.[3] An address delivered on behalf of the Baptist Academical Institution at Stepney
Green, near London, was printed in full, "as calculated to answer
truly valuable purposes in these United States, and as an incentive to
the American Baptists to come forward and do likewise."[4]

At the annual meeting of the Massachusetts Baptist Missionary
Society in Boston in May 1813, the trustees reported that during the
year they had "aided brother Reis from Nova Scotia, who has been
stirred up to leave his family and country to preach the Gospel to the
destitute in New Orleans and adjacent parts of that country." Along
with this account of missionary activity which surmounted the bar-
riers raised by war, the report carried a fervently expressed hope that
hostilities would soon be at an end.

The Shaftsbury Association, too, was anxious to re-establish contact with the churches of Upper Canada. Four of these, Clinton, Charlotte-ville, Townsend, and Oxford, had been connected with that body before the war, receiving fairly regular visits from its missionaries and reporting to it at intervals by sending letters. In 1814, while the war was still in progress, the Association named the Rev. Stephen Olmstead and the Rev. Peter Brown as missionaries to visit Upper Canada if possible.[5] There is no record, however, of their having done so. It was not until 1815 that the first post-war missionary tour was made into this province, after a lapse of nearly five years.

1815

Rev. Stephen Olmstead, Rev. Cyrus Andrews & Rev. Nathan Baker

Though Stephen Olmstead apparently did not get as far as Upper Canada in 1814, the minutes of the Clinton (Beamsville) church make it clear that he and Cyrus Andrews reached there in September 1815. The occasion was the calling of a council to consider the ordination of Samuel Burdick, and Mr. Olmstead and Mr. Andrews were chosen as moderator and clerk, respectively. Invited to a seat on the ordina-tion council was another visiting missionary, the Rev. Nathan Baker, who was present as a representative of the Hamilton Missionary Society of New York State.

The candidate, Burdick, was a member of the Clinton church who had been exercising his preaching gifts in the presence of his fellow members. When the Niagara (Queenston) church was left without a minister by the flight of Elkanah Holmes, Burdick preached there frequently.[6] It would seem that at the beginning he was there on trial, for the Queenston people were asked to report to Clinton on the quality of his services. Unable to decide at first what they thought of his efforts, the Queenston folk at length reported very favourably, with the result that in 1813 and 1814 he was engaged to preach "half the sabbaths" at Clinton, and also to take care of the church building; he received one hundred dollars per year for his services.

Brother Burdick's hope of being ordained was doomed to dis-appointment. The council listened with kindness and pleasure to the statement of his Christian experience and call to the ministry, but on hearing his views of Scripture doctrine decided that it would be un-wise just then to set him apart for the pastoral office:

We have a general satisfaction with respect to the experience of Bro. Burdick, his call to the ministry and his doctrinal knowledge as far as he has been led, but notwithstanding, it is our opinion that his opportunity of acquaintance with the scriptures and with Human Nature in general have not been sufficient to warrant us in proceeding with his ordination at this time. We hope, however, the Chh. will continue to encourage him in his public improvement, and that a little more opportunity and experience may prepare him for the sacred office.[7]

In February 1816, Mr. Burdick, at his own request, was granted a letter of dismission from the Clinton church, and his name disappears from the record. The three missionaries from the United States, so far as is known, went no further into Upper Canada at that time, but returned home when the deliberations of the ordination council were completed.

1816

Rev. John Upfold

In the spring of 1816 the Niagara Peninsula was visited by a representative of the Hamilton Missionary Society, Elder John Upfold, whose career will be considered in more detail in another chapter. Mr. Upfold was a native of England, and well educated. His arrival in Clinton is recorded in the church minute book, and later entries also mention his presence there:

April 6th, 1816 — Elder John Upfold being present on a Mission, we requested him to break bread to us on the following Lord's Day, which was done accordingly.

August 3rd. — Church met by appointment; after prayer proceeded to business. Eld. Upfold being present on a Mission we chose him Moderator. Invite Eld. Upfold to break bread with us the next Lord's Day.

Nov. 9th, 1816 — Chh. met agreeable to appoint. After prayer proceeded to business. fst. — Voted to Receive Elder John Upfold.

The story behind these brief notes is that Mr. Upfold, at the conclusion of his mission that fall, settled with the Clinton church as its minister. On the day that the church voted to receive him he signed the membership roll in his own beautiful handwriting. The name of Jane Upfold appears after his, and against it the word "deceased" (spelled "diseast") has been written by a later hand. Elder Upfold remained nine years at Clinton before returning to the United States.[8]

1817

Rev. Timothy Sheppard & Rev. Charles Lahatt

Very little attention was paid to the Baptist churches in the eastern part of Upper Canada by American missionary societies after the War of 1812-14. Immigration from the British Isles was soon to flow into the Ottawa valley, bringing Baptist people into the new townships that were being opened up from the interprovincial boundary westward along the Ottawa River. Meanwhile the churches in the Bay of Quinte region and northeast of Kingston maintained their existence and sought closer fellowship by re-forming their associational groupings.

In December 1816, a spiritual awakening on a small scale took place in Hamilton, Cramahe, and Haldimand townships, and a number of people were baptized by Joseph Winn. This revival, according to J. T. Dowling,[9] continued for several weeks, in response to the Rev. Timothy Sheppard who had come up from the United States.

About the first of February [1817], Elder Shepherd came as a missionary from the States and baptized many in Haldimand and Hamilton, and many after converts dated their first awakenings to his preaching. About the first of March, a meeting was held at the "Four Corners" (now known as Wicklow), where the Baptist professors in Christ agreed "to form themselves into a church, to walk together in love and unity, and to watch over each other for good." The record of this event bears date of the fourth of March, 1817.

It is not clear from Dowling's account that Elder Sheppard, the missionary from the United States, was actually present at the meeting on March 4, 1817, when the organization of the Haldimand church took place, but it seems plain that its independent existence, as distinct from its earlier status as a branch of Cramahe, was due in large measure to the impulse given by his visit to that neighbourhood. In a report of the Hamilton (N.Y.) Baptist Missionary Society, dated Feburary 24, 1819, the Rev. Timothy Sheppard is named as one of fifteen missionaries who had recently been in the employ of the Society, and his term of service is given as fifteen weeks.[10] The report added, "Some of our missionaries . . . have found their way into Upper Canada and made known the Word of God in the regions around Lake Ontario."

By the year 1817, as we have seen, there were five churches in Upper Canada in fellowship with the Shaftsbury Association, including Talbot Street (Aylmer), which had come into being the year before, and the four earlier ones, Charlotteville, Townsend, Clinton, and Oxford, which had been in the Association before the war. From 1813 to 1816, according to the statistical reports published by the Association, returns from these churches had been very irregular; indeed some of them sent none at all.

Baptist Missionary Tours into Upper Canada

Missionary	Year	Sponsor	Area covered
Andrews, Cyrus	1815	Shaftsbury Assoc.	Niagara Peninsula
Baker, Nathan	1815	Hamilton M.S.	Niagara Peninsula
Blood, Caleb	1802	Shaftsbury Assoc.	Niagara Peninsula, around Lake Ontario probably as far as York
Cornell, Joseph	1803	Mass. B.M.S.	Kingston and Steventown
	1804		Thurlow Assoc., Kingston, and Steventown
Covell, Lemuel	1803	Shaftsbury Assoc.	Niagara Peninsula, Long Point, and Thames River
	1805		Niagara Peninsula and Long Point
	1806		Niagara Peninsula
Gorton, Hezekiah	1804	Shaftsbury Assoc.	Niagara Peninsula and Long Point
Hartwell, Jesse	1807	Mass. B.M.S.	Niagara Peninsula and Long Point
Hascall, Daniel	1810	Shaftsbury Assoc.	Niagara Peninsula and Long Point
Holmes, Elkanah	1801-1808	New York, M.S.	Grand River and Niagara Peninsula
Irish, David	1806	Mass. B.M.S.	Niagara Peninsula and Long Point
Kendrick, Clark	1808	Mass. B.M.S.	Niagara Peninsula and Long Point
Kendrick, Nathaniel	1808	Shaftsbury Assoc.	Niagara Peninsula, Long Point, York, and Thurlow Assoc.
	1809	None	Niagara Peninsula
Lahatt, Charles	1817	Shaftsbury Assoc.	Niagara Peninsula, Long Point, Thames River, and Talbot Settlement
Morse, Asahel	1807	Shaftsbury Assoc.	Niagara Peninsula, Long Point, and Thames River
Olmstead, Stephen	1815	Shaftsbury Assoc.	Niagara Peninsula
Pillsbury, Phinehas	1807	Mass. B.M.S.	Steventown and district
Rathbun, Valentine	1807	Mass. B.M.S.	Niagara Peninsula and Long Point
Roots, Peter P.	1804	None	Thurlow Assoc., Kingston, and Steventown
	1805	None	Niagara Peninsula, Long Point, York, Yonge St., Thurlow Assoc., and Kingston
	1808	Mass. B.M.S.	Niagara Peninsula
Sheppard, Timothy	1817	Hamilton M.S.	Haldimand Assoc.
Upfold, John	1816	Hamilton M.S.	Niagara Peninsula
Warren, Obed	1803	Shaftsbury Assoc.	Niagara Peninsula, Long Point, and Thames River
Witherell, George	1810	Shaftsbury Assoc.	Niagara Peninsula and Long Point

With a view to clarifying the relationship of these churches to the Association, the Rev. Charles Lahatt, one of its most active missionaries, was sent to Upper Canada in the autumn of 1817. References to his visit are found in the minutes of the Townsend and Oxford churches. The Townsend record reads, *"Oct. 7th., 1817* — Conferred with Elder Lahatt a missionary from the States relative to our situation with the Association. Agreed to send a letter." The annual report of the Shaftsbury Association for that year shows that the letter was sent in due course, and that it was delivered by Elder Lahatt in person.

On October 4, 1817, a council had met at Oxford to consider the ordination of Simon Mabee to the ministry, and after proper deliberation resolved to accept him. A few days later Elder Lahatt arrived at Oxford and proceeded to ordain Mr. Mabee.[11] (This event is also described on page 116.) Mr. Lahatt's wide connection with American Baptist institutions is shown by the fact that on this visit he considered himself to be the official representative of at least three missionary organizations: the Northern Missionary Society in the State of New York, the Foreign and Domestic Missionary Society of New York City, and the Missionary Committee of the Shaftsbury Association. His connection with the Foreign and Domestic Missionary Society is explained by the fact that he had spent several years of his ministerial life in the immediate vicinity of New York City. At the time of his visit to Upper Canada he was pastor at Pittstown, one of the leading churches of the Shaftsbury Association.

Lahatt's visit revealed to the bodies he represented that the time had now come for the Canadian churches to establish their own associational relations with each other, and to relinquish their connections with the United States. Even before the War of 1812, the churches in the western part of the province had been accustomed to meet occasionally for conference, and as early as 1810 Clinton was a favourite centre for such gatherings.[12] More formal organization of the "Clinton Conference," raising it to the status of an association in everything but name, took place in 1816,[13] and in 1818 the Shaftsbury Association took specific action to dismiss its five Canadian churches to this new body.[14] In the eastern part of the province, the old Thurlow Association, in existence since 1802, and the first such body to be formed by Ontario Baptists, took on new life and was reorganized as the Haldimand Association in 1819.

With the dismissal of five churches from the Shaftsbury Association to the Clinton Conference in 1818, and the gathering of six more churches, Haldimand, Cramahe, Ameliasburg, Sidney, Thurlow, and Rawdon into the newly formed Haldimand Association in 1819, we reach the end of the first distinct period of development in the history of the early Baptists of Ontario. The American Baptist Home Missionary Society was to spend considerable sums of money in Upper Canada for many years to come, but the era of the itinerant part-time missionary, who left his own work in the United States for a few months each year at the behest of his local association to go on tour into this province, was now practically at an end. From 1820 onwards, we encounter new circumstances and enter upon a different period of the Baptist history.

V

The Missionaries

OF THE TWENTY-TWO MISSIONARIES named in the preceding chapters as having visited Upper Canada before 1820, at least twelve were men of sufficient prominence in the Baptist denomination to warrant more detailed study of their individual careers. Two of the twelve, Elkanah Holmes and John Upfold, became pastors of churches in the province, and biographical sketches of them will be included in the chapter dealing with the work of the first settled ministers. The remaining ten to be considered at this point are Caleb Blood, Joseph Cornell, Lemuel Covell, Daniel Hascall, David Irish, Nathaniel Kendrick, Charles Lahatt, Asahel Morse, Peter P. Roots and Obed Warren. What manner of men were these?

Caleb Blood (1754-1814)

The bearer of this striking name was born at Charlton, in Worcester County, Massachusetts, on August 18, 1754. He experienced conversion at the age of twenty-one and became a church member at that time. The author of *The Pilgrim's Progress* heard a voice suddenly dart from heaven into his soul while he was in the midst of a game of Cat on the Sabbath: Caleb Blood is said to have received his first serious impressions of religion "amidst the gaieties of the ball room." About eighteen months after his conversion he began to preach, and is believed to have been licensed by his home church, whose minister was the Rev. Nathaniel Green.

After a short period of apprenticeship, during which his preaching efforts were evidently acceptable to the churches in the vicinity of Charlton, Mr. Blood paid a visit to the church at Marlow, New Hampshire, where he was ordained in 1777 at the age of twenty-three. Remaining in Marlow for only two years, he then went to Weston in Massachusetts, for another short pastorate of two years' duration. His next move was to Newton, near Boston, in 1781, where a new church had been organized the year before. Here he remained seven years and, during this period, his great powers came to full maturity.

In 1788 he accepted a call to Shaftsbury, Vermont, and in this ministry he gave vigorous leadership to the Baptist cause over a period of nineteen years. In Shaftsbury he organized the Fourth Baptist Church, which grew under his care until it reached a membership of over four hundred. During his pastorate of this congregation, several revivals took place, the most noteworthy being in the winter of 1798-99, when nearly two hundred people were received into the church. In addition to his work as minister of his own congregation, Mr. Blood was prominent in the work of the Shaftsbury Association. Nine times he was elected moderator of this body; on five occasions he was the preacher of the annual sermon to its members, and twice he was appointed to write the Association's circular letter to the churches.[1]

During his years at Shaftsbury, Mr. Blood's name became known far afield, and this reputation was due not only to his great success in his own pastorate, but to his missionary journeys and to service rendered by him beyond the bounds of his own denomination. As an itinerant missionary to outlying settlements he travelled many thousands of miles without thought of monetary reward; often he did not receive enough to cover his expenses. In 1802, as we have seen, he visited Upper Canada, and created such a favourable impression among the people that Nathaniel Kendrick, who followed him six years later over the same route, could report that everywhere Mr. Blood had visited he was "held in grateful remembrance."[2] When the University of Vermont was founded in 1791, Mr. Blood became a trustee, serving in that capacity until 1808.[3] Out of twenty-one names submitted to the legislature for the appointment of the first trustees of this new university, his was one of the ten to be chosen.[4] In 1792 he was asked to preach the Election Sermon before the legislature, and fittingly spoke on the qualities to be desired in magistrates.[5] "A wise magistrate," he advised, "will set a constant guard over the words of his mouth, that, with a becoming moderation, he may express his resentment of injuries done him, and have all his language such as shall tend to prevent others from an uncivil, profane way of treating their fellow citizens."

In 1807 he was invited to take charge of the newly formed Third Baptist Church in Boston, and though handicapped by illness during the three years of his ministry there, he left his mark upon the Baptist life of that city. Jonas Galusha, one-time governor of Vermont, was a member of his congregation, and a son of Jonas, Elon Galusha, entered the Baptist ministry. In 1810 Mr. Blood accepted a call to the First Baptist Church in Portland, Maine, his last charge. There, in 1814, after three months' illness, he died content, saying to his friends, "I have done the work and finished the ministry which I have received." During his Portland ministry a large new building had been erected to house the congregation of the First Baptist Church, and the sermon he delivered at the opening of the new meeting house on July 11, 1811, was afterwards published.[6]

Though Caleb Blood's preaching was of the type that produced revivals in the local church, he had a reputation for discouraging excessive emotionalism. It is said that once, when attending a meeting marked by great excitement, a member of the congregation said to him, "Oh, Mr. Blood, did you ever see such a meeting before?" "No," he replied, "and I hope I never shall again." He prepared his sermons very carefully, but did not read them verbatim, preaching from notes instead. Like F. W. Robertson of Brighton, when he wished to preserve his sermons, he wrote them out in full after they had been delivered.

Calvinistic in doctrine, Mr. Blood seems to have read fairly widely in theology and in the Baptist literature of his time. In addition to the sermons which found their way into print he also wrote *Historical Facts recorded for the Benefit of Youth* (known to us through a later edition reprinted in 1822), and a treatise on Baptist doctrine.[7] To this latter work, published after his death, a foreword was added by an anonymous friend, who summed up his career by describing him simply as "a pious, useful man." This, surely, was modest enough praise for one of his stature and achievements.

Joseph Cornell (1747-1826)

Elder Joseph Cornell may be regarded as an excellent example of a self-educated farmer-preacher, who, through diligent use of his native gifts, came to occupy an honoured place in the full-time ministry of his denomination. Son of Elisha Cornell, he was born at Swansea, Massachusetts, on February 11, 1747. Converted at the age of nineteen, he was baptized and received into the church at Swansea by the Rev. Russell Mason, but fourteen years were to elapse between the time of his joining the church and the date of his ordination at Lanesborough in 1780. From 1780 to 1794 he was pastor of the church in Manchester, Vermont, and it was at a gathering of representatives held in his barn at Manchester that the Vermont Baptist Association was organized in 1785.[8]

In 1794 Mr. Cornell went to the Second Baptist Church in Galway, New York, but it is uncertain how long he remained officially as pastor of that congregation.[9] Two years later, in 1796, we find him at Providence, New York, presiding over the ordination of a gifted young man, by trade a blacksmith, named Lemuel Covell, who was later to give his life while engaged in missionary work in Upper Canada. In 1802, while still living in Galway, Cornell accepted appointment from the newly organized Massachusetts Baptist Missionary Society, and in 1803 he undertook the trip into Upper Canada that resulted in the organization of the church at Steventown, Leeds County, that same year. On his second trip in 1804, accompanied by Peter Roots, he again visited Steventown, as well as the annual meeting of the Thurlow Association, and presided over the ordination of Abel Stevens and Daniel Derbyshire.

There is reason to believe that, after his term of service with the Massachusetts Baptist Missionary Society, he may have held a pastorate of considerable length in Providence, Rhode Island, but here also the records are somewhat conflicting, and it may have been Providence, New York. In any case, by 1812 he was back in Galway, where he remained until 1821. In the latter year he entered the service of the Hamilton Baptist Missionary Society and continued in it until his death in 1826.

It was said of Cornell that "he was wholly self-taught, — notwithstanding this, his language was generally well selected," and certainly his reports to the missionary societies that employed him bear out this estimate of his ability. He knew how to think, speak, and write clearly. His views of churchmanship were logical and sound. He had a high conception of the ministry and would not ordain Abel Stevens and Daniel Derbyshire until it could be done "agreeably to gospel rule." A further tribute paid to him by his friends John Peck and John Lawton is worthy of quotation: "Unlike many of his age and circumstance with reference to literary acquirements, he was a warm and decided friend of education, and of those institutions which have in view the education of persons for the ministry."

It was the good fortune of Baptists in Upper Canada to have had some contact with this sane and devoted missionary during the formative period of church life. His high ideals, and those of men like him, were not, unfortunately, always followed by the Baptists of Ontario in later years.

Lemuel Covell (1764-1806)

This remarkable man was in many respects the most outstanding personality among all the Baptist missionaries who had a part in the evangelizing of Upper Canada. He was born on June 28, 1764, at Nine

Partners, Dutchess County, New York, in a locality where Baptist influence was strong in early days. His father died when he was four years of age, and his mother, who married again, was later murdered by her second husband. Lemuel was reared by his maternal grandfather, whose name was Payne. He was taught to read by his grandmother but, by the time he was fourteen, he had received only six weeks of formal schooling. He was then apprenticed to a blacksmith, and as a part of his training he was given the privilege of attending school for a short course of eleven evenings' instruction in order that he might "learn to cipher."

At the age of twenty-one Covell went into business for himself as a blacksmith at Shaftsbury, Vermont, and remained there for two years. He then went to live for a time with an uncle, Simeon Covell, in Lower Canada, and while there underwent a religious experience which he later described as "a change in heart." In 1789 he returned to New York State and married Clarissa Mather of Galway, intending to make his home in Lower Canada. He gave up this idea, however, and remained in Galway for ten years. He had said to friends at various times that he thought he would like to be a Presbyterian minister, "but not one of those New Lights." Despite these remarks, he joined the Third Baptist Church in Galway, and there he preached his first sermon in 1792. That he had a gift worth "improving in public" was recognized by his fellow church members, and he was licensed to preach by his own church in 1793. From that time on he preached regularly, at the same time supporting himself by his trade. He was invited to become pastor of the Fourth Baptist Church, Galway, in 1796, and was ordained on May 11 of that year, at the age of thirty-two.

Early in 1799 he moved to First Baptist Church, Pittstown, New York, and there he accomplished in seven short years more than many men achieve in a lifetime. Plunging into the work of the Shaftsbury Association, Covell prepared its circular letter in 1799 and was elected clerk in 1800. His church gave him neither salary nor living quarters, and in 1801 he purchased a large house with a small farm adjoining, but his livelihood, such as it was, came from whatever work he was able to do in his blacksmith shop in his spare time. In 1803, as already described, he toured Upper Canada with Obed Warren, preaching almost daily throughout the period of that journey. At Long Point he baptized thirty people and organized the Charlotteville church, which was admitted to the Shaftsbury Association the following spring.

For these long absences from home on missionary work Mr. Covell did not receive enough money to cover his expenses, and in 1805 he found that he was in debt to the extent of seven hundred dollars, a large sum for those days. Aroused to a sense of their responsibility at last, his congregation at Pittstown offered to pay off his debt provided he would promise not to move to another church. To this he agreed, but obtained the one concession from his people that he should be free to accept a call to any church that was willing to refund the seven hundred dollars to Pittstown! His financial burdens lightened for a time, he volunteered to go to Canada again in August that year, and undertook the long tour that kept him away from home until March 1806.

On his return to Pittstown he was called to the church in Cheshire, Massachusetts, which was so eager to obtain his services that it paid off the sum demanded by Pittstown as a condition of his release, and consented to his going on another missionary trip to outlying settlements that same fall. It was on this journey, as we have seen, that he took ill and died at the home of Jacob Beam in Clinton Township, Upper Canada on Sunday, October 19, 1806. He lies buried in the Baptist cemetery at Beamsville, Ontario. It was Nathaniel Kendrick who broke the sad news of Covell's death to the widow and her children, one of whom, a daughter, had attended his school in Lansingburgh. Financial assistance for the bereaved family came from both the Shaftsbury Association, which Covell had served so faithfully, and the nearby Warren Association of Massachusetts and Rhode Island. When Mr. Kendrick visited Clinton in 1808 he reported that Covell's grave was surrounded by a "decent fence," and that a monument had been erected by the people there.

The death of Lemuel Covell at the early age of forty-two, after only nine years as an ordained minister, called forth expressions of sorrow and regret wherever his name was known among Baptist people. Eager, intense, and energetic, he literally wore himself out in the effort to make his life count for the advancement of the Baptist cause. Reading his careful reports of his missionary journeys, written from day to day as he travelled, one realizes that such a schedule could not be followed for very long without serious physical results in any but the strongest of men. A close friend described him thus:

Below common stature, and of good proportions . . . he became very thin and spare . . . complexion dark, and dark blue eyes, of deep and penetrating look, features rather strongly marked, he ever exhibited great neatness and propriety of dress.

Covell's power as a preacher is beyond dispute, and can only be explained by the fact that he strove incessantly to cultivate his talent to the point where his lack of formal education might be to some extent overcome. Credited by his daughter with "an innate sense of propriety which enabled him to speak grammatically," he must have laboured hard to achieve the clarity of style and diction shown in his writings. "Preaching," said a writer in the *Massachusetts Baptist Missionary Magazine,* "was his element. His subjects were judiciously chosen, and his arrangements natural and clear. His voice was clear and majestic, and his address manly and engaging. He lived the religion he professed, and wherever he was known was highly and universally esteemed."

Another commentator, writing twenty-one years after Covell's death, showed again the measure of respect he had earned. "He was indeed a flaming herald of the Cross. There are many yet living who cherish for him a most affectionate and grateful remembrance. He now slumbers in the dust of Canada at Clinton. . . . He died universally beloved and lamented." From all the evidence available, it would appear that Lemuel Covell was an utterly selfless Christian man, who gave his all to the cause in which he so earnestly believed, and in his self-giving he inspired to a remarkable degree the love and respect of his acquaintances.

Daniel Hascall (1782-1852)

The Rev. Daniel Hascall, A.M., who toured Upper Canada on behalf of the Shaftsbury Association in 1810, was born at Bennington, Vermont, on February 24, 1782. His father was a Baptist, and his mother a Congregationalist. The foundations of his theological training were laid at home through his study of the Westminster Confession and catechism under the tutelage of his parents. In Pawlet, Vermont, where the family moved in 1785, he went to school in the winter months and made good use of the small public library in the village. His education was assisted by study at home and, at eighteen years of age, he was able to qualify as a school teacher. Meanwhile, he had been baptized and had united with the church in Pawlet.

In 1803, at the age of twenty-one, Mr. Hascall entered the sophomore class at Middlebury College. He graduated in arts in 1806, and the next two years were spent in teaching at Pittsfield, Massachusetts, and in the private study of theology. In 1808 he was ordained as pastor of the church at Elizabethtown, New York, and took an interest in the work of the Lake Baptist Missionary Society. For this body he not only went on tour as a missionary, but also acted as editor of its magazine, the *Vehicle*, later called the *Western Baptist Magazine*, and ultimately merged with the *New York Baptist Register*.

The Lake Baptist Missionary Society, it will be recalled, was organized in Hamilton, New York, and later changed its name to the Hamilton Baptist Missionary Society. To Hamilton, in 1813, Mr. Hascall went as pastor of the Baptist church; in addition to his ministerial duties he continued to do some teaching, and shared in the editing of a periodical called the *Christian Magazine*. Deeply concerned about the problem of educating young men for the ministry, he began to gather them to his home for instruction in 1815, and the following year he discussed with his friend Nathaniel Kendrick the possibility of establishing a literary and theological institution somewhere in central New York State. In 1817 he and twelve others founded the Baptist Education Society of the State of New York, and in February 1818 the first student, Jonathan Wade, was admitted by the executive committee of the Society to what they termed "the privileges of the institution." Actually, there was as yet no "institution," and Mr. Wade simply studied under Mr. Hascall's personal direction.

By 1819, however, the Baptist Education Society of the State of New York was incorporated by an act of the New York legislature, and a charter was granted for the establishment of a school of learning, which, it was decided, should be located at Hamilton. In May 1820, the school was formally opened in the third storey of a brick building, the two lower floors being occupied by a district school and by an academy. Hascall was elected principal and professor of rhetoric in the new Literary and Theological Institution. He had six students at the time of opening, the first of the many who attended what later came to be called Madison, and still later, Colgate University.

Hascall was able to obtain some help from Professor Zenas Morse, who conducted the academy on the floor below his theological school, and in 1821 he was joined by Nathaniel Kendrick, who became professor of theology. Hascall himself was now appointed professor of ancient languages, and continued to hold in addition the chair of rhetoric. In 1828 he relinquished his pastoral duties entirely, and devoted himself wholly to teaching; at this time he transferred from the chair of ancient languages to that of natural philosophy. By his heroic efforts and under his personal supervision, three separate buildings had been added to the physical equipment of the Institution between 1823 and 1827. In 1835 he left his professorial work at Hamilton and gave his attention to promoting the interests of the academy at Florence, New York, and later, those of the Vermont Baptist Convention. Some years later, in 1848, he again accepted a pastorate, at Lebanon, New York, but the following year went back to Hamilton where so much of his life's work had been done.

In the jubilee volume celebrating the first fifty years of Madison University there is recounted at length the story of the great controversy of 1848-50 which resulted from the proposal to move the Literary and Theological Institution from Hamilton to Rochester. In this debate Hascall, as might be expected, took a leading part: he held firm against removal, and even obtained a court injunction restraining those who wished to take such action. Though his health was failing at the time he prophesied to his friends, "I shall live to see this conflict end and the Institution saved, then I shall die." This proved to be quite an accurate prediction, and death came to him in June 1852. On his monument in the cemetery on the hill overlooking Colgate University are engraved the words spoken by him when he took his stand against the transfer to Rochester:

Illa non movebitur — It shall not be moved.

During his active career as a preacher and teacher Mr. Hascall published several sermons, a treatise on baptism,[10] a small work on theology for family reading, and a little book for use in Sunday schools. His contact with Baptist work in Upper Canada was, in a sense, fleeting, consisting as it did of one brief tour made in 1810, when he was but a young minister, not long out of university. In another sense, his contribution to Canadian Baptist work has been an imperishable one, for it was in the school founded by him that Daniel McPhail and Robert Alexander Fyfe were to receive the higher education that was to equip them for the magnificent work done by them at a later date in this country.

David Irish (1757-1815)

David Irish, who accompanied Lemuel Covell to Upper Canada in the fall of 1806, and who, when Covell fell ill, carried out the main part of that mission by himself, was a man after Covell's own heart. He was born at Paulingstown, New York, on December 21, 1757. At the age of seventeen he joined the Baptist church at Dover, where Elder Waldo was minister; by 1776, when he was but nineteen years of age, he had, as one of his friends expressed it, "settled himself in marriage." Leaving Dover in 1782, he moved to Stillwater, and joined the church of which Lemuel Powers was the minister. The two men formed a close friendship, and encouraged by Mr. Powers, Irish began to prepare himself for the ministry. He preached his first sermon on his thirtieth birthday.

In 1789, at the age of thirty-two, Mr. Irish moved to Lanesborough, where he was ordained as pastor in the following year. He returned to Stillwater, however, in 1791, and gained very valuable experience in the ministry as Lemuel Powers' assistant. This happy arrangement lasted for three years, at the end of which, in 1794, Irish went to Scipio, New York, and founded a Baptist church. From this centre he made many trips into the surrounding country, and did much to evangelize the pioneer settlements on the outskirts of civilization. In the year 1800 he founded another church at Aurelius, a town not far from Scipio, and there he made his home until his death in 1815.

For many years Mr. Irish was in close touch with the missionary committee of the Shaftsbury Association, and it was under their auspices that he went with Lemuel Covell to Upper Canada in 1806. In his ability to preach every day of the week, and at the same time to travel several miles daily on foot, he resembled his doughty companion. He reported that in seventy-two days he had preached seventy times and had baptized thirty-three people, while travelling a daily average of twelve miles. When the Lake Baptist Missionary Society was organized at Hamilton in 1807, it was only natural that such a well-known missionary preacher as David Irish should be elected as one of its original directors.

It is in his own reports of his missionary tours, rather than in the written tributes of his acquaintances, that we catch the most intimate picture of Mr. Irish: of these reports, that of the tour made with Lemuel Covell in 1806 shows him at his best. There is no doubt that by his visits to the infant churches on that occasion, and by his ordaining of Peter Fairchild to the ministry, he gave a sorely needed stimulus to Baptist work in Upper Canada. In view of his enthusiasm and energy, it is not surprising to read of him that "there were few places in western New York and Upper Canada where his name was not known."

Nathaniel Kendrick, D.D. (1777-1848)

One of the most prominent Baptist leaders in the United States to take an interest in missionary work among pioneer settlements in Upper Canada was Nathaniel Kendrick, who was the second professor named to the faculty of the Hamilton Literary and Theological

Institution, and later became its first president when that office was created in 1836. Dr. Kendrick was born at Hanover, New Hampshire, on April 22, 1777, of Congregationalist parents. Reared on a farm, he attended a local academy, and at the age of twenty was teaching school. Through revival services held in a nearby Baptist church, he was converted, and after careful consideration decided to be baptized in 1798.

For the next five years he continued to live at home, helping with the farm work, teaching school, and studying in his spare time. He arranged with the Rev. Mr. Burroughs, of Hanover, for tutoring in some of his studies, and took instruction also in 1802 and 1803 from Dr. Asa Burton, of Thetford, Vermont, and Dr. Emmons, of Franklin, Massachusetts, both of whom were Congregationalist ministers. In 1803 Kendrick went to Boston to receive further training from Dr. Thomas Baldwin and Dr. Samuel Stillman, the two great Baptist leaders of that city. During his stay in Boston he was granted a licence to preach by the Second Baptist Church, of which Dr. Baldwin was minister.

His work in 1804 as supply preacher in Bellingham, Massachusetts, brought an invitation to remain there as pastor, but this he declined. The following year he was called to Lansingburgh, New York, and ordained. There he opened a school, to which came as one of his pupils a daughter of Lemuel Covell, whom he knew as a fellow minister in the Shaftsbury Association. Just as Covell's living was made in the blacksmith shop, so Kendrick's main source of income was the teaching that he did in his spare time throughout the years of his ministerial life. Of his trips to Upper Canada in 1808 and 1809, and of his invitation to stay at Beamsville, we have already heard. After declining the call to Canada, he settled at Middlebury, Vermont, in 1810 and there he remained until 1817, when he took charge of two small churches not far from Hamilton, New York. Here he found his friend, Daniel Hascall, struggling to establish what became Colgate University.

Dr. Kendrick had, by 1820, given up one of his churches and was lecturing with Hascall, his subject being theology. In 1821 he was appointed professor of systematic and pastoral theology and of moral philosophy. Brown University honoured him in 1823 with the degree of Doctor of Divinity, and he spent the rest of his life serving the cause of higher education among Baptists. He was corresponding secretary of the New York Baptist Education Society, and wrote the annual reports of the Hamilton Literary and Theological Institution.

The columns of the *Baptist Register* received a constant correspondence from him on subjects pertaining to the college, and he was diligent in keeping its claims before the churches of New York State.

Impressive in appearance, standing six feet four inches in height, he was a man of great physical strength as well as intellectual power. Though without the benefit of formal university training, the ground work of his education had been well laid, and he built faithfully upon this foundation by his own efforts as the years passed, becoming proficient in Greek as well as in philosophy and theology. His last illness was brought on by an injury to his spine, sustained through a fall on the ice, and after many months of severe pain, he died on September 11, 1848. Respected and liked by the people of the churches in Upper Canada where he visited, he gave to them the remembrance of an unselfish, sincere, and dignified Christian gentleman.

Charles Lahatt (1764-1850)

Charles Lahatt, it will be recalled, was the missionary from the Shaftsbury Association who came to Upper Canada in the autumn of 1817, ordained Simon Mabee at Oxford, and conferred with the churches in that part of the province as to their future associational connections. As a result of his report, five churches in Upper Canada were dismissed from the Shaftsbury Association to the Clinton Conference in 1818.

Mr. Lahatt was born in Germany, in the city of St. Goar, on the banks of the Rhine, on July 2, 1764. His formal schooling was begun when he was between three and four years of age, and at eight-and-a-half years he commenced the study of Latin. At twelve he survived a severe attack of smallpox, and soon afterwards was apprenticed as a medical assistant to a military surgeon. He was to have attended medical school, but was placed on active service in the army, where he spent five-and-a-half years as a boy orderly, attending the sick and wounded under conditions of severe hardship. Tiring of the hard life and harsh treatment, he abandoned his apprenticeship at the first opportunity and, before he was eighteen, had made his way to England where he taught in a German school. The large number of European refugees, especially Germans, who had fled to England during the latter part of the eighteenth century provided opportunities for such work on a considerable scale, and Mr. Lahatt had no trouble in finding employment.

His first trip to America was of a business nature, on behalf of an

Englishman for whom he acted as agent. When his trip was over he went back to England, settled in London, and resumed his teaching. About this time he became an avowed Christian and thereafter he looked back upon this step as a great turning point in his life, since it marked the beginning of the first real happiness in his personal experience. Once established in England, he returned on several occasions to Germany to visit friends and relatives, but before he came to America his people in Europe had all died except one brother and one sister.

It was in 1789 that he went to New York for the second time, again to transact business for a person in England. After two years in that city he joined the First Baptist Church and began to preach almost at once. From 1791 to 1801 he remained in the vicinity of New York City, and his name appears in several places in the minutes of the New York Baptist Association, which was formed in the year of his joining the First Baptist Church. In 1801 he went to Newark, New Jersey, and in 1809 to Pittstown, New York, where he stayed for eight years. It was towards the conclusion of his Pittstown ministry that he made the journey to Upper Canada in 1817.[11]

From 1819 to 1823 Mr. Lahatt spent short periods in New Lisbon and Guildford, New York, and then went to Portland, where he spent the rest of his life. His death occurred on August 4, 1850, in Fredonia, New York, when he was away from home to visit friends. The funeral sermon was preached by the Rev. H. S. T. Griswold of Fredonia, who later published a sketch of Mr. Lahatt's life and work.[12] He left behind him a reputation for being of a cheerful, optimistic temper; shortly before his death he said confidently to a friend, "My mind has not altered on the great subject of religion from first to last."

Asahel Morse (1771-1838)

The Rev. Asahel Morse, who was born in Montville, Connecticut, on November 4, 1771, came of a long line of ministers. His great-grandfather had been an army chaplain in the days when the New England colonists were defending themselves against the Indians and the French. His father, the Rev. Joshua Morse, had been converted under Whitefield during the Great Awakening in 1742; he was ordained at Montville where Asahel was born. In 1779, during the Revolution, the family moved to Sandisfield, Massachusetts, and Asahel's education, begun at home when he was very young, was continued at school. He said in later life that he could not remember the time when he was unable to read, and at a very early age he was introduced to the Bible, Cook's *Voyages,* and Salmon's *Geography.* "I was rarely allowed to sit in the house in his presence," he recalled, speaking of his father, "without a book in my hand."

Morse's religious experience followed the conventional pattern of a very diligent search for the assurance of personal salvation, and at the end of a long struggle, which he described in great detail in later writings, he found peace. In November 1798, he was baptized by the Rev. Rufus Babcock, of Colebrook, Connecticut. For some years before this he had taught school with considerable success in Stockbridge, Massachusetts, and other places. He had pronounced views on many subjects, especially on religion, and these opinions he was not slow to express. "I tried to muster resolution enough to be peaceable with others about religion," he confessed. "However, when I heard others talk, I found it difficult to be silent." In 1799 he was licensed to preach by the First Baptist Church in Sandisfield and was ordained at Winsted, Connecticut, in 1801. He travelled and preached all over Connecticut, averaging six sermons each week, until he was well known in nearly every town in the state. In 1803 he moved to Stratford, Connecticut, for a residence of nine years.

Mr. Morse achieved the reputation of being a powerful advocate of both civil and religious liberty. In the oration which he delivered on Independence Day in 1802 he spoke of the necessity "to draw the line between those rights which are alienable and those which are inalienable, secure to every citizen like privileges in like cases, and put an effectual bar against all legislative encroachments upon rights of conscience." He was very anti-British in his political views, believing that Britain had behaved tyrannically towards the American colonies, but there is no record of his having entered that field of discussion during his trip to Upper Canada in 1807. It is possible that he received a special warning on this subject before setting out on his journey. The Massachusetts Baptist Missionary Society had instructed its missionaries to avoid political controversy, and Nathaniel Kendrick, of the Shaftsbury Association, under whose auspices Morse visited Canada, is on record as saying, "It is important that we send no missionaries into that province but such as have prudence enough to say nothing against their government."

In any case, during that tour, Elder Morse found enough to keep himself busy without entering into political discussions. As a convinced Calvinist, he criticized the Arminian point of view, though he sometimes found his doctrinal sermons were beyond the grasp of his frontier congregations. At the same time, he did not scruple to hold joint meetings at Oxford on the Thames with the Methodists, despite their Arminian theology. He quickly disabused the congregation at Clinton (Beamsville) of any notion they may have held that they were ever a properly organized Baptist church, and saw to it that they adopted a proper covenant and confession of faith before calling a council to give them recognition. Minutes were kept of these proceedings, and he signed them personally before he left.[13] In 32 days in the province he attended 54 meetings, preached 51 sermons, and baptized four persons. He also found enough time to take a sight-seeing trip to Niagara Falls.

In 1812 Mr. Morse settled as pastor of Suffield, Connecticut, where he stayed for nearly twenty years. He was a member of the political convention called in 1818 to draft a new constitution for the state and wrote the article on religious liberty which was adopted at that time. After a few years' absence from Suffield during his period of semi-retirement, he returned in 1836 and remained there until his death on June 10, 1838.

Neither as saintly as Lemuel Covell nor as learned as Nathaniel Kendrick, Asahel Morse was, nevertheless, a very capable, conscientious, and hard-working minister. His pronouncedly anti-British views would hardly have permitted him to take up permanent residence in Canada, even had he been invited to do so, but no one can study the report of his tour of the churches in 1807 without giving him credit for a very solid contribution to the Baptist cause in Canada. His setting in order of the Beamsville church, so that it has been able to maintain an unbroken period of service ever since his visit, was in itself sufficient to earn him a vote of gratitude.

Peter P. Roots (1765-1828)

Peter Philanthropos Roots, who visited Upper Canada with Joseph Cornell in 1804, again by himself in 1805, and in 1808, was the son of a Congregationalist minister, the Rev. Beniah Roots, of Simsbury, Connecticut. Here Peter Roots was born on March 27, 1765, but the family moved to Rutland, Vermont, after a time, and while they were living there the son was converted, in 1783. He was educated at Dartmouth College, graduating with the degree of A.M., and was licensed as a Congregationalist preacher in 1790.

After a careful study of New Testament teaching on the subject of baptism, he went to Boston for conversations with Dr. Samuel Stillman. The result was that Dr. Stillman baptized him and received him into the membership of the First Baptist Church, Boston, in June 1792. Arrangements for his ordination as a Baptist minister were then made, and the event took place on September 4, that same year, in Providence, Rhode Island, on the day before the commencement exercises at Brown University.[14] Participating in the ordination service were Dr. Stillman, who preached the sermon; Dr. William Williams, whose academy at Wrentham, Massachusetts, had matriculated a great many students for entrance to Brown; and Jonathan Maxcy, the brilliant young scholar who had served for a short period as an instructor at Brown, went from there to the pastorate of First Baptist Church, Providence, for one year, and then returned to the university to be made president at the age of twenty-four.

Mr. Roots published a book in 1794 giving reasons for his change from the Congregationalist church to the Baptist,[15] and a few of his sermons have been preserved, some in manuscript and some in printed form.[16] His preaching talents were recognized as being above the average, and his sermons were admired as "evangelical, sensible, plain, and richly stored with Scripture truth." His home life was noted for its happiness, and it was said of him by one who knew him well that, "like a good bishop, he ruled well his own house." From the beginning of his ministry he was especially fond of missionary work: in the winter following his ordination he travelled as far south as Georgia. He rode, on the average, about three thousand miles each year, and preached three hundred sermons.

Having had the advantage of university training himself, Mr. Roots coveted the same privilege for as many ministers as could possibly receive it. He was one of the thirteen men who responded in September 1817, to an invitation to meet at Hamilton, New York, to "converse and pray over the want of a more enlightened ministry," and whose efforts resulted in the founding of the Hamilton Literary and Theological Institution.[17] Despite his own academic attainments, however, he found it no problem to be on intimate terms with men whose background was different from his own. His affection for Joseph Cornell, the farmer-preacher whom he accompanied on tour in 1804, has already been described.

Modest and unassuming, Mr. Roots was satisfied to do his life's work without the reward of fame. Speaking of the ministers of the Baptist denomination who had originated in Connecticut, David Benedict, the historian, referred to Peter Roots as being one of a number of men who were "less known, but of distinguished usefulness."

Obed Warren (1760-1824)

The state of Connecticut contributed another valuable leader to the Baptist denomination in the person of Obed Warren, who was born at Plainfield on March 18, 1760. He became a professing Christian as a very young boy and began to preach at the age of twenty-one. He was ordained at Halifax, Vermont, and then went to Salem, New York, where he remained for twenty years. At Salem he took a very active part in the work of the Shaftsbury Association, especially its missionary endeavours. He accompanied Lemuel Covell to Upper Canada in 1803, when Titus Finch was baptized and the church at Charlotteville was organized.

The cause of higher education had a warm friend in Mr. Warren. He was a strong supporter of the Baptist Education Society of the State of New York, and presided over its annual meetings in 1818, 1820, and 1821. In 1818 he was made a director of the Society, and in 1821 became a member of its executive committee.[18] For a number of years he served as a collecting agent for the Hamilton Literary and Theological Institution. His death took place in 1824, in the forty-third year of his ministry. Dr. Nathaniel Kendrick, his friend and colleague, paid tribute to the qualities which he brought to his work:

> He was favoured through life with a firm constitution, never impaired by sickness or age, nor by the most arduous labours. He had a strong mind, but little cultivated in early life, and never much improved in classical literature, but richly stored with good sense, a well regulated judgment, correct views of national interests and of the doctrine of the word of God. . . . In fine, his whole character and deportment as a man, a Christian and a minister united many excellencies which are worthy of imitation. . . . He had elevated views of the ministry, and spared no pains to expose and remove those who degraded the office.

A review of the lives and characters of the missionaries who gave leadership, encouragement, and counsel to the early Baptist churches in Upper Canada leaves the indelible impression that here was a company of very fine men indeed. Of the twelve whose careers have been sketched above, all were firm believers in an educated ministry and supporters of every effort to supply such a ministry to the denomination. Blood, Cornell, Irish, Roots, and Warren all served on the official boards of various educational institutions. Hascall and Roots were holders of the M.A. degree, the one from Middlebury and the other from Dartmouth. Morse had been a successful teacher on the secondary school level; Hascall and Kendrick were college teachers as well, the latter holding an honorary degree from Brown University.

With the possible exception of Daniel Hascall, all the missionaries named in this chapter were strongly Calvinistic in theology, but this did not detract from the evangelical tone of their preaching. Their churchmanship was clearly defined and had been carefully thought out; it embodied the best results of the inquiries made by earlier generations of Baptists, whose main task had been to arrive at a satisfactory doctrine of the church as set forth in the New Testament.

Their practical wisdom is seen in the remarkable degree to which they were able to reconcile the ideals of local congregational autonomy and the interdependence of all the churches. They showed no fear of the association as a threat to the independence of the local church as some later Baptists have done. Rather, they seemed to insist that the association had a vital role to play in the Baptist scheme of things. Thus the organization of local churches, their recognition *as* churches, the ordination of ministers, and other details of polity were made conditional upon what they called "proper gospel order," or "gospel rule." For the free-lance preacher who took unto himself the authority of the gospel ministry they had nothing but censure. Let such a man produce his credentials, was their ruling, and if he could not, then the churches must be warned against him. With the informal group of believers who desired to call themselves a Baptist church they were equally firm. Let there be a properly framed covenant, even though simple, as a basis of their uniting together. Let there be at least some statement of faith, so that the community at large might know for what the church stood, and let no such group of people call itself a Baptist church until its avowed faith and order were declared acceptable to the Baptist body as a whole, by a council representative of that body through its local association.

Here, in short, were men who, as wise master builders, laid a good foundation. It was no fault of theirs that some who followed them took little heed how they built thereupon. But the work the founders did for the Baptist movement in Upper Canada was never wholly undone, even though at times there were grave departures from the course they had mapped out. The main stream of Baptist polity has now flowed strongly and steadily for a century and a half in the province. Disruptive forces have crept in at times, but have always been successfully thrown off by the general health of the body. Ever and again the saving formula has been that of "proper gospel order," and in times of denominational danger the one remedy needful to restore equilibrium has been the ancient one of searching the Scriptures "to see whether these things were so."

VI

The Churches in Upper Canada: East

FROM THE INCEPTION of Baptist meetings in the pioneer settlements, whether sponsored by local families without the help of any pastor, by licensed preachers or ordained ministers living in the community, or by visiting missionaries, the aim was to raise each congregation to the status of an organized church. According to generally accepted Baptist polity, this meant that five conditions must be fulfilled:

1. Adoption of a covenant, setting forth the basis on which the members agreed to be formed into a church. This did not usually lay down specific rules for the governing of personal conduct, but did include a promise to be loyal to the church and to behave in a Christian manner.

2. Adoption of a statement of faith, declaring the beliefs which the church proposed to propagate, and the principles for which it stood.

3. Recognition of the church by a Baptist association on behalf of the Baptist body in general.

4. Appointment of appropriate officers, including deacons, clerk, and pastor, the latter being first ordained as an "elder."

5. Provision for the regular observance of the ordinances of baptism and the Lord's supper, and for stated times of public worship.

By the year 1819 twenty organized churches had been established, twelve in the eastern, and eight in the western part of the province, and though some of them enjoyed but a short life, they all contributed to the progress of the denomination. A short account of the churches in both parts of the province will be given in this and the next chapter, following the chronological order of their organization.

Hallowell (West Lake), 1796

In 1794 a licensed preacher named Reuben Crandall, a native of the state of New York, came to the Bay of Quinte area in Upper Canada. In 1795 he was joined by another licensed Baptist preacher named Joseph Winn, also from New York State, who settled near West Lake, in Prince Edward County. Though both of these men had a part in establishing the Baptist church in Hallowell Township, it was Winn who remained on the field and served the congregation as its settled minister. By 1796 Crandall had moved to Northumberland County, taken up land in the township of Cramahe, and begun to hold services there. Winn, meanwhile, had visited the United States long enough to be ordained and had returned to West Lake, where he was still living and preaching when Joseph Cornell and Peter Roots made his acquaintance in 1804.

It has been questioned whether the church in Hallowell was ever completely organized, but there are good reasons for believing that it was. In 1799, for example, a council met at Hallowell to ordain Mr. Crandall to the ministry, and Joseph Winn himself presided as moderator. The facts regarding this ordination are recorded in the minute book of the Cramahe-Haldimand church, and though brief, the record shows that everything was done in an orderly manner. Delegates were present from the Thurlow church as well as from Cramahe-Haldimand, and it seems unlikely that Hallowell, the entertaining church, with Winn as its pastor, could have been any less thoroughly organized than the other two.

The three churches whose representatives participated in Reuben Crandall's ordination in 1799 again co-operated in 1802 to form the Thurlow Baptist Association.[1] Since the first meeting of the Association was held at Thurlow, and the 1804 meeting, according to the minutes, was held at Haldimand,[2] it is practically certain that in 1803 the Association met in Hallowell, even though no actual statement to that effect has been found. Recognition of the Thurlow Association, with its three constituent churches, by the Massachusetts Baptist Missionary Society is a strong reason for crediting Hallowell with being a fully organized church. The missionaries who represented the Society were, as we have seen, quite strict about matters of church order. Joseph Cornell and Peter Roots, who met with the Association in 1804, would not likely have countenanced any recognition by that body of a church that was not properly organized. Cornell reported to the Massachusetts Society after his visit that Mr. Winn's work at West Lake was being "favoured with a glorious revival of religion."

After a time, Joseph Winn moved from the immediate vicinity of West Lake to the Carrying Place in the township of Ameliasburg, and from then on, apparently, the work in Hallowell declined. For whatever reason, the church does not seem to have survived the War of 1812, though it was listed by Michael Smith along with fourteen other Baptist churches in the province shortly before the war began.

Its early demise should probably be blamed on the scarcity of Baptist ministers in Upper Canada at that time.

Thurlow, 1796

The township of Thurlow, north of the Prince Edward district, was surveyed in 1787, and in 1789, according to William Canniff, a party of settlers, unable to secure land along the lake front, ascended the Moira River as far as the fifth concession, where they "proceeded to take possession of such land as struck their fancy."[3] By 1794 the people in Thurlow had set up a rudimentary system of municipal government, and from then until 1797 they held joint town meetings with the township of Sidney, which lay immediately to the west. An entry in the Sidney Township Record Book for the year 1798 states, "This year the township of Thurlow holds its first annual meeting by itself."

Among the settlers who ascended the Moira River in 1789 was a Baptist preacher named Asa Turner. He held services in the homes of the people, notably at Gilbert's house in Sidney, and at Colonel Bell's, Hayden's Corners, Reed's and Ross's in Thurlow. Finally, he gathered a congregation which met regularly at the home of Mr. Ross, and from this small group of about a dozen worshippers the Thurlow Baptist church was organized. The date of this event is not on record, but it would appear to have been in 1796; the Thurlow church was therefore about the same age as the one in Hallowell.

The building put up to house this congregation has long since disappeared, and neither the date of its erection nor its exact location is known. It is said to have been thirty feet square, and situated on the bank of the Moira in the fifth concession of Thurlow, which would place it between the present villages of Corbyville and Foxboro, near the Reed cemetery. It was here that Upper Canada's first association of Baptist churches met in 1802, and, as the minutes show, again in 1805.[4]

In 1804 Joseph Cornell reported that upwards of twenty persons had been baptized during the previous year in Thurlow, and that the number of additions to the membership of the church had been considerable. The Rev. Peter Roots, on his travels through Canada in 1805, visited the Thurlow church, arriving just after the Association had concluded its sessions.

Around 1810 or 1811 Mr. Turner left Canada to accept a pastorate in Scipio, New York, and not much is known of the Thurlow church after that. It was probably without any minister during the War of

1812, and it seems to have suffered greatly over that period. When Isaac Reed became its pastor after the war there were very few members left, but the work revived under his care. In the month of Feburary 1819, when the Thurlow Association was reorganized as the Haldimand Association, the Thurlow church was represented at the meeting, and from later reports of the Association we learn that it was in fairly good condition in 1837. By 1858, however, the same source of information shows that its life had sunk to a very low ebb, and by 1867 it had passed out of existence. To take its place, a church was organized in Belleville in 1873.

Cramahe-Haldimand, 1798

Baptist work in Cramahe and Haldimand began in earnest with the arrival of Reuben Crandall as a settler in the former township in 1796. It is quite probable, however, that he had paid occasional visits to the locality from the time when he first went to Prince Edward County from New York State in 1794. Fortunately, the minute book of the Haldimand church, though somewhat mutilated, contains some records dating back as far as 1798, and from this and other sources a number of facts regarding the Baptist cause in the two townships can be gathered.[5]

On June 23, 1798, in Cramahe, according to the Haldimand minute book, "Brethren and sisters assembled for the purpose of obtaining fellowship with sister churches, and entered into solemn covenant with each other before God, to walk together in love and fear of God, Christ strengthening them; and to watch over each other for good, and to be for God and no other; to maintain family and public worship on the Lord's Day; to attend conference every two weeks, to set in order the things that are wanting in the church of Christ."

The expression, "for the purpose of obtaining fellowship with sister churches" should not be overlooked. It points to the fact that there were other Baptist churches in the area already, and leads to the conclusion that the Baptists of Cramahe and Haldimand were endeavouring to complete the organization of a church so that they might become associated with Hallowell and Thurlow. In 1802 this purpose was realized with the formation of the Thurlow Association.

On October 27, 1799, sixteen months after the organization of the Cramahe-Haldimand church, Reuben Crandall was ordained by a council which met at Hallowell. The record of this event was later transcribed into the Haldimand minute book, and the transcription was certified as a true copy by Benjamin Ewing. It states that Joseph Winn presided as moderator, examined Mr. Crandall as to his principles, preached the ordination sermon, and delivered the charge to the candidate. Asa Turner of Thurlow offered prayer and welcomed Mr. Crandall to the ministry by giving him the right hand of fellowship. The clerk of the council was Moses Clark, a member of Crandall's church.

On the roll of the new church were such names as Moses Clark, Benjamin Ewing, Moses Hinman, and members of the Wait and Wyatt families. Moses Clark came to Hastings County from Connecticut in 1798, and took the oath of allegiance to the Crown before Samuel Sherwood, J.P., on October 30, 1809. He served in the War of 1812, was captured by the Americans along the Thames River, and was allowed to go home on parole in November 1814, after promising "not to bear arms against nor do anything prejudicial to the interests of the United States" until he had been regularly exchanged as a prisoner. When he petitioned for land in 1823 he gave his residence as the township of East Gwillimbury.[6] Benjamin Ewing, born in 1776, was a native of Massachusetts. He came to Canada in the year 1800 and served in the War of 1812 as a quartermaster. Later he was commissioned as a lieutenant in the Northumberland militia, 1st Regiment, and ultimately became a magistrate.[7] For his services in the war he received a grant of four hundred acres in the second concession of Alnwick. Moses Hinman joined the church on October 18, 1799, having just come from Vermont that year with his wife and infant son, Truman. The latter, according to an inscription in the Fairview cemetery at Wicklow, was born in Vermont on May 11, 1799. Mr. Hinman died in June 1837, at the age of eighty years, and was buried at Wicklow. His descendants have been prominent in the Baptist denomination for several generations. The Wait family has also continued to be represented in the vicinity of Haldimand down to the present time (1956). One of its members, the Rev. David Wait, was for many years a minister in that area before removing to the state of Michigan. He served as corresponding secretary of the Haldimand Association, and the destruction of his house at Vernonville by fire in 1858 unfortunately meant the loss of many important records of the early churches in that region.

Services of the Cramahe-Haldimand church for a number of years were held alternately in both townships. In February 1804, the Thurlow Association held its third annual meeting at Haldimand, and Joseph Cornell, who was present, wrote, "Elder Crandall had had

YORK, THE NEW CAPITAL OF UPPER CANADA

As it appeared in the autumn of 1803. Several of the missionaries visited York during their tours. (From a painting in the Public Archives of Canada)

A CLEARING IN UPPER CANADA

Water colour by Lt. Philip John Bainbrigge. Early settlers in Upper Canada coming from populous areas of the United States found themselves isolated in a vast forest and almost entirely dependent upon their own resources for survival. (Bainbrigge Collection, Public Archives of Canada)

a comfortable season in the year past. The church is increasing in numbers, and we thought in graces likewise."[8] (This meeting, which Peter Roots also attended, has been described on page 44.) For a period of sixteen years after taking up land in Cramahe, Mr. Crandall continued to build up his church and to travel throughout the district, going as far as Rice Lake and Kingston. In 1812 he resigned and went westward to Townsend. The coming of war, which meant that many of the male members were away on military service, coupled with the lack of a regular minister during the period of hostilities, imposed a severe hardship on the church, and no record of its activities during those years has been preserved.

In 1816, however, the members who resided in Haldimand began once again to carry out the terms of their covenant, and to meet fortnightly for "conference." The home of Mr. Wyatt was the scene of these gatherings, and a reawakening of interest was the result. (The revival is also described on page 60.) Joseph Winn visited the field in January 1817 and baptized Ephraim Doolittle, Mr. and Mrs. Henry Steel, and Polly and Lucy Batty. In February the Rev. Timothy Sheppard, of the Hamilton Missionary Society of New York State, held meetings in the townships of Haldimand and Hamilton, baptizing several converts.

The Haldimand branch of the church now felt strong enough to assume a separate existence and in the first week of March 1817 it was reorganized at Wicklow. The Rev. Peleg Card, formerly of the Black River Association in New York State, became its pastor in 1818. His tombstone in the cemetery at Wicklow records that he died in 1837 at the age of sixty-nine, and that three weeks later his wife also died at the age of sixty-seven. By 1824 the Haldimand Church had erected the commodious building which still stands at the "Four Corners" of the township, on No. 2 Highway at Wicklow. It is probably the oldest Baptist church building in Ontario.

At about the same time that the Haldimand congregation was separately organized the Baptists in Cramahe also reorganized, and continued as a church for many years. As the township of Cramahe developed, the old original church gradually disbanded and gave place to new causes at Brighton (called First Cramahe), at Morganston (Second Cramahe), and at Colborne. The last named, according to the late Rev. J. T. Dowling, who became its minister in 1883, was, more than either of the other two, the continuation of the life which began in the first Baptist congregation established in Cramahe by Reuben Crandall.

Steventown (Bastard or Philipsville), 1803

That there were Baptists in Leeds County as early as 1789 is shown by the fact that James Stark, of Elizabethtown, petitioned the commissioners of the Land Department on June 24 that year, praying that he might "be indulged with His Majesty's bounty of land and other privileges of the British Government." Mr. Stark described himself as a Baptist minister who had "in consequence of his attachment to the British Govt. suffered imprisonment and loss of property in the States." His application was supported by Philip Philips and Jabez Sanders, who stated that they had known Mr. Stark since 1778 as a loyal subject, and that he had been persecuted in the United States "for praying for the King and not praying for the Congress."[9] Stark and Philips, along with Abel Stevens, Thomas Knolton, and Obadiah Reed, all of whom declared themselves to be Baptists, petitioned Lieutenant-Governor Simcoe in 1796 to grant ordained Baptist elders the right "to administer the ordinance of marriage."[10]

James Stark does not appear to have continued his career as a preacher in Canada, and no real impetus was given to the Baptist cause in the general region of Leeds County until the arrival of Abel Stevens in 1794. Stevens, after somewhat lengthy negotiations with the government, had received a grant of land in Scarborough Township in 1793, but he was not satisfied with it and turned eastward towards Kingston, ending his journey in the region of Bastard and Kitley townships. Here he embarked on a long and arduous scheme of settlement and development of the country, the details of which may be read in his numerous letters to the government. Though his labours as a pioneer colonizer were prodigious, his main love was for the Baptist church, of which he was a licensed preacher. In the township of Bastard, in the settlement which was called Steventown after him, he co-operated with Daniel Derbyshire in gathering a congregation of baptized believers.

As a result of the visit of Elder Joseph Cornell in 1803, the Baptists around Steventown were formed into a church on February 12 that year.[11] Though a partial organization had already been attempted, the people decided, after the visitor had looked into their congregational affairs, that they "had moved in many respects not agreeable to gospel prudence." The organization meeting was held at the home of Benjamin Huntley, and Cornell presided as moderator. The impressiveness of the event shines through even the mis-spelt words and halting sentences of the record kept by the clerk on that occasion. There is a solemn grandeur in his statement that Cornell, their "beloved brother and father in the gospel," gave them the right hand of fellowship and bade them welcome "as a sister church in relation to all the babtis [Baptist] churches in north america."

Though the church was founded in February, it was not until September, at a meeting presided over by Daniel Derbyshire, that an official list of members was drawn up and recorded in the church book. The names of Batchelor, Bresee, Bullard, Burgess, Churchill, Cross, Day, Derbyshire, Edmonds, Huntley, Knapp, Mott, Nichols, Parish, and Stevens appear among the families of the church during its early years.

In 1804, Joseph Cornell paid his second visit to Steventown, accompanied by the Rev. Peter P. Roots, and the two missionaries ordained Daniel Derbyshire and Abel Stevens on the first day of March. The service was held at the home of Richard Day, and Cornell preached the ordination sermon from I Timothy 5:21, 22, a passage containing the warning to "lay hands suddenly on no man." Roots delivered the charge to Abel Stevens and Cornell gave him the right hand of fellowship to the ministry. Derbyshire's ordination then followed, with Cornell giving the charge to the ordinee and Roots extending the hand of fellowship. Stevens offered the closing prayer and Derbyshire led the singing of the concluding hymn. Cornell's declaration in his report about the solemnity of this ordination service has been referred to in the account of his missionary tour (see page 45).

A few weeks after the ordination of its two leaders, the church decided to plant a field of corn "for to support the gospel meeting." Most of the services were held at Benjamin Huntley's during the first two years, with an occasional meeting at the home of William Parish. In Feburary 1806, it was resolved to meet half of the time at the middle of the township, one quarter of the time at Benjamin Huntley's, and one quarter of the time "at the mill."

In 1807, the Rev. Phinehas Pillsbury visited the church, reporting that Daniel Derbyshire was still pastor, and that the church was "somewhat low, but not altogether discouraged." Pastoral leadership at Steventown itself seems to have devolved almost entirely upon Mr. Derbyshire until his death sometime after 1808.[12] Abel Stevens, continuing as a member, did considerable itinerant preaching in adjoining settlements, but devoted much of his time to his work of colonizing, including the building of roads and the establishment of industries.

In 1809 Jesse Brown joined the church by letter, was soon given a licence to preach, and shortly afterwards was appointed pastor by a formal agreement (see page 127). In addition to various sums of money contributed by certain members, fifty acres of land were given to him for his use, which were to become his personal property if he remained as pastor for six years.

The records show that during the next decade the church maintained a vigorous existence. Delegates went from it to the meetings of the Thurlow Association. Pastor Jesse Brown was given a letter commending his work as a preacher so that he might visit other churches in that capacity. Abel Stevens, on a journey to York on business in December 1809, delivered invitations to several ministers along his route, including Joseph Winn, to visit Steventown at their convenience. In 1812 George Ebberson united with the church, and five years later was ordained to the ministry at Gananoque. In 1818 Elder Carson, not long out from Scotland, joined the church (see page 128), and soon afterwards, along with a number of others, helped to form a church in the township of Augusta. A visitor to Steventown on one occasion during 1818 was the Rev. Peleg Card, of Haldimand, who, having presented his credentials to the church on the last Saturday in June, was invited to preach the next day.

When in 1803 Joseph Cornell organized the first Baptist church in Leeds County at Steventown, he prayed that the "little vine" which he had planted might be saved from the ravages of "the wild boar of the wilderness." His prayer was answered and the vine flourished. Its branches spread to Delta, Athens, Plum Hollow, Augusta, Gananoque, and Crosby. But important as these results near at hand might seem, they were outshone by the work of one member of the Steventown church, named Samuel Day.

This young man's father was Capt. Jeremiah Day, who had been one of the signatories to the agreement establishing Jesse Brown as pastor at Steventown.[13] In 1829, Samuel left his native county of Leeds for Hamilton, New York, to study for the ministry at Madison University. In 1835 he travelled to India, where he established what has since become the great mission field of the Canadian Baptist Foreign Mission Board in that country.[14] Day and his wife went out as missionaries of the American Baptist Convention and their first term lasted for twelve years. After a furlough of two years in the United States to recover their health, they went out again in 1848 and stayed until 1853, when their foreign service came to an end. Establishing his residence at Homer, New York, Mr. Day travelled about as a foreign mission representative of the American Baptist Convention, and in that capacity he visited his native Canada on several occasions.[15] It was Day, perhaps, more than any other, who first inspired Baptists of Ontario and Quebec to take an interest in missions abroad. In 1867 they entered into partnership with American Baptists in sending missionaries to the Telugu people of India, and by 1873 they were ready to launch out on their own at Kakinada. Samuel Day, however, did not live to see this final result of his efforts, for he died in 1871 at Homer, New York, after a trying illness.

Percy, c. 1804

That a Baptist church came into existence in the township of Percy early in the nineteenth century we know for certain, but beyond this one fact we know very little. Michael Smith in his book, *A Geographical View of the Province of Upper Canada,* which was published in 1813, stated that the Baptists of the province had one church in Percy. When did this church come into being?

The Rev. Peter Roots provides an approximate answer to this question. Writing to the Massachusetts Baptist Missionary Society in April 1805, he reported his failure to reach Thurlow in time to attend the annual meeting of the Association on the second Friday in February of that year, and stated that in the following year, 1806, the Association would meet at Percy on the first Friday of February.[16] From this we may reasonably conclude that the Percy church was represented at the 1805 meeting, and must therefore have been in existence in 1804.

How long the church survived, and who were its ministers, are facts not yet uncovered. It is probable, however, that it went out of existence during the War of 1812-14, since there is no mention of it in the accounts of the reorganization of the Association in 1819.

Rawdon (Stirling), 1806

Prominent in the municipal affairs of the townships of Sidney, Thurlow, and Rawdon in early days were two men named Samuel Rosebush and Barse Chard. Rosebush was appointed in 1796 collector for Sidney and Thurlow, which held joint town meetings from 1794 to 1797. Thurlow Township held its own meeting in 1798, but from 1799 to 1805 Sidney combined with Rawdon. At the town meetings of 1799 and 1800 Mr. Chard was appointed pathmaster for Rawdon.[17]

Both Rosebush and Chard were Baptists, and on June 6, 1806, at the home of the former, the Rawdon Baptist church was organized. David Couch was one of its leading members, and an itinerant preacher, Elder James Hulse, seems to have provided a certain amount of pastoral oversight. Records of 1825 definitely list him as the minister of this church.

The Rawdon church was represented at the meeting at Haldimand Four Corners in 1819 when the Thurlow Association became the Haldimand Association, and its name appears two decades later in the 1844 minutes of that body. The membership did not increase greatly and in 1858 the Association felt obliged to note that "Rawdon is in a low state yet she will not lie down and say there is no hope." In 1860, however, a church was formed at Stirling and the Rawdon church was absorbed into the new congregation. Stirling, in turn, with its branch at Hubble Hill, ceased to report to the Association in 1911.

Ameliasburg (Murray), c. 1809

The founding of the "First Baptist Church in Ameliasburg," as it was officially called, must have occurred at about the same time that Elder Joseph Winn moved from West Lake, in Hallowell, to the Carrying Place, where he seems to have lived for the rest of his life. Winn was still at West Lake in 1804, and the Ameliasburg church had not yet appeared on the list of churches in the Thurlow Association in 1808. In 1809, however, Abel Stevens, of Bastard, when on a trip to York, visited Winn, and invited him to preach at Steventown, so it seems likely that Winn was then living at the Carrying Place (later known as Murray). If we set 1809, therefore, as the approximate date of the organization of the Ameliasburg church, we shall not be far wrong.

Though Winn himself exercised a wide influence not only among Baptists but throughout other denominations as well, his little church at the Carrying Place never attained any great strength. Michael Smith mentioned it in his list of Baptist churches in Upper Canada in 1812, but placed it incorrectly in the township of Sophiasburg. It was represented at the founding of the Haldimand Association in 1819. When Benjamin Farmer was ordained at Haldimand in 1825, Elder Joseph Winn, Deacon John Winn, and Bro. William Beals were present from Ameliasburg. In 1832 the membership of the church numbered just twenty-one, and in 1837, though two had been baptized during that year, its numerical strength was only twenty-two. The minutes of the Haldimand Association for 1837 refer, pathetically, to the Ameliasburg church as "a little band," and in 1845 they record that the "small band remains much the same." In that same year, 1845, the Murray church, as it was then called, reported that during the previous year its former pastor, Joseph Winn, had been "called away to his eternal rest." It was not long before the church itself passed out of existence.

Sidney, c. 1809-1812

The present church in Sidney Township dates from 1829, but it was preceded by an earlier church whose fortunes were very closely linked with those of Thurlow. Indeed, the origins of the two churches are so interwoven that it is difficult to separate them. Nevertheless, that an organized church existed independently in Sidney before the War of 1812 seems beyond dispute.

Canniff says that when Asa Turner first began to hold services in the district north of Prince Edward County in the late 1790's, one of his preaching stations was at the Gilberts' house in Sidney. It appears that for some time the congregation in Sidney was regarded as a branch of Thurlow, and did not assume a separate and distinct existence as a church in its own right until later. Nathaniel Kendrick, in 1808, reported that the Thurlow Association consisted of six churches.[18] These can be identified as Hallowell, Thurlow, Cramahe-Haldimand, Markham, Percy, and Rawdon, and it can be concluded, therefore, that Sidney was not yet counted as a church.

Michael Smith, however, in his book published in 1813, stated definitely that there was a Baptist church in Sidney, and that it had been organized by that time seems quite probable. By 1819, Sidney was certainly constituted as a separate church, since it was represented in its own right, along with Thurlow and the others, at the founding of the Haldimand Association.[19] In the decade following 1819 it must have declined and been revived again, for in 1829 we find James Hulse and Isaac Reed co-operating in its reorganization. New strength was added at that time by the dismissal of sixteen members from Thurlow: these belonged to the Turner, Faulkner, Wright, Guffin, Sarles, Lines, Fraser, and Fairman families. It is possible that some of them, if not all, had joined the Thurlow church while that at Sidney was dormant, and were merely returning to their proper church home when its organization became active once more.

Breadalbane, 1817

The township of Lochiel in Glengarry County, at first a part of Lancaster, was separated and named after the chief of the Camerons when large numbers of that clan arrived from Scotland. The first group of about forty families came to the new township in 1794. There were no Baptists among them[20] and we do not hear of any arriving until after the turn of the century. In 1815 thirteen Baptists from Perthshire decided to emigrate to Canada, and they reached Lochiel in the spring of 1816. Five of them came from a Baptist church in Lawers and eight from a church in Killin.[21] Both of these places are on Loch Tay, Perthshire, in Breadalbane District. The churches in Lawers and Killin were established as a result of evangelistic campaigns held in central and northern Scotland by the great Edinburgh preacher, James Haldane. In 1802-3, according to his biographer, Haldane's preaching in Breadalbane District had produced a notable revival and though Haldane himself was not a Baptist at that time, he attracted to himself many followers, who, when he did become a Baptist in 1808, imitated his example. From those followers Mr. Haldane was able to establish more than thirty Baptist churches in Scotland.[22]

The thirteen Baptists who reached Lochiel, Upper Canada, in 1816 were Donald McLaurin and his wife Catherine, Duncan Campbell and his wife Catherine, Peter McDougall and his wife Catherine, John McDougall and his wife Catherine, Allan McDermid (or McDiarmid), Janet McDermid (Allan's sister-in-law), Margaret McDermid (Allan's mother-in-law), Susan (Mrs. I.) McLaurin, and Peter Stewart. They had held services in the Gaelic language on the ship while crossing the ocean, and continued the same custom regularly in their new settlement, which they named Breadalbane after their native district in Perthshire. On August 2, 1817, they constituted themselves into a church, appointing Allan McDermid and Peter McDougall as elders, and Duncan Campbell and Donald McLaurin as deacons.

In line with the views preached by Mr. Haldane in Scotland, the polity of the Breadalbane church emphasized the independence of the local congregation. Little stress was laid on the importance of an ordained ministry or on the desirability of the church being recognized by the Baptist body in Upper Canada through the calling of a council. The fact that the members spoke Gaelic almost exclusively may have made them hesitant about consulting the English-speaking Baptists farther west around Steventown. At the same time, it is hard to imagine the Breadalbane church adopting any such rule as was laid down by the church in Oxford Township, which read: "None to administer the ordinances except those who have been publickly set apart to preach the gospel by prayer and laying on of the hands of the presbytery."[23] Instead, the Breadalbane church, without consulting anyone, gave its own elders authority to administer the ordinances, as well as to preach. Soon several converts were baptized, and by 1818 the membership had more than doubled, reaching a total of thirty.

The two ruling elders developed differences of opinion on doctrine, and in 1821 the congregation divided into two sections, each with its own leader, and each claiming to be a church. Nevertheless, both factions increased in numbers, until in 1826 they were united again. Gradually, as other churches sprang up in the Ottawa valley, Breadalbane came into closer touch with a wider fellowship, but four more years were to pass before the congregation was to enjoy the leadership of an ordained minister.

Fortunately for the Baptists of the Ottawa valley, there arrived in Canada in 1819 a man named John Edwards. Also a native of Scotland, he had belonged to James Haldane's open membership church in Edinburgh, but had later been baptized in Portsmouth, England, while employed in the shipyards there. Settling first at Kingston, Mr. Edwards moved to Clarence on the Ottawa River in 1822. He was an active promoter of Baptist work, and had much more mature views of church polity than the simple folk at Breadalbane. For one thing, he recognized a need for trained leaders. In 1829 he went to Britain and persuaded two capable ministers to come to Canada the next year. The Rev. John Gilmour of Aberdeen went to Montreal, where a group of Baptists desired to form a church, and the Rev. William Fraser, of Invernesshire, took charge at Breadalbane.[24]

Mr. Fraser was an ideal man to lead the people to whom he ministered, and during his pastorate of nineteen years he made a great contribution to the welfare of Lochiel Township. He was active in the affairs of the Ottawa Baptist Association, and commanded the complete loyalty of his own congregation. At the time he and some of his flock decided to migrate westward to Bruce County he declared, "I never heard an oath or saw a glass of liquor drunk in Breadalbane." This was a rare tribute, even to such a godly and temperate people as the Gaelic-speaking Baptists from Perthshire.

Augusta, 1818

The township of Augusta, which faces the St. Lawrence River just east of Brockville, was one of the thirteen royal townships laid out for loyalists and disbanded troops in 1783. The first mention of Baptist activity in Augusta is made in a report submitted by the Rev. Phinehas Pillsbury to the Massachusetts Baptist Missionary Society in 1807.[25] Mr. Pillsbury preached a number of times there on his tour along the St. Lawrence, and baptized a young woman. As there was no church in the township, he gave the candidate a certificate of her baptism in order that she might be received into church membership at a later date.

The minutes of the Steventown church provide some information about the work in Augusta. In December 1817, a Baptist minister from Scotland, Elder Carson, appeared in the vicinity and joined the church in Steventown. He was closely examined as to his views, but, championed by Abel Stevens, who had consulted other "elders," Mr. Carson and his wife were both received in June 1818 on presentation of letters from their home church in Scotland. On July 27, 1818, "Elder Carson presented a letter from a number of brethren and sisters at Augusta, requesting a dismissal from this church. We then voted to grant the request by giving them letters of dismission."

The church in Augusta had been organized on March 8 of that same year by Abel Stevens, and now in July it received a considerable addition to its strength by the transfer of a group from Steventown. In 1828 the Augusta church took the lead in forming the Johnstown Association and the first meeting of that new body was held there on February 6. At that time the church membership numbered forty-two. A revival in 1832 resulted in twenty-four baptisms, and by 1835 the membership had increased to seventy. Yet the shortage of ministers was an acute problem. In the 1830's the Johnstown Association had only three ordained pastors. At that time Augusta was cared for by two licentiates, Samuel Reed and Adam Hillis. In 1845, with Rev. J. Fay as minister, it reported 117 members, which made it the largest church in the Johnstown Association. Before many years had passed, however, this once flourishing pioneer church had succumbed to lack of leadership and to the effects of migration westward on the part of many families.

Gananoque, 1819

In the minutes of the church at Steventown there is an entry dated August 30, 1817, which reads:

Took into consideration a request of a number of Brethren from Gananoque that we should send Elder Stevens down there in order to ordain Bro. George Ebberson. Then voted that Elder Stevens and Brother Abel Stevens and

Brother Nicholas Bresee should go and examine Bro. Ebberson's principles and belief and if they found him to possess a sound mind then to proceed and ordain him to the ministry of the gospel.

From this we learn that Baptists at Gananoque had been holding services, and that George Ebberson, who had joined the Steventown church in 1812, had been so acceptable as a lay preacher that they were willing to have him ordained as their minister. The ordination took place as planned and Mr. Ebberson exercised an effective ministry over many years. In subsequent reports of the Johnstown Association, formed in 1828, his name is shown as pastor at Steventown as late as 1835.

At the time of Ebberson's ordination, the group in Gananoque were not yet organized as a church. In June 1819, however, one of their number, Thomas Howland, wrote on their behalf to Steventown "requesting a delegation to sit in council to organize the brethren there into a church." Again Elder Stevens was sent to Gananoque as head of a delegation consisting of Brethren June, Tryon, Baker, and Peter June Jr. The church was duly organized on July 1, and continued for a number of years. At the first meeting of the newly formed Johnstown Association it reported thirty-five members, but seven years later it had not increased in size.

The Baptists in Gananoque received help over many years from the missionary societies of the denomination, but their numbers still did not grow. As late as 1878 a student from Woodstock College was busy trying to revive the cause at the beautiful "Gateway to the Thousand Islands." The Principal of Woodstock, Dr. R. A. Fyfe, holidaying in Gananoque that summer, preached on two occasions, his second sermon in the town hall being the last he ever delivered.[26] In the following summer the student reported that the membership had dwindled to thirteen. "It is now felt," he wrote, "that the remaining faithful few are too much separated from each other; and many being absent on excursion boats during the summer, progress in the future will be very slow."[27] In the early 1880's the church went out of existence.

VII

The Churches in Upper Canada: West

THE BAPTIST WITNESS first appeared in the western part of Upper Canada in the area around Long Point, where the demand for land grants was quite brisk, even before the first three townships had been surveyed in 1796. Word of the region's many advantages as a place of settlement reached the ears of certain New Brunswick loyalists and their friends who had grown dissatisfied with the rocky land assigned to them in that province. They therefore left their holdings on the Nashwaak River, a tributary of the Saint John, and arrived at Long Point in 1798, to apply for grants in Upper Canada. Among them was Titus Finch, a former soldier in the Prince of Wales' American Regiment (see the biographical sketch in chapter VIII), who was an earnest lay preacher. He was given land in Charlotteville Township, and was soon busy promoting the cause of religion in his neighbourhood.

Charlotteville (Vittoria), 1803

Baptist influence seems to have been present among these newcomers to Long Point from the time of their arrival in 1798, and Finch himself, though unbaptized as yet, had evidently accepted Baptist views. The fact that in the year 1793 Edward Manning had conducted Baptist revival services in the Saint John River valley of New Brunswick may account for the opinions held by Finch and some of his companions who had lived there at the time.[1] Whatever the explanation, we know that by 1802, when Caleb Blood first visited Upper Canada, there were thirty or forty candidates ready for baptism at Charlotteville and that the people were waiting for the arrival of an ordained missionary to administer the sacred ordinance.

Mr. Blood was unable to visit Long Point that year, but twelve months later, Lemuel Covell and Obed Warren went to Charlotteville, representing the Shaftsbury Baptist Association. Thirty people, including Titus Finch, were baptized by them, and a church was organized during the second week of October 1803. (These events have been presented in the reports of the missionaries on pages 37 and

40-3). Finch was commended by the visiting missionaries for the work he had done in the community, and following his baptism he was given status as a licensed preacher by the church which he had helped to found.

Charter members of the Charlotteville church were Mr. and Mrs. Titus Finch, Mr. and Mrs. Lawrence Johnson, Mr. and Mrs. John Gustin, Mr. and Mrs. Peter Teeple, Mr. and Mrs. Oliver Mabee, Mr. and Mrs. Richard Lanning, Mr. and Mrs. Joseph Merrill, Mr. and Mrs. Samuel Smith, Mr. and Mrs. Robert Shearer, Mr. and Mrs. Abraham Smith, Mr. and Mrs. Andrew McCleish, Mr. and Mrs. Levi Montross, Mr. and Mrs. Peter Fairchild, Mr. and Mrs. James Corliss, Thomas Smith and Solomon Smith. Other early members were Isaac Smith, Jesse Smith, Dr. Troyer and Mrs. Julia Beemer, who later married the Rev. Reuben Crandall.

The church was received into the Shaftsbury Association at its annual meeting in June 1804, and reported that eleven members had been added since its organization. In the autumn Hezekiah Gorton, a Shaftsbury Association missionary, spent some time at Charlotteville and baptized seven persons. In January 1805, it was visited by Rev. Peter Roots and in the fall of that year by Lemuel Covell for the second time. On this occasion Mr. Covell ordained Titus Finch to the ministry; at the end of his visit in November he reported that the church had fifty-two members. Seventeen had been added during the year, twelve had been dismissed to the recently formed church in Townsend, three had been excluded, and one member (probably Mrs. Abraham Smith) had died.

Our next glimpse of the church is given by the record of David Irish's visit in October 1806, when he preached at Deacon Oliver Mabee's. By 1807 the membership had grown to fifty-two, and an acre of land was purchased from Mr. Mabee as a site for a church building and a burying ground. Trustees of the newly acquired property were Peter Teeple and Lawrence Johnson; witnesses to the sale were Richard Lanning and Joseph Merrill. The progress achieved thus far was sufficient to satisfy even so exacting a critic as Asahel Morse, who reported in October 1807 that "the church appears to be in a prosperous state. They have collected materials, and are building them a decent meeting-house." Added prestige had been given to the Baptist cause through Titus Finch's receiving his licence to perform marriages from the Court of Quarter Sessions at its meeting in June that year.[2]

Between 1807 and 1810 the church reported regularly to the Shaftsbury Association and received visits from various missionaries, including Nathaniel Kendrick (1808) and George Witherell (1810). In 1808 a group of members moved to Oxford township and were incorporated as a branch of the Townsend church, forming the nucleus of what became the Oxford church in 1809. The Charlotteville church building, begun in 1807, was completed in 1809, and this commodious structure, with a gallery on three sides of the auditorium, continued to be used until 1851.

From the minutes of the Townsend church we learn that Charlotteville, Clinton, and Townsend conferred on the subject of joining the Thurlow Association in 1809, and that the delegates, on the suggestion of Elijah Bentley, the Association's special representative, actually agreed to withdraw from the Shaftsbury Association in order to join the Canadian body. Though Charlotteville seems to have taken no formal step to withdraw from the Shaftsbury Association at this time, reports to that organization after 1810 were very sketchy. In place of its connection with the Shaftsbury group a closer relationship with its Canadian neighbours was developed through periodic "conferences" with Clinton, Oxford, and Townsend.

The War of 1812 caused a certain amount of disruption in Charlotteville as in other places. Not only was religious activity interrupted but a raid by American forces terrified the settlers. The conflict also confirmed the movement of the Charlotteville church away from the American association. Finally, in 1817, Elder Charles Lahatt came from the Shaftsbury Association and discussed the relationship of the churches in Upper Canada with that organization. Charlotteville, along with four others, formally requested dismissal in 1818, and this was granted in 1819 so that these churches might officially join the Clinton Conference.

Beyond this point in its career we are not permitted in these pages to trace the story of this illustrious church. Suffice it to say that of all the Baptist churches in Upper Canada it has enjoyed the longest continuous and active existence. In its records are preserved with great clarity some of the brightest pictures of the religious aspirations and achievements of our pioneers.

Markham, 1803

Baptist church directories of more recent years contain the information that there have been at least two churches in the township of Markham. That known as First Markham was founded in 1837, and after belonging to the Toronto Association for fifty-two years was transferred to the Whitby-Lindsay Association on its formation in 1889. The Second Markham Baptist church came into being in 1846, and continued as one of the member churches of the Toronto Association until 1927. Both of these churches withdrew from the Baptist Convention of Ontario and Quebec during a violent controversy in the denomination in the late 1920's.

But the church called First Markham was by no means the earliest Baptist church to exist in that township, for a congregation of baptized believers was established there very early in the nineteenth century. In the year 1800 several members of a family named Bentley came from Rhode Island and New Jersey into Markham and applied for land. One of these was a Baptist lay preacher named Elijah Bentley, who received title to a grant in the township in 1801.[3] By 1803 he had established a congregation, and the story of its brief life can be partly traced, not through its own written records, but through references gathered from various sources, the chief of these being the career of Elijah Bentley himself (see chapter VIII).

The minutes of the Thurlow Association for 1804 state that a fourth church had been added to the original three that comprised the Association when it was founded in 1802. Though the name of the church is not given, a careful process of elimination leaves Markham as the church most likely to have been received that year. In 1805 Mr. Bentley was ordained at a service attended by Reuben Crandall, Joseph Winn, and Abel Stevens, a fact which further establishes the connection between Markham and the Thurlow group. In 1806 Bentley applied to the Court of Quarter Sessions of the Home District for a certificate authorizing him to perform marriages, and his application was supported by seven members of his church whose names were William Bentley, Brig. Harrington, Joshua Wixon, Andrew Thomson, Amos Prescott, John Williams, and John Marr.[4] Here, then, we have a short list of some of the earliest Baptists in Markham.

In 1808 Nathaniel Kendrick attended a meeting of the Thurlow Association which he said took place "seventeen miles back of Little York." This meeting must have been at Markham, the location of the only Baptist church known to have been in existence in that vicinity at the time. Bentley's active participation in the affairs of the Thurlow Association is further revealed by his appointment in 1810 as special representative to visit all the churches of the Association. From the minutes of the Philipsville and Townsend churches we learn that he sought to enlarge the Association by persuading other churches to join it.

The arrest of Bentley in 1813 on the charge that he had used seditious language in a sermon, and his subsequent imprisonment, seem to have struck the little church a mortal blow, for it apparently did not survive the War of 1812-14. Nearly twenty-five years had to elapse before the Baptists of Markham Township were able to join once more in the fellowship of an organized church. Even then they were not free from the stresses imposed by political disturbances, for the bitterness engendered by the 1837 rebellion tried them sorely. That, however, is another story.

Townsend (Boston), 1804

The records of Townsend Baptist church, situated in the village of Boston, constitute a social and historical document of great interest. Here, better than anywhere else in the annals of Ontario Baptists, is mirrored for us a picture of congregational life in pioneer days. The original records were in possession of the church until recently, when they were given to the Public Archives of Canada at Ottawa. From them, and from other sources, this narrative is drawn.

To the township of Townsend in 1793 came a New York loyalist by the name of Peter Fairchild. He and his wife, Sarah, both baptized believers, associated themselves with the group of Baptists led by Titus Finch in the nearby township of Charlotteville. When the Charlotteville church was established in 1803, Fairchild, though he lived sixteen miles away, became a member, and took an active part in its affairs, serving on occasion as lay preacher. In 1804, Townsend also received as settlers James Corliss and his wife Sarah, Baptists from the state of New Jersey, and soon after their arrival they too joined the Charlotteville church.

On Sunday, October 21, 1804, some of the Baptists living in Townsend met at the home of George Cunningham for worship, and after hearing a sermon by Mr. Fairchild they agreed to meet again the following Saturday to discuss the organization of a church. At the meeting that took place on October 27 Peter and Sarah Fairchild and James and Sarah Corliss were the only Baptist church members present, but Uriah Corliss and Barzillai and Peggy Beal, who also attended, were described as "new converts." These seven got as far towards forming a church as to adopt a simple covenant, and they continued to meet each month thereafter, adding slowly to their numbers. Julia and Joseph Beemer, Champion and Isabel Schovel, and Rachel Fairchild were "received" into their fellowship between October 1804 and August 1805. On August 25, 1805, Elder Joseph Winn visited the little congregation, and administered the ordinance of baptism to seven people: Barzillai Beal, Champion Schovel, Joseph Beemer, Uriah Corliss, Peggy Beal, Mahitabel Corliss, and Rachel Fairchild.

At their meeting on October 26, 1805, the Townsend congregation sent word to Lemuel Covell, who was then at Charlotteville, that they would like him and a group of brethren to visit them, "to look into our order, and if they shall think it expedient, to give us fellowship as a church in gospel order." The council assembled on November 9, with Lemuel Covell as moderator and Titus Finch as clerk. Its action is recorded in businesslike fashion, a model of procedure for all bodies called for a similar purpose:

1st. A number of brethren and sisters living in this place who are members of the church at Charlotteville manifested their desire to be set off as a church by themselves on account of their living at such a distance that it is very inconvenient for them to perform the duties of Religion in that church.

2nd. Their articles of faith and practice were presented and read, and a number of questions were asked them on points of doctrine and practice and their answers given to said questions.

3rd. Their written covenant read, and to which they all agreed to.

4th. The brethren composing the conference entered by themselves and after mutual consultation agreed unanimously to give them fellowship as a church in sister relation with us.

5th. Voted that Eld. Covell preach a sermon to them and give them the right hand of fellowship.

Signed on behalf of the conference

LEMUEL COVELL, Moderator
TITUS FINCH, Clerk.

After this meeting the organization of the church continued. On Tuesday, November 12, the members met to elect its officers and Uriah Corliss was appointed clerk. Application was made to the Shaftsbury Association for membership in that body. On November 20 four members were named to go to Charlotteville for further conference with that church. Lemuel Covell again presided at a congregational meeting on December 5, at which a confession of faith was adopted and Peter Fairchild was granted a licence to preach. When Covell left in December the church had twenty-four members. It is noteworthy that Fairchild did not assume the responsibility of administering the ordinances even after he was a licensed preacher. Several converts were baptized in February 1806 by Titus Finch, who had been ordained the previous autumn.

Rev. David Irish of the Shaftsbury Association visited Townsend in October 1806. He was to have been accompanied by Lemuel Covell, but the latter's illness prevented his going past Clinton. Since Covell's last visit the people had been asking for Fairchild's ordination, and arrangements were made for this event to take place on October 21. Elder Irish acted as moderator of the ordination council, and Lawrence Johnson served as clerk. The record states that "their beloved Peter Fairchild" was set apart "to the office of the ministry by prayer and laying on of hands." Mr. Irish remained in the vicinity for several weeks, until after November 7, with an interruption at the time of Lemuel Covell's death. The success of his work has been described on page 49.

By April 1807, the church was ready to make plans for the erection of a house of worship. An acre of land was purchased for six pounds from "Sister" Cunningham, and it was agreed that the building should be twenty-four feet square. In this year, again, travelling missionaries from New England came to the young church. The Rev. Jesse Hartwell and Rev. Valentine Rathbun visited it in August on behalf of the Massachusetts Baptist Missionary Society, and in October Asahel Morse of the Shaftsbury Association made a brief visit, after which he said he thought the church was "better informed in doctrine than in discipline." At the end of the year the membership stood at fifty-six.

In 1808 the church barely held its own as far as membership was concerned, for while thirteen were added, twelve were excluded during the year. The exclusion of twelve persons so soon after Elder Morse's visit may have been the result of his pointed remarks about church discipline. The year 1808, however, was marked by some events of special importance, one being a visit by Nathaniel Kendrick and another being the formation of a branch congregation in Oxford. This group, which included several members of the Charlotteville church, as well as eight from Townsend, formed the Oxford Baptist church in the following year.

As the result of a visit in 1809 from the Rev. Elijah Bentley, who represented the Thurlow Association, Townsend resolved to unite with that body and to withdraw from Shaftsbury. No further reports were sent to the latter, but formal dismissal did not take place for another ten years. In 1810 the church was strengthened by the addition of a group of Baptists living in Ancaster. In that year, too, there was held the first of a series of informal meetings which gave rise to the organization known as the Clinton Conference. The minutes of the church show that delegates to this gathering were named in 1810, 1811, 1816, and 1817. During the same period, the church maintained its membership in the Thurlow Association.

The death of James Corliss, one of the founders of the church, occurred in 1812. Towards the end of that year Elder Reuben Crandall and his wife, Lydia, who had moved to the district from Haldimand, were received as members. Mrs. Crandall died soon after she went to Townsend, and in December 1813, the church was rocked by the excitement attendant upon Mr. Crandall's marriage to Julia, the widow of Joseph Beemer. It was alleged by some that Elder Crandall and "July" Beemer had been guilty of "indecent and unworthy travel . . . in regard to their great haste to marry," and special meetings were held to give the Elder an opportunity to explain his conduct. He, however, stood his ground, refusing to acknowledge that the church had any right to question him on the matter. It is recorded that on January 18, 1814, "the church met to settle the above accusation, and Eld. Crandall not seeing it his duty to confess, the church agrees to bury it."

The urge to keep watch and ward over the matrimonial affairs of its members was strong in the Townsend church. In 1817 Sarah Fairchild, the minister's wife, passed away, and after an interval of a year and a half Fairchild was married again, this time to a non-Baptist. Great was the indignation, and the man who had once been described as "our beloved Peter Fairchild" found himself out of favour with the congregation he had laboured so hard to establish. An entry in the minutes dated August 22, 1818, tersely, and somewhat cruelly, states, "considering the case of Eld. Fairchild we concluded there was no hope of a reconciliation taking place, therefore we withdrew our fellowship from him for marrying an unbelieving character and justifying himself to our dissatisfaction."

As a result of Charles Lahatt's visit in 1817 (reported on page 62), the Shaftsbury Baptist Association took formal action at its 1819 meeting to dismiss Townsend to the Clinton Conference. Despite a decline in membership in 1816 and 1817, the church maintained its life and work, and was assisted in 1819 by visits from Elders Moore and Alward. With its roots deeply established in the community of which it has been a part from pioneer days, the church has lived on for a century and a half. Along with some others, it withdrew from the main Baptist body in the 1920's, and united with the Fellowship of Independent Baptist Churches of Canada.

Clinton (Beamsville), 1807

In view of the many statements that have been made regarding the very early founding of the Clinton church, it is necessary to trace with care the facts that have been ascertained. The reader is referred to the account of the settlement of the Niagara Peninsula given in chapter II, and to the statements made by Lemuel Covell and Peter Roots regarding the Baptist cause in Clinton and vicinity in 1803 and 1805. Covell's report in 1803, that there had once been a Baptist church in Clinton, but that it had practically disappeared though some of the members still resided there, raises the question as to when that earlier work had been attempted and what had happened to it in the meantime.

Fortunately, Elder Asahel Morse, who visited Clinton in 1807, went into this matter thoroughly, and his report casts a good deal of light upon the problem. It will be remembered that when Caleb Blood first toured the Niagara Peninsula in 1802, he found the people very suspicious of itinerant missionaries because they had been imposed upon by "vicious characters who had been among them in the profession of preachers." It was just such an impostor, reported Mr. Morse, who had attempted to organize a church in Clinton some years before. His name was Tims, and he called himself a Baptist, but his theology was Arminian and he gave the church neither covenant nor articles of faith.[5] Morse quickly told the Clinton people that they had never, in fact, been a properly organized gospel church, and under his leadership a council met on October 16, 1807, to establish one that could be accepted into a Baptist association. Mr. Morse did not say just when Tims had tried to form his Arminian church, but in all probability it was during the 1790's. Those who set 1796 as the date when this church began have this much at least to support them.

Misunderstanding regarding the beginning of Baptist work in Clinton is undoubtedly due in large measure to the garbled and contradictory account which appeared in Page's *Atlas of Lincoln County* in 1876. There, for example, we are told that "the first church [was] built in 1776 by the Baptists in what is now the village of Beamsville." This statement, however, is contradicted in the next paragraph, which informs us that the first preaching in the township was done in 1782 or 1783 by Rev. William Holmes at the home of Staats Overholt. The date of 1776 for the founding of the church is further contradicted by the same writer when he states that one of the first settlers in Clinton was William Walker of Virginia, who arrived in 1780, at which time the township was still "in its wildest state."

It must be pointed out that if Walker settled on Thirty Mile Creek in 1780, he did so in defiance of the express orders of the commandant at Niagara, who had been instructed not to allow settlers to enter Indian territory until a proper treaty had been made with the Indians; this did not take place till 1784. It will be remembered, also, that in

1782, according to Colonel Butler, there were only sixteen families in the Niagara settlement, and their names are all known. The Niagara authorities apparently knew nothing at that time of any settlers farther west in the peninsula. But if we accept the statement that Walker was there in 1780, we must still ask how, if the township was in its "wildest state" when he came, it can be seriously maintained that a Baptist congregation had been established four years before he arrived.

The statement in the *Atlas* that the first preaching in Clinton was done in 1782 by Rev. William Holmes at the house of Staats Overholt has been widely circulated, and some have been led to set 1782 as the date of the founding of the Clinton church. This cannot be supported by verifiable facts.[6] There is no authentic record of any Baptist minister named William Holmes in Canada or the United States at that time. There was, of course, the well-known minister named Elkanah Holmes, of the New York Missionary Society, who did come to Clinton, but not until after 1800, and the details of his career are on record. During the American Revolution (i.e., until 1783) he was serving as a chaplain with a New Jersey regiment and was known for his extreme revolutionary views. It was said of him by one who knew him well that "he variously urged and aided the valiant resistance which the American colonists were then making against tyranny." It is surely impossible that such an ardent revolutionist, who not only preached to the troops, but fought with them as well, could have been at Clinton in Upper Canada, preaching to loyalist settlers, and founding a church among them while the war was still on. Yet the legend that he did so has stubbornly persisted, thanks to the article in the *Atlas*. After the war ended, Holmes preached in Hackett's Town, N.J., North Stamford, Conn., Bedford, N.Y., and then founded a church on Staten Island. There is no evidence that he ever came near Canada until 1800 or 1801, and his contact with the Baptists of Clinton was made even later.

Although the names of House and Kentner appear in the early annals of the Niagara settlement (1787), and are also found at a later date on the membership roll of the Clinton church, the Baptist cause seems to have arisen with the coming of the Overholt and Beam families. The date of Staats Overholt's arrival is not known. In the petitions signed by him that are on file in the Ontario Bureau of Archives and in the Public Archives of Canada he does not give that information, and the earliest petition of his that has come to light is dated 1791. However, from the account book of the land surveyor, Augustus Jones, as mentioned in chapter II, we learn that Jacob Overholt, a son of Staats, was employed on a surveying party in December 1788, when the township was being surveyed, and it seems reasonable to assume that the Overholt family arrived that year or shortly before.

That Jacob Beam settled in Clinton in 1788 is confirmed by statements made in several of his petitions to the government. He had been a farmer in Sussex County, New Jersey, and had assisted the British in various ways during the Revolution. He had, for instance, recruited twenty men to serve as soldiers for General Skinner. For "harbouring and subsisting Captain Moody when he came out of New York, and for aiding and assisting British soldiers to make their escape from imprisonment" he was imprisoned and fined five hundred pounds. In addition he suffered the loss of some of his property.[7] After the war, he moved to Mansfield, in southern New Jersey, where he is said to have come under Baptist influence; he helped to form a Baptist church there in 1786, a small one of only eighteen members. Two years later, at sixty years of age, he arrived in Upper Canada with his wife and six children. In time he received land grants for himself and his family which amounted to almost one thousand acres. He built mills on Thirty Mile Creek (but complained that there was often not enough water to turn them) and became a prominent citizen in the community. In 1808 he gave land for a church and burying ground, and died in 1812 at the age of eighty-four.

The commencement of Baptist services in the Overholt and Beam homes we can picture in imagination. Visiting preachers of all sorts and descriptions, the Arminian Baptist, Tims, among them, would no doubt play their part, and the attempt at establishing a church would follow in due course, probably in the 1790's. Caleb Blood preached in the vicinity in 1802, and Lemuel Covell and Obed Warren in 1803. By this time Elkanah Holmes was established at Tuscarora on the American side of the Niagara River, and had made some contacts with Baptists in Canada. Covell also mentions "an old Baptist brother named Sloot" who travelled with them for a week. The minutes of the Clinton church reveal that at times the members contributed to the support of Brother Abraham Sloot, and it is possible that he may have been a local preacher who played a part in establishing and maintaining the church there. Twenty years later a younger Abraham Sloot, probably a member of the same family, helped to found a church in Westminster Township.[8]

Hezekiah Gorton passed through Clinton in 1804, and both Lemuel Covell and Peter Roots visited there at different times in 1805. The

Baptist group was not a large one in these years but by 1806 there were signs of a re-awakening among the Baptists of Clinton, and David Irish baptized three converts in the month of October. Covell's death at that time in the home of Jacob Beam, the coming and going of Elkanah Holmes, who preached Covell's funeral sermon, and the visits of David Irish, must all have made an impression on the people. "Some," Mr. Irish reported, "are forsaking their Arminian schemes." When Jesse Hartwell and Valentine Rathbun visited Clinton in late August 1807, interest was such that Hartwell preached to a congregation so large that the service had to be held outside.

October 1807 brought the inspection visit of Asahel Morse. Taking Elder Morse's advice, the Baptist people in Clinton requested the two churches of their persuasion in that part of Canada to form a council for the purpose of granting them recognition. This was done, and Peter Fairchild, with two other members, James Corliss and Joseph Beemer, came from Townsend, while Robert Shearer represented Charlotteville. Mr. Morse himself acted as moderator and presided over the gathering. Articles of faith and a covenant were read and carefully explained to the people. After they had assented to each item by saying "Amen" in unison, Mr. Morse extended to them the right hand of fellowship on behalf of the Shaftsbury Association. Psalm 116 was then sung and Peter Fairchild pronounced the benediction. There were twenty charter members: Jacob Beam, Christian Buchner, Arthur Gray, Samuel Corwin, Daniel House, Isaac Overholt, Staats Overholt, Robert Shelley, James Vanatah, Catherine Beam, Elizabeth Gray, Anna Corwin, Susannah Overholt, Alice Kitchen, Polly Root, Mary Overholt, Esther Stafford, Anna Overholt, Susanah Overholt, and Mary Beam.

Following the formal meeting of the council, the church itself met to receive applications for membership. John Gray was the first to be accepted, and after being baptized in the lake in front of the Overholt house on the next day, he was immediately appointed clerk of the church. From the records kept by him we obtain a fairly accurate account of the church's career after its organization in 1807. The first deacon to be appointed was Arthur Gray, who presided at the business meetings, which were usually held at his house.

In 1808 Christopher Overholt informed the church that he felt called to preach the gospel, and he was given leave to "improve his gift." The effect of his amateur discourses on the congregation may be judged by the fact that one month later it was recorded, "We have heard Br. Overholt and do not think his gift profitable, therefore we desired him to stop and he likewise did." The Shaftsbury Association gave formal recognition to the church in June 1808, at its annual meeting. In September Nathaniel Kendrick spent some time at Clinton while on his tour of the province; he reported that the church was "small and destitute," and depended on Elkanah Holmes for part-time oversight. This is confirmed by the minutes, which state that on December 10, 1808, "finding that Elder Holmes was settled in this Province [the members] took into consideration to call him to our assistance as much of his time as he could find duty." At the same meeting they decided to give an offering to the Missionary Society and instructed Arthur Gray to finish the church building, lay the floors, put in a stove, and fix the windows.

In April 1809, Holmes told the church that he could no longer provide the part-time oversight he had been giving them, and it was decided that they should invite Nathaniel Kendrick to become their settled pastor. Mr. Kendrick visited them in the late fall but concluded that he could not accept their invitation and returned home in November. His refusal of the call was a blow to the Baptist cause as a whole as well as to the church at Clinton. A leader of his stature might have done much in those early days to establish the denomination firmly.

Mr. Holmes continued to render part-time service at Clinton, but it is plain that a stronger, wiser leadership than his was needed to guide the church towards greater usefulness. Many meetings were devoted solely to settling disputes between members. Some degenerated into noisy squabbles, and even Christopher Overholt, the erstwhile would-be minister, was accused of "brawling and railing" at a church meeting held in the home of Jacob Beam. Holmes was constantly being ordered by vote of the church to read this person or that out of the membership. The vote on such a matter was nearly always taken on a week-night, but the real "dirty work" had to be done by the preacher who was called on to make the public announcement at the Sunday service.

Daniel House was more than once charged with being drunk in public, at which times he was given to taking off his shirt and offering to fight anyone who would accept his challenge. His wife Sally was also disciplined for quarrelling with Susannah Singer, and after resisting the judgment of the church for some time she yielded and expressed repentance. Mrs. Catherine Merrel, who had left the Baptist fellowship about 1804 to join the Methodists, applied for membership in 1812, but before being admitted was required to sign a document admitting her errors and abjuring her misconduct in having attended Methodist services and in having taken communion with them. One member accused Deacon Gray of taking his oxen and working them. Another charged Jacob Beam Junior with defaulting on a debt of seventeen bushels of rye. Deacon Gray was ordered to pay seventeen shillings to the owner of the oxen and Mr. Beam, under protest, obeyed the church's command to deliver the rye. One member signed a promissory note to another for three dollars, but when it was due claimed he owed three shillings. The church admonished him for his "disgracefully refusing to pay" his debt.

Pacifist sentiment on the part of Staats and Isaac Overholt and their wives led to prolonged discussion of this subject. It is possible that the Overholts, like the Beams, may have come of Mennonite stock, and retained their Mennonite pacifism after becoming Baptists. The affair ended by their withdrawing from the church, "for," says the record, "they could not walk with us because we bore arms."

Despite the turbulent business meetings, a strong current of spiritual life still flowed beneath the surface, and new members were constantly received, either by baptism or by transfer. The Rev. George Witherell baptized two candidates when he and Daniel Hascall visited Clinton in 1810. Offerings were taken for both the New York and Massachusetts Baptist Missionary Societies. Samuel Burdick was granted a licence to preach, and entered into part-time duty as pastor in August 1810. In December Jonathan Wolverton applied for membership, saying that he had once belonged to the Baptist church in Kingwood (New Jersey), but when that church had divided over "universalist" doctrines he had gone with the universalist group. He now recanted, and desired to become a Baptist once more.

Jonathan Wolverton had come to Upper Canada from New Jersey with his wife and four children in 1798. In 1800 he took the oath of allegiance before Robert Nelles, J.P., and on the outbreak of the War of 1812 he repeated the oath as a proof of his loyalty. In 1819 he applied to Sir Peregrine Maitland for a grant of land as a settler.[9] Mr. Nelles, in a letter now deposited in the Public Archives of Canada, strongly recommended Mr. Wolverton as a "good neighbour, a sober and industrious man." He went on to say that in the War of 1812-14 Mr. Wolverton, though sixty years old, had driven his team in the service of the government, going once, in 1813, as far as Sandwich with a detachment of the 45th Regiment. From the time when he became a member of the Clinton church in 1811 he took an active part in its affairs, and his surname is still prominent in the denomination.

In 1810 and 1811, the preaching at Clinton seems to have been shared by Samuel Burdick and Elkanah Holmes, both of whom also preached at Queenston. Mr. Burdick and his wife became members at Clinton, and he continued to serve the church throughout the war years. Holmes, who had always been strongly pro-American in his loyalty, left Canada during the war, and the last time that his name appeared in the minutes of the church was when he presided at a meeting in October 1812. The only reference to the conflict itself which occurs in the record is a statement that on account of the "troubles of the wars" no meeting was held from June 4 to September 24 in the year 1814. On April 1, 1815, the church resolved to hold a public meeting on the first Thursday in May "to render thanks to Almighty God for His blessing of peace." At the same time a letter was sent to the Shaftsbury Association asking that a missionary be sent to visit them.

In the summer of 1815, the renewed activity brought a request on August 24 to Townsend and Charlotteville to send delegates to a council. This met on September 9. Rev. Stephen Olmstead and Rev. Cyrus Andrews came from the Shaftsbury Association, and Rev. Nathan Baker represented the Hamilton Missionary Society. The council, as described elsewhere (see chapter IV), refused to ordain Mr. Burdick, and he and his wife left Clinton in February 1816. Shortly after Mr. Burdick's departure, the Rev. John Upfold, of the Hamilton Missionary Society, visited Clinton, and that fall, as has been reported (chapter IV), became their minister, remaining with them for nine years. A new era in the life of the church was begun when this well-educated and capable minister assumed charge of its affairs.

Niagara (Queenston), 1808

The Baptist missionaries who crossed the Niagara River into Canada during the early years of the nineteenth century found a welcome in the homes of several settlers living in the townships of Stamford, Niagara, and Grantham. Archibald Thomson (a Presbyterian), Isaac Swayze, Rose's and Slater's are mentioned in the reports of the missionaries as people in that area who had shown them hospitality and opened their doors for services.

When Elkanah Holmes settled at Fort Schlosser in 1800 he soon made contact with Baptists on the Canadian side of the river, and in 1803 he assisted Lemuel Covell and Obed Warren in their preaching to the settlers around Niagara, Queenston, and Grantham. By 1807, according to Nathaniel Kendrick, Holmes was preaching to a small congregation at Queenston, in a "house pleasantly situated on the banks of the Niagara River." Mr. Kendrick went on to say of the house, "It is the property of a gentleman of liberality, who had made the Baptists welcome to hold meetings for a year past. Here Mr. Holmes has frequently preached with much acceptance to the people, with considerable success."[10]

Mr. Kendrick spent two Sundays with Holmes in October 1808, and while he was there a church was constituted with nine charter members. Most of these had been baptized by Holmes himself since he began to preach in the vicinity. Kendrick was impressed by the manner in which the organization was carried out, saying that the people showed a better understanding of the covenant and articles of faith than the members of many long established churches. Holmes divided his time between the church at Queenston and other congregations that called for his services, the chief of these being that at Clinton; he had also given several weeks that fall to preaching in New York State. Already plans were being made to erect a church building at Queenston.

Further information about the Queenston church is found in the minutes of the New York (city) Baptist Association, of which Holmes was a past moderator. In April 1809, he wrote to the Association reporting on his work in Upper Canada, and the clerk was in turn instructed to reply to his letter. The Queenston church applied for admission to the New York Association in 1810, and the clerk was told to write that it had been granted admission. The church was reported to be "increasing and flourishing" under Holmes's ministry.

In 1811 the report to the Association showed that there were only eighteen members in the Queenston church. The New York Baptist Missionary Society, however, reported to its annual meeting that the church at Niagara, Upper Canada, was making progress: "Unity abounds — zeal for knowledge increaseth — both male and female members have met once a week the past year to assist each other in reading the scriptures. An opulent and generous man [Mr. W. H. Young] has given four acres of ground on which to build a meeting house." The Society then named Elkanah Holmes and Mr. Young to act as agents to solicit funds on its behalf for the erection of the said meeting house.

The minutes of the New York Association for 1812 record that a letter was received from the Queenston church, but no delegate attended. There was no reference to Holmes. From 1813 onward the minutes of the Association make no reference to the church at Queenston, but the 1813 edition of David Benedict's *History of the Baptists* states that "the church at Niagara, Upper Canada, under Elder Elkanah Holmes, has a seat in the New York Association." With the departure of Holmes from Canada in 1813, oversight of the Queenston church devolved upon the licensed preacher, Samuel Burdick, who preached there and at Clinton on alternate Sundays.

The fortunes of the Queenston congregation after the war are obscure. Its membership in the New York Association ceased, and evidently the church became dormant for a time. By 1832, according to I. M. Allen's *Annual Baptist Register,* there was a church at Queenston with forty-two members, fifteen of whom had been received during the previous twelve months. William Stillwell, a licensed preacher, was in charge. This church, however, according to later editions of the *Year Book* of the Baptist Convention of Ontario and Quebec, came into being in 1831, so it would appear that the earlier Queenston church barely survived the War of 1812.

It is well to remember that the church founded in 1808 received its name from Niagara Township, and is not to be confused with later churches which bore that name because they were situated at Niagara Falls. The original Queenston church had a struggle to survive the War of 1812; the reorganized church that succeeded it in 1831 succumbed during the First World War. By 1916 its membership had declined to five, three of whom were non-resident, and in 1917 it reported to the Niagara Association for the last time.

Oxford, 1809

The land which now comprises the three townships of East, West, and North Oxford was originally assigned to Thomas Ingersoll and his associates in 1793.[11] Two years passed before he was able to make his way through the woods to the site he had selected for his home, but at length he arrived at the place where the town of Ingersoll now stands, and began to clear away the trees. In the end, Mr. Ingersoll and his friends were treated in the same way as the majority of settlers, each receiving a deed to one township lot. By 1806 a great many settlers had entered Oxford; the Canfield, Mabee, Teeple, Scott, and Burtch families were among those that became identified with the Baptist church.

The Canfields were members of the original party associated with Thomas Ingersoll, and so, apparently, was Elizabeth Scott. Peter Teeple, known as "Squire" Teeple, had been a lieutenant in the British army during the American Revolution and was married to Lydia Mabee, daughter of Frederick Mabee. He and the Mabees had settled in Norfolk County in 1793, but he later moved to the Thames River in West Oxford Township. His brother-in-law, Simon Mabee, also moved from Norfolk and settled nearby in the same township. Peter Teeple's daughter Susan married Archibald Burtch, a son of Zachariah Burtch. The latter had come from New York State in 1798 and is said to have built the first log house in what is now the city of Woodstock.[12] Archibald Burtch later became well known throughout the denomination for his generous support of the Canadian Literary Institute; on one occasion he mortgaged his farm to help the college over a critical period.

In the fall of 1803, Lemuel Covell and Obed Warren visited the Baptists of Oxford Township during their missionary tour. The people were overjoyed to see them and a number of baptisms took place. In 1806 the Rev. David Irish also visited Oxford for the Shaftsbury Association and several more were baptized. He regretted that there was no minister in the place. Mr. Irish was followed in 1807 by another Shaftsbury Association missionary, Asahel Morse, who stayed four days in the vicinity and preached ten times at six different places including the homes of Captain Sweat, Mr. Sage, and Mr. Haskins (see also page 51); some of his services were held jointly with the Methodists of the region. One of those whom he baptized was Zachariah Burtch.

In July 1808, Elder Peter Fairchild, of Townsend, visited Oxford and conferred with a group of Baptists that included Peter Teeple, Simon Mabee, Zachariah Burtch, Deborah Sales, Abigail Burtch, and Elizabeth Scott. Abigail Mabee, wife of Simon Mabee, was baptized on this occasion, and out of this conference, held at the home of Peter Teeple, came certain decisions that were to lead to the formation of a church. As a beginning, those who had assembled at Mr. Teeple's agreed to live according to the generally accepted tenets of Baptist discipline, and to hold a covenant meeting on the second Saturday of every month. On September 24, the same autumn, Mr. Fairchild again visited the little group, this time accompanied by Nathaniel Kendrick, who was on a missionary tour representing the Shaftsbury Association, and it was decided that they should ask for recognition as a branch of the Townsend church. The addition of Samuel and Lucy Canfield had increased their numbers to nine.

Within twelve months the little congregation had developed sufficiently to seek recognition as a separately organized church. On October 5, 1809, a council was convened with Titus Finch as moderator and Samuel Burdick as clerk. The result of its deliberations was that the First Regular Baptist Church of Oxford came into being, with nineteen charter members. In June 1811, it was received into the Shaftsbury Baptist Association, and the latter's reports for that year and the next give the membership as twenty-two. During the next five years, the Association continued to list its membership at that figure, owing to the fact that during the War of 1812-14 no reports were sent.

In July 1812, Simon Mabee was granted a licence to preach, and throughout the war years it was to him that the church looked for its pulpit ministry. Though not yet ordained, he devoted a great deal of his time to preaching, and his ministerial status was quite generally recognized. Michael Smith, writing of Oxford in 1812, said that in the township there were "1 divine (Baptist), and 3 religious societies (2 Methodist and 1 Baptist)."

Following the War of 1812-14, when contact between the churches of Upper Canada and those in the United States was again established, Oxford seems to have made no attempt to communicate with the Shaftsbury Association to which it nominally belonged. It was still listed by the Association in 1817, but its membership figures had not been revised since 1811. In 1817 the Association despatched Charles Lahatt to visit Upper Canada to clarify the relationship between the organization and its member churches in the province. He arrived at Oxford early in October, to discover that on the fourth day of that month a council of delegates from Clinton, Charlotteville, and Townsend had agreed to ordain Simon Mabee as soon as a really representative gathering could be convened. Mr. Lahatt's visit provided the occasion for this meeting, and he ordained Mr. Mabee in the presence of a large congregation.

The name of the Oxford church disappeared from the Shaftsbury Association statistical report in 1818, and in 1819 it was formally dismissed to the Clinton Conference of Upper Canada. In that same year of 1819 it was divided into three sections, one east of the Governor's Road, one in the River Settlement, and one at the South Oxford Settlement. Deacons Trees, Tims, and Kings respectively were to supervise these three divisions and services were held in school houses. In 1820 Darius Cross, Nicholas French, and James Harris were licensed to preach.

Although the First Baptist Church in Oxford Township was Calvinistic in doctrine and "regular" in polity, it was soon affected by "Free Communion" and "Free Will" influences. Several of its leading members, including Darius Cross and James Harris, were to withdraw in 1822 when a Free Communion Baptist church was formed in the town of Oxford (Woodstock). This Free Communion church, to which Archibald Burtch belonged, became known in time as the First Baptist Church, Woodstock. The original First Regular Baptist Church of Oxford, which arose in West Oxford Township in 1809, continued its life in what was later called the Thames Street Baptist Church in Ingersoll.

Malahide (Talbot Street, or Aylmer), 1816

When the township of Malahide began to fill up with settlers under the direction of Thomas Talbot, the familiar denominational patterns of religious life appeared there as in other pioneer communities. Methodists and Baptists were especially active in itinerant preaching, and one religious "inquirer," who had not yet decided what his church affiliation was to be, wrote of these two groups, "I was invited by both sides, 'Come with us and we will do thee good.' " The writer of these words was Samuel Baker, who, shortly after his marriage in 1815 to Elizabeth, eldest daughter of Deacon Oliver Mabee, had moved from Charlotteville to Malahide.[13] He and his wife sorely missed the regular services and social contacts of the church they had left behind, though neither of them had at that time become a church member. "I felt very much the loss of our Sabbath privileges," he recalled in his memoirs, and went on to say, "These were dull Sabbaths, far from gospel preaching and from loved friends."

Though the Bakers felt very lonely at their pioneer farm on Talbot Street, the township of Malahide was by no means destitute of preaching. About the time of their removal to that vicinity the Rev. Stephen Olmstead, of the Hamilton Missionary Society, preached at the home of Joseph Davis, and Mr. Baker said he and his brother travelled eight miles to hear him. There was yet no organized Baptist church holding regular weekly services, but one was to be formed on October 1, 1816, as a result of frequent visits made to the community by Titus Finch, Simon Mabee, and especially Reuben Crandall. Several Baptist families had moved westward from the Long Point district to Malahide, and the new church that was organized on Talbot Street had twelve charter members: Mr. and Mrs. William Teeple, Mr. and Mrs. William

Davis, Mr. and Mrs. Joseph Davis, Mr. and Mrs. Stephen Leek, Kate and Polly Mann, Daniel McKenney, and Mrs. John D. Brown.

Present at the time of organization were Reuben Crandall, Nicholas French of Oxford, and the Rev. John Upfold, who had just come to Clinton. Solomon Smith, who joined the church by letter from Charlotteville, acted frequently as lay preacher, but in 1817 Mr. Crandall was invited to become the settled pastor and from then on made his permanent home in Malahide. In 1818 the Shaftsbury Association voted to receive the "Baptist church in Talbot Street (U.C.)," and its statistical report shows that the church had nineteen members. Samuel Baker and his wife were baptized by Mr. Crandall in 1819, and other additions during Crandall's pastorate brought the membership up to thirty by the time he left to resume an itinerant ministry again. The date of the termination of his full-time ministry is not clear, but it can be fixed as some time in the early 1820's.

For several years after its organization the Malahide or Talbot Street church met in Teeple's barn, near Orwell, west of Aylmer, or in the school house at Rodger's Corners. After Reuben Crandall relinquished the pastorate it depended upon visiting ministers and local lay preachers. Samuel Baker, who had served the church quite regularly for some time, became a licensed preacher in 1825, and in 1828 he was ordained to the full-time ministry. By 1843 a chapel seating three hundred people had been erected in the town of Aylmer, and there the church has remained ever since. Like Charlotteville, Oxford, Townsend, and Clinton, it was formally dismissed from the Shaftsbury Association in 1819.

Bayham (Port Burwell), 1819

According to an historical sketch written in June 1944, when the church at Port Burwell was celebrating its 125th anniversary,[14] an introductory page of an early minute book kept by the church reads as follows:

January 19th, 1819. A number of Baptist Brethren living in the township of Bayham, in the county of Middlesex, in the district of London, and province of Upper Canada, met together at the house of Dennis Downlands to consult together the better how to keep up the Visibility of Christ's Kingdom. Opened meeting by solemn prayer.

1. Requested Elder Simon Mabee, a missionary from the Upper Canada Domestic Missionary Society, and brother Teeple from the Baptist Church in Oxford, and Deacon Samuel Smith from the Baptist Church in Charlotteville, to sit in Council with us.

2. Choose Elder Simon Mabee Moderator and Joseph Merrill, Clerk.

3. Proceed to examine the brethren's letters and write down the names of those we found in good standing, which are as follows:

James Russell	Elizabeth Russell
Thomas Hollywood	Sarah Hollywood
Jesse Smith	Elizabeth Smith
Joseph Merrill	Rebecca Merrill
Isaac Smith	Mary Griffin

4. Proceeded to take the names of those that offered themselves as candidates for baptism.

Samuel Edison	Nancy Edison
John Sibley	Elizabeth Sibley

Elder Mabee baptized them.

5. Elder Mabee gave the right hand of fellowship as a Sister Church. The church made choice of Thomas Hollywood and James Russell as our deacons.

The same account relates that a church covenant, eleven articles of faith, and eleven articles of practice were adopted. Meetings were held once a month to renew the covenant. The ordinance of baptism was administered by visiting ordained ministers when the opportunity offered, Elder Alward, who visited Townsend in 1819 and Charlotteville in 1820, being one who assisted in this way. Elder George Ebberson of Gananoque and Steventown was another minister who baptized candidates at Bayham. A building was erected soon after the church was organized.

Joseph Merrill, who acted as clerk at the organization meeting, was a native of New Brunswick who had moved to Upper Canada in 1804 and had lived at Charlotteville, where he married Rebecca Fairchild, daughter of the Rev. Peter Fairchild, the U.E. Loyalist minister of the Townsend church. Merrill received a grant of two hundred acres of land in Malahide Township, and his wife, as the daughter of a loyalist, received the same amount.[15] He was chosen to be the first pastor of the Bayham church, was ordained as an elder, and served in that capacity until his death in 1842.

The fact that some of the Edisons were connected with the Bayham church is of special interest because of the fame achieved by one of their descendants, Thomas A. Edison, the inventor. His great-grandfather, John Edison, had served on the British side in the American Revolution; indeed he had actually been sentenced to be hanged in the United States but escaped. He went to Nova Scotia in 1783, where he bought some land and lived until his family were grown up. In 1811 he moved to Upper Canada with his three sons, Thomas, Moses, and Samuel, and his three sons-in-law, James Wilson, Peter Weaver, and Dennis Dowling, accompanied them.[16] It was in the home of the last named that the Bayham church was organized.

John Edison's son, Samuel Edison Senior, was married and the father of eight children when they moved from Digby, Nova Scotia.[17] In 1812 he was commissioned as a captain in the 1st Regiment, Middlesex Militia, and commanded a battalion company in which at least two other Edisons served as privates. Thomas Talbot himself commanded the regiment, and signed the muster rolls of Samuel's company.[18] Many of the Edisons, it may be added, received their grants of land through Colonel Talbot, and from his recommendations attached to their petitions, they appeared to be on good terms with him. When the Baptist church was organized at the home of his brother-in-law, Dennis Dowling, Samuel Edison and his wife were the first to apply for baptism.

One of the eight children whom Samuel Edison brought with him from Nova Scotia was his son, Samuel Junior. He married Nancy Elliott in 1828, and became an innkeeper in the London District. Unlike his father and his grandfather, Samuel Edison Junior adopted a hostile attitude towards constituted authority in Upper Canada, and was indicted for high treason during the days of the rebellion.[19] His name appears on a list of sixty-one persons indicted but not brought to trial because they had left the country, and so it was that Thomas Alva Edison, his sixth child, was born in the United States, in 1847.

Whether Samuel Junior was ever a member of the Bayham church is not clear, nor is it clear how long Samuel Senior continued to be a member after his baptism in 1819. There is reason to believe that the elder Edison's membership ceased after he was disciplined by the congregation for some infraction of the church's rules. The frequency with which he was prosecuted in the Court of Quarter Sessions on charges of assault and battery would indicate that he was not the type of man to endure church discipline patiently.[20]

Like the church in Charlotteville, the Bayham church was strongly reinforced in early times by people of loyalist stock who had been influenced by Baptist ideas in Nova Scotia. It was fortunate in the pastor chosen to lead it, and continued to flourish. Two other churches in the same township, Lakeview and Calton, were later formed from the original parent, and all three have continued their active service to the present time.

VIII

The Baptist Ministers of Upper Canada

before 1820

THE TITLE GIVEN to the leader or overseer of the local congregation was Elder or Minister, or occasionally, Pastor, the first of these being used much more generally than either of the other two. While Baptists in all parts of the world have agreed that the elder or pastor is equivalent to the New Testament bishop, the latter term was hardly ever used to describe a Baptist minister in these provinces. Even under the most primitive pioneer conditions, the churches adhered to the pronouncement of the Philadelphia Confession that "the way appointed by Christ for the calling of any person . . . unto the office of bishop or elder, is that he be chosen thereunto by the common suffrage of the church, and solemnly set apart by fasting and prayer, with imposition of hands of the eldership of the church. . . ."[1] No instance has come to light of any minister being ordained by a local congregation without the presence and participation of some ordained missionary or representative of an association. Only those already ordained to the eldership could in turn lay hands upon a new ordinee.

Proof of a man's fitness for ordination lay not in his formal training or educational qualifications, but in whether he possessed sufficient natural gifts to justify the church in setting him apart. In order that he might "improve" his gifts through practice, it was customary to grant a promising layman a "licence to preach." Such a licence could be revoked if it became apparent that the candidate had no aptitude for the work of preaching. Licensed preachers frequently acted as assistants to ordained elders whose work was too much for one man to do. At times the licentiate found himself in full charge of a congregation, through lack of a qualified minister, but even in such circumstances he was not permitted to administer the ordinances of baptism and the Lord's supper.

Typical of the point of view that governed in such cases is the answer given by the Warren Association of Massachusetts and Rhode Island to a query addressed to its annual meeting by one of its member churches in 1805:

Query: "Is a licentiate in the Ministry to govern himself by the commission of Christ, Matt. 28:19, to teach and baptize; or be subject to the prevailing custom of the churches, to teach and not baptize?"

Answer: "We think that a brother does not officially receive the commission to teach and baptize, until he receive the imposition of the hands of the presbytery; but in order that the church may gain the evidence that he has the appropriate qualification for the office of a Bishop, it may be necessary that they should license him previously, to improve his gift."[2]

Where a church called to its pastorate an elder who had already been ordained, it was customary to hold a service of installation or induction. Thus in 1785 the church in Pittsford, Vermont, of which Abel Stevens was a charter member, as soon as it had called Elder Elisha Rich as its first minister, sent to neighbouring churches for "elders to install Elder Rich over this church." After a service of worship which included a sermon, Elder Eastman conducted the ceremony of "prayer and laying on of hands," Elder Skeels delivered a charge to the new minister, and a member of the church, Caleb Hendee, gave Elder Rich the right hand of fellowship.[3] Baptists of the twentieth century who consider the holding of an induction service to be an innovation in Baptist circles should note this event which took place on March 17, 1785!

The high ideal set forth in the Confession that "it is incumbent on the churches to whom they the pastors minister . . . to communicate to them of all their good things, according to their ability, so as they may have a comfortable supply, without being themselves entangled in secular affairs" was incapable of fulfilment. Most ministers found it necessary to do secular work of some kind in order to support themselves, though there were some exceptions. John Upfold of Clinton seems to have lived entirely on what the church provided.

The problem of the itinerant preacher, who, without credentials of any kind, went from one pioneer community to another calling himself a Baptist minister, was at times a vexing one. The churches were warned against such men by the associations, who labelled them "impostors," and laid down rules by which they could be identified and exposed. The records of the Canadian churches show that care was taken to examine the credentials of any newcomer who claimed to be a Baptist elder.

The right of Baptist ministers to solemnize marriage in Upper Canada was long under dispute in some quarters. By an Act of the Upper Canada legislature in 1798 (38 George III, cap. IV) marriages could be solemnized by "ministers of the Church of Scotland, Lutherans and Calvinists, and by their own right," but the minister had first to obtain a certificate of authority from the Court of Quarter Sessions in his district. To obtain such authority he had to give three months' notice of his application, and then appear in court with seven members of his congregation to prove that he had been appointed as their minister. He had also to present proof that he had been ordained.

As Baptists were not named in the Act, they, as well as Methodists, often had difficulty in obtaining the necessary authority from their district court. In some districts there was no trouble if the minister followed the rules laid down for Presbyterians, Lutherans, and Calvinists. Reuben Crandall obtained his licence in the Newcastle District in 1805, and Titus Finch in the London District in 1807. Even Presbyterians, however, could have difficulty if a court official was determined to be obstructive, and William Bell, the Presbyterian minister at Perth, has told of his trouble with the clerk of the court in the Johnstown District.[4] An interesting contention on the part of some Baptists was that though they were not specifically named in the Act of 1798, they could properly be included under the name "Calvinists," since in doctrine and polity they were Calvinistic. This argument was set forth by John Upfold in his letter to Sir Peregrine Maitland in 1821.[5] At no time, however, did Baptists of that period ever suggest that unordained licensed preachers should be allowed to solemnize marriage. To use the language of the petition sent by Abel Stevens and others to Lieutenant-Governor Simcoe in 1796, this was a privilege that was sought only for "regularly ordained elders."

From the many sources of information on Baptist work in Upper Canada before 1820 a list can be made of at least eighteen ordained ministers who lived and worked in the province in that early period. Those whose names are known were Elijah Bentley, Jesse Brown, Peleg Card, "Elder" Carson, Reuben Crandall, Daniel Derbyshire, George Ebberson, Peter Fairchild U.E.L., Titus Finch, Elkanah Holmes, James Hulse, Simon Mabee, James Stark, Abel Stevens U.E.L., Alex. Stewart, Asa Turner, John Upfold and Joseph Winn. Not all of these remained in the province throughout the entire period under review, and in the cases of James Stark and Alex. Stewart there is no definite information regarding their work among the churches. Nevertheless, each name recalls a story of some kind, and those who carry on the work begun by them do well to see that they are not entirely forgotten.

Elijah Bentley

The background of Elijah Bentley may be gleaned from an unofficial family history kept up over the years by interested relatives and descendants, to which reference is made by Reuben Butchart in *The Disciples of Christ in Canada since 1830*. Like most family histories, this one contains a certain amount of folklore mingled with the facts, and some of the facts have been misplaced chronologically. Thus, while it seems probable that the founder of the American branch of the Bentley family was Benjamin Bentley of Rhode Island, we cannot accept the statements made in the family history that he was a member of Bunyan's church in Elstow, England, and that he later joined Roger Williams in helping to found First Baptist Church, Providence, Rhode Island. When the church in Providence was founded in 1639, John Bunyan was only eleven years old, and he did not begin to preach until eighteen years later.

Be that as it may, several of Benjamin Bentley's great-grandchildren, including William, a son of Caleb Bentley, and Elijah, a son of Samuel Bentley, moved into Markham Township in the year 1800. They were a gifted family, and nearly all were Baptists. One of their cousins, another William Bentley, a son of Thomas Bentley, was a very successful Baptist minister in the United States.[6]

Elijah received his land patent in 1801.[7] Like his cousin in the United States, he felt the call to preach, and his friends and relatives assisted him in organizing a Baptist church in Markham in 1803. Ordination came in 1805, and the minutes of the Court of Quarter Sessions for the Home District[8] relate his attempts to obtain the authority that was necessary before he could perform marriages:

8th Oct. 1805.
Read a notice of Elijah Bentley, that he will apply at the next general sessions for a Certificate to authorize him to celebrate the ceremony of marriage as a Calvinist minister.

14th Jan. 1806.
Elijah Bentley of Markham, having notified on the 8th day of October last, that he would apply at the present General Quarter Sessions of the Peace for a certificate to enable him (as a Minister of the Calvinist congregation of the said Township of Markham), to celebrate the Ceremony of Matrimony, appeared in person and made application for the said certificate, stating that the persons required by the Statute in such case made and provided, were also present.

On this occasion the court adjourned without dealing with his application, because only four judges were present and six were required by law to hear such cases.

The story is resumed, however, three months later, when he presented his certificate of ordination and renewed his request for a licence.

8th April, 1806.

Elijah Bentley, calling himself a preacher of the Calvinist congregation in the Township of Markham, personally appeared; and produced a paper, of which the following is a copy —

'Percy, Feb. 10, 1806'

'This certifies to whom it may concern that I, Reuben Crandall, of the first Baptist Church of Christ, in Cramahae, Upper Canada, by request, did sit as a member of the Council of Mr. Elijah Bentley's ordination on the Eleventh Day of August last with Elder Joseph Winn and Elder Abel Stevens. In confirmation I have hereunto affixed my hand and seal.'

(signed) REUBEN CRANDALL.

9th April, 1806.

Elijah Bentley appeared. Ordered that his certificate, read yesterday, be returned to him, and that it cannot be admitted as a sufficient Testimony of his ordination as a Calvinist Minister under which denomination he presents himself. The said Certificate being under the signature of one who states himself a Baptist.

Bentley was not the only Baptist minister of those times to try to take advantage of the clause in the statute that provided for the issuing, to "Calvinist" ministers, of the authority to perform marriages. As we have seen, these ministers argued that since they were Calvinistic in doctrine they properly came under the terms of the Act, even though their denominational name was Baptist. In some places the argument worked, but evidently not in the Home District!

In 1810 Mr. Bentley was named as a special agent of the Thurlow Association to visit all the churches in Upper Canada and to persuade any of them that had not yet joined the organization to do so. In that capacity he visited Steventown, and the church minutes record that a dispute between him and the pastor, Jesse Brown, had been "settled." It is also clear from the Steventown minutes that the Association paid Bentley's travel expenses and that each church was expected to pay its share. Earlier, he had been successful in persuading the Townsend church to leave the Shaftsbury Association and to join the Thurlow group.

The dispute between Bentley and Jesse Brown is not the only instance on record of Bentley's managing to get himself into trouble through unwise speech; in June 1813, the minutes of the Home District assizes state that "Elijah Bentley, Anabaptist preacher, was convicted by a jury of using seditious language in a sermon preached in Markham Township on May 2nd." He was sentenced to six months in county gaol and had to give bonds to keep the peace for five years. Whether the sentence was deserved or not it is difficult to tell, for many such charges were laid without much foundation. In any case, it effectively silenced a very energetic man who had been active for a decade among the pioneer Baptist churches, and from that time on he disappears from Baptist history.

Later generations of Bentleys played a part in the development of the denomination known as Disciples of Christ, which, in Upper Canada, drew heavily from the ranks of Baptist churches, especially those of the "Scotch" type in such townships as Markham, Dunwich, Aldborough, and Eramosa.[9] Some of the later Bentleys, also, were under a cloud for suspected disloyalty during the days of the Upper Canada Rebellion in 1837. It was a Baptist minister, the Rev. A. Stewart, who intervened on their behalf at that time when he became convinced that some of them were being unjustly punished, so that Elijah Bentley's services to the Baptist cause in an earlier day did not go entirely unrequited.

Jesse Brown

The minutes of the Steventown church may serve to introduce the account of this pioneer minister. They inform us that at a meeting held on February 25, 1809, with Abel Stevens presiding,

Beloved Brother and sister Brown gave in their relations and presented a recommend from the branch of the Baptist church to which they belonged, to the full satisfaction of the Brethren and sisters of this church. But for the obtaining of other credentials and further acquaintance it was thought proper not to join in covenant bonds at this time. Considered the case of Brother Brown as teacher in Zion, and after hearing a brief relation of his life and experience, together with the acquaintance that we have had with him, thought it expedient for him to preach with us, which was manifested by a vote of the church and society.

The facts behind this entry seem to be that Steventown had lost its minister, evidently through death, and was now in need of a preacher. Jesse Brown was a newcomer amongst them, but his preaching had been so acceptable that they were willing to have him continue, even though they were cautious about receiving him and his wife as members of the church. However, just a month later, we are told that "Brother Brown and sister Brown came forward and joined the church, having letters from other churches." Then followed negotiations between the congregation and Mr. Brown which must be almost unique in Baptist annals. Anxious as they were to obtain his services as their settled pastor, they first had to consider how they would provide for his support. As a start, they purchased fifty acres of land to be a sort of "glebe" for the minister, and Obadiah Reed, Rebekah Reed, and William Parish gave money donations "to support Jesse Brown, minister of the gospel." On June 2, 1809, according to the old minute book, arrangements were completed in a signed agreement.

A committee of the Baptist church and society met according to appointment at the house of Jesse Brown for the purpose of settling the said Brown in the ministry, and agreed if the said J. Brown shall continue a faithful leader of the church six years, the said farm, estimated at fifty pounds shall be his and his heirs for ever. If he wishes to leave the place at any time he may by paying back to the church and society that which they have put into his hands with a deduction of one sixth part of the fifty pounds yearly for his improvements. And if the said J. Brown shall die at any time short of the six years the said property shall be the property of his present wife to be at her full disposal.

(signed) THOMAS KNOLTON
PETER BRESEE
JEREMIAH DAY
ABEL STEVENS, JR.
ELIJAH GORDON

The said Jesse Brown manifested a hearty assent and full agreement to the same agreement and proposals, whereunto he has also set his name.

(signed) JESSE BROWN.

For the next two years Mr. Brown's name appears constantly in the church records. He went with Abel Stevens and Sheldon Nichols to the Thurlow Association. He was given a letter of recommendation by his people to other churches as a preacher. He aired his differences with the Association's representative, Elijah Bentley, before the church, and reached a settlement that was satisfactory. What happened after 1811? Did Brother and Sister Brown give up their little farm and return to the unnamed Baptist church from which they had come? The record ends abruptly.

Peleg Card

According to notes written by Mr. Platt Hinman, whose family had belonged to the Haldimand church from a very early date, the Rev. Peleg Card went to Haldimand in 1818. This statement agrees with other accounts and sources of information. It is recorded in the Steventown minutes, for example, that Mr. Card visited that church and preached on the last Sunday in June 1818. David Benedict, in his *History of the Baptists,* lists him as one of the ministers who had been very active in the Black River Baptist Association of northern New York State. I. M. Allen, in the *Triennial Baptist Register* for 1836, states that Mr. Card was at Haldimand the year before, and that another minister, the Rev. John Butler, and a licensed preacher, William Hurlbert, were associated with him. Finally, a tomb stone in the Fairview cemetery at Wicklow, Ontario, where many members of the Card family have been buried, gives the information that the Rev. Peleg Card died on June 4, 1837, at the age of 69 years, 10 months and 19 days.

Elder Carson

In the month of December 1817, a Baptist minister from Scotland made his appearance in the vicinity of Steventown and presented himself to the church, not only to apply for membership for himself and his wife, but to obtain the church's approval of his ministerial credentials. Accordingly the church, cautious as usual, resolved on December 27 that "Elder Stevens should consult the minds of some elders with regards to Elder Carson's principles and practices." Whether any of the other ministers in Canada were acquainted with Mr. Carson or not we cannot tell. Perhaps Abel Stevens and the other members merely desired to discover, if they could, whether Elder Carson, coming from across the ocean, might be expected to preach and practise the views held by Calvinistic Baptists of the "regular" type. After the warnings of men like Joseph Cornell and Peter Roots they would not likely be willing to run the risk of admitting an Arminian to their midst.

At the end of six months' probation on his part and diligent inquiry by the church, Elder Carson passed the test. On the last Saturday in June 1818, he "presented his letters of recommendation from the church he belonged to in Scotland, his native country, after which he told his experience and joined the general fellowship. Then sister Carson told her experience and she gained a general fellowship and joined the church."

By this time Mr. Carson had been working among the Baptists in the neighbouring township of Augusta, where missionaries had preached and occasionally baptized as early as 1807. On July 27, 1818, the Steventown minutes record, "Elder Carson presented a letter from a number of brethren and sisters at Augusta requesting a dismissal from this church. We then voted to grant the request by giving them letters of dismission." The church thus begun in a few years outgrew all others in the area, but disappeared before the century was out. As for Elder Carson, all that we know of his work is contained in the brief references to his short career at Steventown and Augusta.

Reuben Crandall

Among the more than four thousand descendants of Elder John Crandall of Rhode Island, the founder of the Crandall family in America, no fewer than twenty-one have borne the Christian name of Reuben.[10] It is small wonder, then, that there have been conflicting accounts of the personal history of Rev. Reuben Crandall, who founded the churches at Hallowell, Haldimand, and Aylmer, Ontario. One tradition asserts that he originated in a place called Nine Partners, supposed to have been in Saratoga County, New York State, and that he came to Prince Edward County in 1785 as a youth of eighteen, but already a licensed preacher.[11] This tradition we must reject in favour of one that is more strongly supported by ascertainable facts.

Actually, from information contained in the Crandall family history, from the census reports of the United States and Canada, from the minute book of the church in Aylmer, Ontario, and other authoritative sources, a fairly accurate outline of Reuben's career can be made. He was born in 1767 in the township of North East, Dutchess County, New York. He was married to Lida Mace, and shortly after the birth of his fourth child, in New York State in June 1794, he came to Hallowell Township in Upper Canada.[12] In his native township a Baptist church had been founded in 1751, and by it, or some other church that he had attended, Reuben had been licensed to preach. Accordingly, he began at once to hold services around West Lake in Hallowell, and was assisted by Joseph Winn, who arrived about the same time as himself.

In 1796 he was granted Lot No. 28, in the second concession of the township of Cramahe, and went to reside in that place. Here too, he held preaching services and in 1798 he was able to organize a Baptist church with two branches, one in Cramahe and one in Haldimand. In 1799 his ordination took place at Hallowell (see page 83); only two other ministers were present, Asa Turner of Thurlow and Joseph Winn of West Lake. Six years later he was granted authority to perform marriages by the Court of Quarter Sessions for the Newcastle District, sitting at Cobourg on April 9, 1805.[13]

For seven more years Mr. Crandall travelled widely throughout the province as a missionary preacher, though still retaining the oversight of his church in Northumberland County. In 1812, however, he moved to western Ontario, and he and his wife Lydia were received as members of the church at Townsend. Of his first wife's death followed by his second marriage to Julia (Smith) Beemer, and his independent stand against his congregation's criticism on that occasion, an account has already been given (page 105). By 1816 he had established his permanent residence in Malahide and had organized a church on the main road running through the Talbot Settlement.

In 1820 Mr. Crandall was arrested and tried at the spring assizes of the London District for having performed marriages without proper authority. There was no doubt as to his guilt, though he had broken the law through ignorance, supposing that the authority that had been granted to him in Newcastle District was valid in all other districts of the province as well. The Attorney-General, John Beverley Robinson, pressed for conviction and for the imposition of the full penalty. The judge, D'Arcy Boulton, on the other hand, while acknowledging that the statute allowed him no choice but to impose the fourteen years' banishment demanded by the law, felt that such a sentence was too severe, and recommended that the Lieutenant-Governor grant Crandall a special pardon. This the grand jury supported unanimously, and Crandall was despatched next day to York bearing the judge's recommendation and the jury's petition on his behalf. He also carried a letter from Robinson to the Lieutenant-Governor's secretary, in which the Attorney-General sought to prevent the judge's recommendation from being acted upon. The determination of the prosecutor, the calm detachment of the judge, the contrition of Crandall himself, and the staunchness of the jurors who stood by him are all revealed in the following letters.[14]

Mr. Crandall's petition for the royal pardon reads:

The Humble Petition of Reuben Crandall of the Township of Malahide, an Anabaptist Preacher, Most Humbly Sheweth

That at the present assizes for the District of London your petitioner was found guilty of solemnizing matrimony unlawfully and is now under sentence of banishment from this province.

That your petitioner was really ignorant of the penalty of the Law, until after the conviction of Henry Ryan, since which he had entirely desisted from the practice of solemnizing matrimony.

That your petitioner begs leave humbly to approach the feet of Your Excellency and to pray that Your Excellency will be graciously pleased to bestow upon him His Majesty's pardon, and that your petitioner promises most solemnly never again to offend the Laws.

And your petitioner as in duty bound will most humbly pray.

Charlotteville, 9th
September, 1820.   REUBEN CRANDALL

On the back of this letter fourteen members of the grand jury subscribed their names to the following statement:

The subscribers, believing the petitioner to be an ignorant man, and that he is useful in his neighbourhood, beg leave humbly to recommend him to the clemency of His Excellency the Lieutenant Governor.

Knowing what was afoot, the Attorney-General made haste to send a note to Major Hillier, giving his version of the case as follows:

MY DEAR MAJOR —

Reuben Crandell, or Elder Crandell, the bearer of this letter is an Anabaptist preacher who was convicted here the other day of solemnizing marriage without licence or publication of banns —

He had resided many years ago in the Dist. of Newcastle and obtained from the Quarter Sessions there a certificate under our Stat. of 1798 enabling him to marry persons of his own congregation residing there — Which certificate of course conveyed no authority out of the District in which it was given, and he was therefore not competent to solemnize marriage here had he pursued the prescribed forms. He pretends, however, that he ignorantly supposed it did, and he rested the vindication of his conduct entirely upon that ground, omitting to touch upon the material circumstance that had his authority to marry been unquestionable, he exercised that authority in this instance directly contrary to law, for he neither published banns, nor had a license, and had any ordained Minister of the established church done the same thing he would quickly have come within the Statute. (26 Geo. 2ᵃ)

Whether his ignorance was so unbounded that he really knew not the necessity of these forms I cannot say — He did indeed urge in his defence that Preacher tho' he was, he could scarcely read and could not write.

This man's case is distinguished from that of Mr. Cook and Mr. Ryan and the other preachers complained of in this — that thus assuming an authority which they had not [they] pretended to solemnize matrimony pursuing the legal forms.

This man, equally without authorʸ (tho' he may perhaps have supposed he had it), solemnized matrimony in a manner that could not have been legal whatever his authority.

The judge having no discretion was obliged in the words of the act to transport, or (as it is with us) to banish the man for 14 years — The law seems to be thought severe and he goes to York I believe with much interest made in his favor.

His character I believe is nothing remarkable. This short statement I have given you privately for His Excʸ's consideration. The only official report must come from the judge.

We finished here yesterday (Saturday) and have a week to travel to Sandwich.

The Man is waiting —

> Yours very
> sincerely
> JNO. B. ROBINSON.

The judge's report to the Lieutenant-Governor, however, expressed admirably the gist of the case, and led to the pardon which Mr. Crandall prayed for:

Charlotteville, 10th Sepr 1820

SIR

I have the honour to communicate to your Excellency that the Bearer Reuben Crandell was indicted, at the assizes holden here last week for marrying a couple witht Banns or Licence contrary to the Statute — he is an Anabaptist Minister and bears an universal good character — The prisoner was found guilty and I have banished him for 14 years according to the express Direction of the Statute. It appears to me most clearly that the man has acted purely from Ignorance and misinformation and as the Law is extremely severe and no person hitherto suffered Punishmt (which I learn from Mr. Attny Genl), I feel it my duty to recommend the man to your Excellency's consideration — the object of this Prosecution is a marrd man with a Family and is a loyal subject.

I have the honour to be
Your Excellency's
most obedient humble servant
D'ARCY BOULTON J.

His pardon obtained, Mr. Crandall continued his itinerant ministry; he gave up the pastoral oversight of Aylmer, but continued to make his home there. In 1832 he was pastor at Dumfries, and his address was given as Galt, Ontario, but he was resident there for only a short time. We hear of him delivering a sermon in 1833 at the organization of the First Baptist Church in Brantford, and later in the thirties he returned to Aylmer to retire. The census of 1841 shows that he was then living on a two-acre plot of ground in Malahide, that he kept two horses and four sheep, and had grown a small crop of potatoes, turnips, and carrots that year. He stated that he had come to Canada from the United States about fifty years before. The 1851 census shows that he was living in the same place, and that his manner of life was frugal. His age was given as eighty-five years. In the minute book of the Aylmer church an entry dated September 28, 1853, reads:

Elder Reuban Crandall, who has been a member of this church from its commencement, died to-day at the age of 86. Mark the perfect man and behold the upright, for the end of that man is peace.

Daniel Derbyshire

Despite the prominence of the Derbyshire family name in the county of Leeds, little is known about the Rev. Daniel Derbyshire except what is contained in the brief references made to him in missionaries' reports and in the minutes of the Steventown church. He was serving as a lay preacher when Joseph Cornell visited that place in 1803, and was ordained as pastor, along with Abel Stevens, in 1804. It is recorded in the county registry office at Brockville that in 1805 he bought a parcel of land (part of fifty acres), from Isaac Palmer in Elizabeth-town for the sum of £27. He made a will on April 15, 1808, a memorial of which was registered on March 17, 1827, by his widow, who, after his death, had married Jedediah Wing, of Yonge. His oldest son was James Derbyshire, who in 1835 disposed of some of the land he had inherited from his parents.

Mr. Derbyshire was, without doubt, the recognized pastor of the Steventown church for some years after his ordination, but the church's negotiations with Jesse Brown to become their preacher in 1809 would indicate that they had been deprived of his services by that date. Church records from December 1806 to December 1807 are missing because the clerk "withheld the book." The minutes for 1808 make no reference to Mr. Derbyshire, though he may have been in charge at that time. He was certainly still on duty in 1807 when Phine-has Pillsbury visited him. There is no record of Mr. Derbyshire's hav-ing travelled among distant communities on preaching tours, as was so common in those days. He seems to have given his whole time to farming and preaching in his own neighbourhood.

George Ebberson

The first mention of George Ebberson is dated the "last Saturday of August, 1812," when the Steventown church agreed to take him under its "watch care." On December 30, 1815, he was given a "letter of recommendation." His was but one of a great many such letters given around that time, and the significance of it is not clear. It is quite definite that he had been preaching fairly frequently in surrounding communities, for on August 30, 1817, a group of Baptists in Gananoque requested that he be ordained as their minister. The ordination was conducted by Abel Stevens and the church at Gananoque was organized. Later Mr. Ebberson became the pastor at Steventown, and is so listed in the Johnstown Association reports for 1832 and 1835.[15] Though he spent most of his time in the immediate vicinity of his home, he did go on occasional preaching tours, and is reported to have baptized several people as far away as Bayham.

Peter Fairchild, U.E.L.

Rev. Peter Fairchild was one of two Baptist ministers whose names are found on the official United Empire List for Upper Canada. His petition asking that his name be placed on the list reads as follows:

To His Excellency Francis Gore, Esquire, Lieutenant
   Governor of the Province of Upper Canada, etc. etc.
      in Council.

   The Petition of Peter Fairchild, of Townsend, Yeoman Humbly Sheweth

   That your petitioner was born in the Province of New York (now the
state of New York), in America, and resided near the Head of Lake George
at the breaking out of the Rebellion, that he joined the Royal Army under
General Burgoyne in the year 1777, that he bore arms, and remained with
the Army until the capitulation — when he returned to his Father's House
which was at that time within the British lines.
   That your Petitioner resided in this Province in the year 1793, and has
continued to reside in it ever since.
   Wherefore your Petitioner prays that your Excellency may be pleased to
order his name to be inserted on the U.E. List.

And petitioner will ever pray,
Peter Fairchild

York, 11 February 1808

Mr. Fairchild's petition was referred to the Executive Council on
February 12, and was recommended for approval. On May 10, 1808,
an Order-in-Council was passed to insert his name.
   The place of his birth is thus established as the state of New York,
and the date of his coming to Canada is fixed as 1793, despite a somewhat different version of his early history that has been widely circulated.[16] He was a Baptist when he arrived in the country, and was
acting as a lay preacher when the Shaftsbury Association missionaries
first visited the Long Point area in 1803. He and his first wife, the
former Sarah Fuller, were among the charter members of the Charlotteville church when it was organized that year. In 1804, when more
Baptists settled in Townsend, Mr. Fairchild began to hold preaching
services in his own neighbourhood. Beginning with only a few baptized believers, he made a number of converts who were baptized in
August by the Rev. Joseph Winn, and that fall, in November, the Rev.
Lemuel Covell helped to organize the Townsend church.
   In October 1806, Mr. Fairchild was ordained by the Rev. David
Irish (see page 104), and he served as pastor of Townsend church
until 1818. In this year, despite his long and successful service, his
congregation was incensed by his second marriage to a woman who
was not a Baptist and he was excluded from the church (see also page
105). According to the inscription on the stone marking his grave in
the cemetery at Boston, Ontario, he died on June 26, 1828, in his sixty-
sixth year.

Titus Finch

Time and again in the annals of the early settlers of the London District, especially those of Norfolk County, we come upon the name of Elder Titus Finch, of Charlotteville. He has been variously described as "the old soldier preacher . . . who came with his regiment to America to fight for old King George III" (E. A. Owen),[17] as "an evangelist from the United States" (A. H. Newman),[18] and as one of the two first ministers to be ordained in Upper Canada (E. R. Fitch).[19] None of these statements is strictly true, though all have some foundation in truth.

Titus Finch seems to have come from New York State, where the name was very common. According to his own account, he did not come from England with his regiment to fight in the American Revolution, but "joined the Royal Standard in U.S. at the commencement of the Revolution."[20] Fortunately many of the records of the Prince of Wales' American Regiment in which he served are still intact, and from the muster rolls, pay states, and other documents of his unit we can put together some of the facts of his career as a soldier.[21] He belonged to No. 12 Light Infantry Company, but during much of the time from November 1777 to February 1778 he was absent from his unit on public employ as an armourer. In November and December 1779, when the regiment was at Lloyd's Neck, and again in March 1780, when his company was at Flushing-fly, Finch is shown as present. Musters held between February 23, 1781, and February 24, 1783, indicate that he was absent, as a prisoner of war, for the whole of that two-year period and he did not rejoin his company until his release in April 1783. A pay list shows that soon after his return from captivity he drew 304 days' back pay and the three suits of clothing that were owing to him.

On being discharged in 1783, Finch accompanied other members of the Prince of Wales' American Regiment to New Brunswick, where they received grants of land in the valley of the Nashwaak River, a tributary of the Saint John. Six years later, on February 6, 1789, he attempted to increase his holdings by the method disclosed in the following petition:[22]

To His Excellency Thomas Carleton, Esquire, Lieutenant Governor and Commander in Chief of the Province of New Brunswick, etc., etc., etc.,

The Memorial of Titus Finch of / The late Prince of Wales Reg[t].
  Humbly Sheweth
  That your Memorialist has a lot on the Nashwaak which he has improved

and having a large growing family is desirous to provide for them which will be difficult on his small farm.

Your Memorialist informs Your Excellency that there is a vacant piece of land in the Block No. 5 adjoining his Land — formerly possessed by one Silvanyus Bishop who has left the Country intending not to return. Your Memorialist humbly prays that Your Excellency will grant him the said Lot, and he as in duty bound will ever pray etc. etc.

TITUS FINCH

From the York County (N.B.) records of deeds it has been ascertained that in 1787 Finch had bought some land in Block 7 of Lyman's grant from William Turner for £6, 5s., and that in 1794 he bought six hundred acres from John Barrett for £100. On their departure for Upper Canada in 1799, he and his wife sold part of their land to Richard Murphy. By 1801 he had been granted four hundred acres in the new province, half of which consisted of Lot 19 in the 4th concession of Charlotteville Township; the rest he was to receive later.

As several people by the same name figure in Baptist activity at the time, Titus Finch's leaning towards Baptist principles may have been the result of family influence. In addition, as has been said earlier, it is known that Edward Manning, a Baptist preacher in the Maritimes, had conducted revival services up the Saint John valley in 1793. It seems quite clear that after Titus Finch went from New Brunswick to Long Point in 1798-99, he held religious services among the settlers, and that Peter Fairchild, the lay preacher from Townsend, assisted him. By 1802 their efforts had resulted in thirty people being ready for baptism, and these Lemuel Covell and Obed Warren, who went to Long Point in 1803 representing the Shaftsbury Association, baptized as a group. The candidates included Finch himself, who had not submitted himself to the ordinance until then. On the same visit Covell and Warren organized the Charlotteville church.

Licensed to preach by formal action of the church soon after his baptism in 1803, Finch was ordained by Lemuel Covell in 1805, and for nearly thirty years he followed the dual career of farmer and minister. He erected a mill near Port Dover, which was burned by the Americans in a raid during the War of 1812, and for which he received £265 in compensation.[23] He was given authority in 1807 by the Court of Quarter Sessions, London District, to solemnize marriage,[24] and the district marriage register, now in the Public Archives of Canada, contains records of marriages conducted by him as late as January 1833. He did considerable travelling away from his own neighbourhood to preach, and participated constantly in ordination and recognition councils, in conferences, and other church meetings.

On occasion, he held municipal offices, and was not entirely aloof from neighbourhood quarrels, for the court records show that he was sued at law.

It has been said by some that his death occurred in 1821, and the stone at his grave in the Charlotteville cemetery sets the date as 1827, but it is plain that he lived for several years after even the latter date. In June 1829, he petitioned Sir John Colborne for a piece of land in Zorra Township, saying that part of his grant was still owing to him, that he was too old to settle in an isolated place, and for that reason would like the parcel he had asked for, which his son would help him to develop. The land in question was indeed a choice location, on the Thames in what is now the city of Woodstock, but he did not get it because the government had reserved it for special purposes. Being on the river, it had a "broken front" and was less than one hundred acres.

In the spring of 1832 Mr. Finch preached in the newly established church in Lobo Township, baptized several converts, and was asked to remain for a year.[25] Though he was listed in the report of the Western Association for 1832 as the pastor at Lobo, his address was shown as Oxford: apparently he was considered to be in Lobo only temporarily.[26] As it happened, he did not complete his twelve months' term of service at Lobo, but was succeeded there before the year was up by William Rees, a Welsh minister employed by the American Baptist Home Missionary Society. This, together with the fact that his last recorded act was to perform a marriage in January 1833, leads to the belief that his death occurred that year.

Elkanah Holmes

Elkanah Holmes was born in December 1743, in Canterbury which was then in Massachusetts, but was later transferred to New Hampshire.[27] At the age of sixteen he joined the army serving under Colonel Rogers and Colonel (later General) Putnam, and saw action during the fighting against the Indians and French along the Canadian frontier;[28] he was present when Ticonderoga fell to the British in 1759. His military career continued in the war against the Spaniards in Cuba, during which he witnessed the capture of Havana. In Cuba he became very ill, was nursed by a Roman Catholic Spaniard, and left the army at Havana to return to New York.

He was married in that city when he was twenty-one. The two sons and one daughter born of that marriage all predeceased him. In 1769 Mr. Holmes was baptized in Kingwood, New Jersey, by the Rev. D. Sutton, and joined the church in that place, where he was granted a licence to preach. He is believed to have been ordained about 1773, when he was thirty years old, but by whom or where is not known; the event probably occurred in New Jersey. During the American Revolution he served as chaplain to a New Jersey regiment, "to whom he frequently preached and with whom he sometimes fought."

On resigning his chaplaincy, Holmes preached at Hackett's Town, N.J., then held pastorates at North Stamford, Conn., Bedford, N.Y., and on Staten Island. At Bedford, he was married for the second time; two sons, the younger of whom predeceased him, were born of this second marriage. The church on Staten Island was said to have been "raised chiefly under his ministry," and continued to be the scene of his labours from 1791 till after 1800.[29] In April 1791, he played a prominent part in the forming of the New York Baptist Association, and in October of that year, when organization of the Association was complete, he was elected the first moderator.[30] He helped to write the Association's circular letters, served on various committees, preached the annual sermon in 1793, and in 1796 he told the Association "that he had for some time past been inclined to travel, and preach the gospel in the western parts of the state; that invitation had been received by him from an Indian chief of pious character among the Six Nations to preach among them also; and that the church of which he is pastor approved his design."

The Association supported with enthusiasm his suggestion of travel, and resolved: "we recommend to him attention to this smiling invitation of providence, and pray the great Head of the church to favour his labours with abundant success." We may speculate that the "Indian chief of pious character" who invited him to preach to the Six Nations was Joseph Brant, but this is not necessarily so. The Tuscarora Indians were part of the Six Nations, having been adopted by the Iroquois in 1722, and it may have been one of their chiefs who had communicated with Holmes at this time. In 1797 he reported to the Association that he had visited the Brotherton and Stockbridge Indians. The Association received letters from the Tuscarora and Caughnawaga tribes in 1798, and Mr. Holmes brought a gift of wampum from Stockbridge. In 1799 he reported that the previous fall he had visited the Brotherton, Tuscarora, Oneida, and Stockbridge tribes but could not stay long among them and had been handicapped for want of an interpreter. Meanwhile he had published a small book on Christian doctrine, including a model church covenant, the whole of which he said that he had "adopted . . . as my present creed."[31] The nature of his political creed we can judge by the exclamation in the New York Association circular letter of 1800 which he helped to edit, "with what gratitude should we behold with increasing lustre, the wisdom and goodness of God in our separation from the British Empire."

In 1800 Holmes was appointed by the New York Missionary Society (joint Baptist and Presbyterian) to its North West Mission. He was to work among the Tuscarora Indians near Fort Niagara and the Senecas near Buffalo Creek. He had not yet resigned his pastorate at Staten Island, for during his missionary journeys in 1799 and 1800 the New York Baptist Association had provided preachers to supply his pulpit during his absence. The circumstances of his appointment to his new missionary post are described in letters written by him from Fort Niagara during his first year there.[32]

In the circular letter of the New York Association in 1801 he reported optimistically on work already done or in prospect among the Tuscaroras, Senecas, Onandagas, Cayugas, and Mohawks. In addition he preached to the white settlers in Buffalo (then called New Amsterdam).[33] Mention of the Mohawks is a reminder that early in 1801 he visited Joseph Brant, as shown in a letter written by Brant and carried by Holmes to the Rev. Samuel Miller of New York,[34] which reads in part:

Grand River, Feb. 9, 1801.

SIR

I feel a particular satisfaction that I have now had an opportunity of answering your letter by the Rev. Mr. Holmes. . . . I cannot omit acknowledging the satisfaction I feel from what the Rev. Mr. Holmes has acquainted me with respecting the generous intentions of your society for diffusing religion and civilization among the Indian nations in general. I would be happy to hear from you, how far your society may propose to extend their goodness with respect to the education of Indian youths that might be well recommended to them. And also if they would be willing, and it might be consistent with their constitution, to assist some Indians who have yet claims on lands in the United States, such as the Nantikokes in Maryland, and the Munsees near Minisink who have requested me to make their application. The Rev. Mr. Holmes can more particularly inform you on this subject. . . .

When he attended the New York Baptist Association in June, Holmes not only presented the Missionary Society with Brant's letter, but set before them his plans for building two Indian schools, one in Tuscarora village, near Lewiston, and the other at Buffalo.[35] On his return from New York, he carried a letter from the Missionary Society to Joseph Brant, along with the Society's financial statement and a volume containing the sermons that had been preached before it, in order that Brant might form a correct opinion of their aims.[36]

In 1802 Holmes attended the June meeting of the New York Baptist Association as usual, and while there he arranged to have his church membership transferred from Staten Island to First Baptist Church,

New York City. Two weeks later, on June 26, he was married in New York to his third wife, the widow of James Bingham, and she returned with him to his mission field. That autumn he was visited by Caleb Blood, of the Shaftsbury Association, who spent several days with him.

He did not attend the Association in 1803, but wrote them a letter about his work and they praised him highly in their circular letter, urging him to "go on, dear Brother, in the strength of the Lord." Meanwhile, his employers, the New York Missionary Society, had set his salary at $500 per annum and gave him an annual expense allowance of $125, on the understanding that he would not be away from his charge more than six months in any one year. In September he was visited by Lemuel Covell and Obed Warren, who met him in Buffalo. Later, in October, he crossed over to the Canadian side of the Niagara River and preached with them among the white settlers.

Similar contacts with missionaries are recorded for the years 1805 and 1806, when he preached Lemuel Covell's funeral sermon at Clinton. In the latter year he was visited by the Rev. Rosewell Burrows, of the Groton Union Conference, an open communion Baptist organization which later united with the "regular" Baptists. In 1806, also, Joseph Landon wrote of hearing Holmes preach in Buffalo, and described the difficulty experienced by the people there in raising their share of his salary. Pledges had been taken, and individual contributions were wrapped in paper bearing the donor's name.[37]

The year 1806 brought division in the ranks of the New York Missionary Society, and the Baptist element withdrew to form an independent organization. For a time this new all-Baptist group, aided by the Massachusetts Baptist Missionary Society, maintained Mr. Holmes as their missionary at Tuscarora, but friction arose when the Presbyterians sent a representative of their own, the Rev. A. Gray, among the Indians, many of whom now deserted Holmes. In 1809 the Baptist Society sent out a long letter explaining the difficulty, and reporting that it had been thought expedient for Holmes to move to the Canadian side of the Niagara River where he had already begun a promising work. They would continue to provide half of his support, and the Massachusetts Society would provide the other half. Nathaniel Kendrick's report to the latter organization in 1808 gives much the same information.

Already in 1807 Mr. Holmes had begun to gather a small congregation at Queenston in Niagara Township. When the new church was organized he and his wife were given letters of transfer from First Baptist Church, New York, to join it. The Niagara church applied in 1810 for admission to the New York Baptist Association, and this was granted. From 1808 to 1812 Mr. Holmes gave part-time service to the church at Clinton, as described in the account of that congregation already given, but his work in Upper Canada ended abruptly with the outbreak of war in 1812.

The period 1812-14 was, as we have frequently seen, a "time of troubles" for Baptist organizations. Neither the Shaftsbury Association nor the Massachusetts Baptist Missionary Society was at all enthusiastic about the war. In the minutes of the New York Baptist Association during the war years there is no mention of Elkanah Holmes, and this association ceased to contribute to the work of the New York Baptist Missionary Society after 1812.[38] As for Holmes himself, his attitude from the beginning of the war was one of thoroughgoing pro-Americanism. When the Americans entered Canada at Niagara in 1813 he gave them all possible aid and comfort, and entertained the officers at his own table. In December 1813, the Americans were compelled to give up Fort George, which they had captured in May, and they burned Newark as they retreated; when they reached Queenston they attempted to take Holmes and his family with them. The ordeal must certainly have been strenuous for the veteran missionary, now seventy years of age. He and his household were overtaken by the British and held captive for a time in an inn near the British lines. Lieutenant Colonel Cyrenius Chapin, whose daughter had married one of Holmes's sons, effected his rescue by a sudden raid in which two hundred men took part, and he was taken across the river to Buffalo.[39]

Even when he reached Buffalo, Holmes was not safe from British wrath. On December 30, 1813, in retaliation for the burning of Newark, the British burned both Black Rock and Buffalo. Chapin was taken prisoner and Holmes was obliged to flee once more. For a time he lived near Canandaigua, and then went to New York City to visit old friends. He rejoined the First Baptist Church there in 1817 and continued to be a member of it till his death, though for the last thirteen years of his life he lived in Bedford with one of his sons.

It is said that during his closing years he was reluctant to enter into debates, though he was still very determined in his ideas, both political and religious. He avoided preaching engagements, but was gifted in public prayer. We hear, for instance, of his offering prayer on Sunday, October 2, 1831, at the "yearly meeting" in Bedford. He died soon after from a fall in which he suffered a broken hip on January 17, 1832, in the "eighty-ninth year of his age and the fifty-ninth of his ministry." After a public funeral service conducted by the minister of First Baptist Church, New York, his son, Samuel L. Holmes, of Bedford, arranged for the publication of the sermon preached at the funeral, and from that source many of the facts of his life have been gathered.

James Hulse

In his account of the churches that were formed in the townships of Sidney, Thurlow, and Rawdon, J. T. Dowling wrote, "The name of Hulse is also associated with these churches. He had been an old revolutionary soldier, and itinerated on horseback. By the annual sale of a colt he was enabled to clothe himself for his year's work." Another version of what seems to be the same tradition is found in William Canniff's *History of the Settlement of Upper Canada*, where we are also told that "One, Elder Holts [Hulse?], also preached around the Bay, but a love of brandy hindered him. Yet he was an attractive preacher. This was probably about 1794."[40]

Whatever truth there may be in these rather vague references, the records show that in 1825 James Hulse was the minister at Rawdon. In 1832 and 1835 the printed reports of the Haldimand Association list him as the minister at Thurlow and give his address as Belleville. Thus it is established that Elder James Hulse played a part in the work of those churches during the 1820's and 30's. His activities during the earlier years of those settlements would seem to be more a matter of legend than of history. The visiting missionaries from 1803 onwards made frequent mention of Elders Winn, Crandall and Turner, but they never referred to Elder Hulse. We may perhaps hazard a guess that his soldiering (if any), was done, not during the Revolution, but during the War of 1812, and that he became active as a preacher in the post-war period.

Simon Mabee

Simon Mabee was the second son of Frederick Mabee, a loyalist who had first settled in New Brunswick, but emigrated to the Long Point district in 1793. The date of Simon's birth is variously given as 1776,[41] 1778,[42] and 1779,[43] but the same three sources agree that his marriage to Abigail Gustin took place when he was twenty years of age. It was about the time of his marriage that he made his first profession of religious faith, and he united with the Methodist church. Later he was baptized, and became a charter member of the Charlotteville church when it was organized by Lemuel Covell and Obed Warren in 1803.

Mr. Mabee owned land at various times in the townships of Charlotteville, Walsingham, and Oxford. His participation in public affairs is clearly indicated in the records of the Court of Quarter Sessions for the London District, where we learn that he served as constable in attendance on the grand jury and also as foreman of that body. He acted as crown witness in a court case in 1805 and was made a justice of the peace in 1808. In 1814 he was appointed assessor for Oxford Township. At times he was himself involved in litigation, being prosecuted by the Crown in 1801 for an unspecified offence, and forced to pay a fine of five pounds in 1806.[44]

When the Townsend church formed a branch in Oxford in 1808, the first person to apply for baptism was Abigail, Simon Mabee's wife. A year later the First Regular Baptist Church of Oxford came into being. Mr. Mabee was given a licence to preach in July 1812, and was ordained to the ministry in October 1817; he continued to serve the Oxford church. Though he had never enjoyed the advantages of formal education himself, he became a capable student of the Bible and was a strong believer in ministerial training. He followed with great interest the work of Adoniram Judson and other foreign missionaries, supported the Sunday School movement, and promoted the efforts of the Bible and Tract Societies.

One of Mr. Mabee's circle of friends has said that though the Oxford church was prosperous, its members gave him inadequate financial support. Nonetheless, he was noted for his lack of envy, and for his evident satisfaction at the success of others. In later years he travelled considerably in other parts of the province, and is credited with having baptized nearly a thousand converts. His death occurred in Oxford, at his home, on January 3, 1843, and a tribute to his life of service was written in the columns of the *Montreal Register* in May of that year by the Rev. William Rees, of Simcoe.

James Stark

In the year 1796 five Baptists in Leeds County sent the following petition to Lieutenant-Governor Simcoe, on a theme by now familiar to us:

To His Excellency John Graves Simcoe, Esquire,
Lieutenant-Governor, Major-General and Commander-in-Chief of His Majesty's Province of Upper Canada in Council etc.

This Petition Humbly Sheweth

That your petitioners now inhabiting the Province of Upper Canada, and loyal subjects of His Majesty King George the 3rd, have been educated in and are professors of the Baptist Religion, and wish not to intermeddle with the affairs of any other Denomination, therefore pray to be indulged and protected in the enjoyment of such privileges as His Majesty's good subjects of any other Denomination in this province enjoy. Particularly we pray that those which are now or hereafter shall be regularly ordained Elders in any Baptist Church in this Province shall be fully empowered to administer the ordinance of marriage, and that a certificate from the Ordaining Council shall be their sufficient Warrant, and your Petitioners will ever pray.

ABEL STEVENS
JAMES STARK
THOMAS KNOLTON
PHILIP PHILIPS
OBADIAH REED

Bastard, 12th May, 1796

It is apparent that the five petitioners knew exactly what they wanted and must have been men of intelligence. Of Abel Stevens a good deal is known, and we shall consider his career in a moment. Thomas Knolton and Obadiah Reed served on the grand jury of the Eastern District in 1798, but there is little information about them other than that. Philip Philips ultimately gave his name to the settlement that began as Steventown, and is called Philipsville to this day.

But who was James Stark? That he had been active as a Baptist preacher before coming to Canada is evident from the following depositions of the preceding decade, which tell their own story, as far as it goes:

To the Hon. Commissioners of the land Department.

The Memorial of James Stark, Baptist Minister, humbly showeth:

That your memorialist, in consequence of his attachment to the British Govt. has suffered imprisonment and loss of property in the States —

Your memorialist therefore prays that he may be indulged with his Majesty's bounty of land and other privileges of the British Govt.

Your memorialist as in duty bound shall ever pray —

JAMES STARK

Elizabethtown
June 24th 1789.

Philip Philips being duly sworn deposeth that he was acquainted with Mr. James Stark since the year 1778 and knew him to be a Loyal man and that he suffered imprisonment and banishment from the place of his residence to another district where he was confined under 200 £ bond for his attachment to the British Govt.

PHILIP PHILIPS

Sworn before me
the 24th June 1789
Justus Sherwood J.P.

Jabez Saunders being duly sworn deposeth that he was acquainted with
Mr. Jas. Stark since the year 1778 and knew him to be a loyal subject, that
he was persecuted for praying for the King and not praying for the congress,
that he was imprisoned, and Banished to King's District where he was
confined under Bonds.

JABEZ SANDERS

Sworn before me
this 24th June 1789
Justus Sherwood J.P.

Mr. Stark's continued interest in Baptist affairs is evidenced by his
signing of the petition regarding marriages in 1796, but his active
career as a preacher seems to have ceased with his coming to Canada.

Abel Stevens, U.E.L.

Abel Stevens was the son of Roger and Mary (Doolittle) Stevens,
who had settled at Pittsford, Vermont, soon after the lots in that place
were surveyed.[45] Abel's brother, Roger Stevens Junior, was very active
as a spy and scout in the employ of General Haldimand and the British
during the American Revolution.[46] Roger's estate was confiscated, and
all his assets were sold, with the full knowledge and co-operation of
Roger Stevens, Senior, who actually received a fee for assisting the
American authorities.[47] Abel, meanwhile, seems to have managed to
serve the British and to assist his brother's comings and goings without incurring the wrath of his fellow townsmen. In 1779 he married
Eunice Buck, of Pittsford, and bought some land from his father. Here
he and his wife lived for fourteen years, and eight children were born
to them.

When the Baptist church of Pittsford was established in 1784, Abel
Stevens and his wife were among its charter members. The church
appointed deacons in 1786, and he was one of the three men selected
for that office. He achieved a local reputation for religious zeal, physical courage, and skill as a hunter. On at least one occasion he was
credited with emerging victorious from mortal combat with a hostile
Indian.[48]

In 1793, Mr. Stevens sold his Pittsford farm to Ichabod Cross, and
applied to the newly formed province of Upper Canada for a township to be granted to himself and several associates, on the ground
that they desired to establish a Baptist settlement and live under the
British flag. His first petition asked for thirty thousand acres on the
Thames River near the Moravian settlement.[49] Not receiving an immediate reply, he again requested a township for himself, his father,

and four others, all from Pittsford. This petition was read in Council the day after it was submitted, but was ruled inadmissible.[50] Instead, he was told that he could receive two hundred acres for himself and each of his eight children, whose names and ages were given at that time as Uriah (21), Abel Jr. (18), Betty (16), Marian (14), Unice Jr. (12), Isaiah (10), Sarah (6), Alfred (4), and Elihu (1½).

Following this decision, he was granted two hundred acres in Scarborough Township, but the minutes of the Council reveal that he was dissatisfied with this location, and made his way eastward to the new townships of Bastard and Kitley, in the county of Leeds.[51] In this locality Stevens became the leading member of a pioneer community, which for a long time was known as Steventown. He joined forces with Daniel Derbyshire to form the Baptist congregation which was organized as a church in 1803, and he was himself ordained as a minister in 1804.

In addition to his activities as a preacher, Abel Stevens' efforts as a colonizer were prodigious.[52] He brought in many settlers from Vermont, some of whom received grants of land direct from the Crown, while others settled on lots that had been assigned to earlier claimants but had not been taken up. Of special interest to Stevens, as to other alert pioneers, were the waterfalls along the Gananoque River which had possibilities as mill sites.[53] His most ambitious scheme as a would-be industrialist was to erect a foundry on the river and to use the bog iron from the adjoining marshes as a source of ore. Frustrating delays tormented him in his attempts to achieve this aim. In 1798 he appeared before the Land Board at York to explain his plan, which involved not only a site for the foundry, but large grants of timber land to supply fuel for his furnaces. The Board was polite, directed the Surveyor-General to reserve the required amount of land as near to his wishes as possible, but said it could not make the grant until new regulations had been established.

A long letter from Stevens to the government in 1799 outlined the cost of setting up his proposed factory. Anvils, hammers, and at least fifty workmen would have to be brought from the United States. Generous land grants would be necessary to attract workmen to the enterprise, and this would also be true of potential investors, whose co-operation was required to provide capital of at least three thousand pounds. The government was not satisfied with his plan, and gave him six months to prepare a better prospectus. It was to include the names of all his associates in the scheme and also those of reliable references. Stevens was unable to fulfil these conditions, and the option on the reserved land was transferred to Matthew Wing.

The main purpose of the iron works was to supply armament for vessels on Lake Ontario, but this was never achieved in Stevens' day, and in the end the Rush-Bagot Treaty between Britain and the United States rendered such a purpose obsolete. Whether he could have launched the project successfully had he been given more co-operation at the critical period it is hard to say. For him, despite his heroic effort, it was to remain a vision of his imagination always. At any rate, his own description of what he hoped to accomplish makes interesting reading even yet. The great forge, with its four fireplaces, each with seven master workmen and twenty assistants, is a picture to excite the imagination, and his account vividly presents the master bloomer and master collier at each fire, attended by blacksmiths, carpenters, stokers, coal carters, and wood cutters.

The failure of his most ambitious secular project, however, did not dampen Stevens' enthusiasm for other schemes connected with colonization and settlement, nor did it cool his ardour for religious activity. He cleared land, built roads, brought in more immigrants, and above all, promoted the welfare of his chief love, the Baptist church. Though he never occupied the pastorate at Steventown himself, he continued as a member there for the rest of his life and did much preaching in surrounding districts. His contacts with other Baptists in the province were extensive, especially in Northumberland County, where other families from Pittsford, notably the Ewings and the Doolittles, had settled.

In his appearances at York before the Executive Council he had established to their satisfaction his service to the British cause during the Revolutionary War, so that his name had been added to the United Empire List of Upper Canada. Apparently some doubt had been cast upon his status as a genuine loyalist, for in December 1806, the minutes of the Council assert that there was read a petition from

Abel Stevens of Bastard, stating that he resided in the British colonies in America at the breaking out of the rebellion, and joined the Royal Standard, previous to the Treaty of separation in 1783, which was proved by Lieut. David McFall before Governor Simcoe, upon which his name was entered upon the U.E. List . . . but trouble having arisen as to his having joined the Royal Standard, he cannot obtain his Patent for lands without payment of fees, until it is determined whether he did or did not join the Royal Standard before the Treaty of separation, and praying that his Name may be continued on the U.E. List.

Council recommended that his name should be continued on the United Empire List, and there the matter rested.[54]

Statements that Stevens died in 1816[55] do not square with the records of the Steventown church, which show that he and his son, who was also ordained, both went to Gananoque in 1817 to take part in the ordination of George Ebberson. The entry makes a definite distinction between them: "Voted that Elder Stevens and Brother Abel Stevens and Brother Nicholas Bresee should go and examine Bro. Ebberson's principles and beliefs, and if they found him to possess a sound mind then to proceed and ordain him to the ministry of the gospel." Subsequent references to "Elder" Stevens as late as 1824 do not make clear whether father or son is referred to, and the identities are all the harder to determine because Abel Stevens Junior spent his life in the same vicinity. The location of the father's grave is unknown, but the son's burial place is in the little cemetery near Daytown, and a carved monument records that he died in 1858 at the age of seventy-nine. Their descendants are to be found in the neighbourhood still, as well as in many parts of Canada and the United States.

Alexander Stewart

The Rev. Alexander Stewart was educated in Edinburgh, Scotland, according to his own account, and came to Upper Canada by way of Quebec in the year 1818. His name is not connected with the founding or progress of any Baptist church before 1820, but his part in the educational controversy of that period and of the following decade makes his career of special interest.

In 1816 the Upper Canada legislature had passed the Common Schools Act, by whose provisions a group of citizens in any township could receive a grant of up to £25 ($100) towards a free school, provided they had twenty pupils and were prepared to subscribe whatever additional funds were needed. Many common schools were started as a result, and when Mr. Stewart arrived in York from Scotland in 1818 he was immediately appointed as teacher in a new school which had just been built at the southeast corner of College Square. Here he continued to teach until 1820, receiving the government grant regularly, and when he moved in that year he was replaced by a Mr. Thomas Appleton, who had come from England in 1819. Mr. Appleton was a Methodist.

When Mr. Stewart reached his new school in Toronto Township in 1820, he found that no government grant was forthcoming. In response to his appeals and inquiries, he was told that the number of teachers in his township had been limited to three, and he was not one of them. This he found hard to believe, as he knew of other townships where there were as many as six common schools, but he seems to have made no protest, and to have accepted the reduced salary provided by his school's supporters.

Mr. Appleton, his successor in York, also found that his grant was discontinued, for the reason that Dr. Strachan and certain members of the Executive Council desired to use part of the funds voted by the legislature to support a school in which Church of England principles would be taught. Their plans were carried out, a teacher was brought from England, and Mr. Appleton's school was closed. He, however, did not accept the decision of the Council without a struggle. Supported by the trustees of his school, of whom Jesse Ketchum was one, he succeeded at the end of seven years' effort in having his case reviewed by the legislature. Many witnesses were called, including the Rev. Alexander Stewart.[56] The legislature condemned the action of the Executive, and there began the long struggle between the two branches of government which continued over many years. Education was to be a subject of controversy from that day to this, the argument breaking out afresh in the 1850's over the provincial university, and at various times over the relationship between public schools and separate Roman Catholic schools.

Mr. Stewart gave up his school in Toronto Township in 1826, and thereafter seems to have devoted himself to the ministry; unfortunately details of his service among the churches are lacking.

Asa Turner

Not much can be told of the career of Asa Turner, though his name abides in the Bay of Quinte area and he was the first ordained Baptist minister to start work in the province. With a party of settlers he went up the Moira River in 1789, and held services in the pioneer homes of Thurlow and Sidney townships.

His first regular congregation met at the home of Mr. Ross in Thurlow, and a church was organized about 1796. In addition to his preaching, Elder Turner played his full part as a citizen in the affairs of the new municipality, as the Sidney Township record book discloses.[57] In 1807 he served as pathmaster of the fifth concession of Sidney, and later he was one of the three road commissioners of Hastings County who laid out a new road from the second concession of Sidney ("back of David Marshall's") to the front road of Thurlow. In 1810 he was pound keeper. He moved back to the United States in 1811.

The last reference to Mr. Turner that has been found is in David Benedict's *History*, where the author states that Elder Turner, then in Scipio, New York, had given him much of his information regarding the Baptists of Canada.

John Upfold

John Upfold was a native of Surrey, England, where his father, George Upfold, was a farmer near the village of Cranley. He was born in the year 1766, and as a young man was employed in the government service as an excise officer. He is said to have been converted at a "dissenting" place of worship in Midhurst, Sussex, and it is known that at about the time the London Missionary Society was formed he applied to that body for service as a foreign missionary. He changed his mind, however, and emigrated to America in 1801, when he was thirty-five years old.

While staying in Boston, Mr. Upfold witnessed a baptismal service conducted by Dr. Thomas Baldwin, of the Second Baptist Church in that city, and was deeply impressed. Later he was himself baptized in Portland, Maine, by Rev. Benjamin Titcomb, founder of the First Baptist Church, Portland. Soon after his baptism, the church in Portland granted Mr. Upfold a licence to preach, and he was ordained at Fairfield, in Herkimer County, New York. He held various pastorates in the United States until the year 1816, when he went on a missionary tour into Upper Canada, and as a result became pastor of the church at Beamsville.[58]

An Englishman by birth, and a loyal British subject, Mr. Upfold was unhappy in the United States during the War of 1812-14, as the following letters will show. It is a tribute both to his personal character and to the broad-mindedness of the congregation he served during part of the war period, that the church in Fabius, New York, should write so unreservedly of their esteem for him at that time.[59]

The Baptis'd Church in Fabius, to any other Gospel Church to whom these presents may come, sends greeting:

Whereas Elder John Upfold came to reside in this town some more than two years since, clothed with ample and satisfactory credentials (as a Gospel minister) which had previously been given him by various churches to whom he had recently belonged, and associated himself with this church as pastor.

During his residence with us, his deportment, life and conversation has been consonant with his profession, and we believe him an able, faithful minister of the New Testament. *As such we unanimously recommend* him wheresoever God in his providence may call, and sorrow most of all that we cannot still enable him to tarry longer with us.

Signed by order of
the ch–h.
Fabius, Oct. 15, 1813   JAMES PETTIT
Ch–h Clk. pro tem.

On arriving in Canada to reside in 1816, Mr. Upfold submitted this letter of recommendation from his former church to Robert Nelles, J.P., of Grimsby with an accompanying explanation which is worth reading.

DEAR SIR:

Having, in the kingdom of divine providence left my native country England, and resided in the United States of America as an alien for more than fifteen years, and whereas I have lately moved from the United States to the Province of Upper Canada with an expectation of devoting my future life to the service of the Church and Society at Clinton in the district of Niagara as a minister of the gospel of Christ, I shall be exceedingly glad to enjoy the privileges of this country.

I have long since been convinced that it is the duty of Christians to obey magistrates, and to pray for Kings and all that are in authority over them, and I hope to conduct myself accordingly. Whereas I have long since been an alien in a strange land, and whereas I am once more placed under the government of my own native country, I write to request you to use your influence with his Excellency, Governor Gore, for me to enjoy the privileges of this country as a citizen.

In order for your information and satisfaction I have enclosed two letters of certificates, one written by Dr. James Pettit of Fabius, in Onondaga County and State of New York, in the behalf of the Church certifying my standing as a minister of the gospel; the other was written by his brother George Pettit Esq. of the same place, certifying that I returned myself to the civil authority of the state of New York as an alien enemy at the commencement of the late war between Great Britain and the United States. Both the subscribers I believe, are distant relations to the Pettits that live in your neighbourhood. Perhaps it is necessary for me just to add to the above that I was born in the Parish of Cranley, in the County of Surrey, about 37 miles south of London, and about 9 miles Southeast of the noted Burrough Town of Guildford, on the River Wye.

I remain your obliged servant.

JOHN UPFOLD
Clinton, Nov. 28th 1816.

Justice of the Peace Robert Nelles forwarded Mr. Upfold's correspondence to the Lieutenant-Governor's private secretary, saying in his accompanying note, "From the short acquaintance I have had with Mr. Upfold, I take him to be a worthy, good man," and the word "granted," endorsed on the back of the letter, indicates that the pastor of Beamsville was acknowledged to be a loyal subject of the Crown.

Mr. Upfold's negotiations with the church and his pastorate in Clinton have been described in the accounts of the missionary tours (see page 59). His superior education and wise leadership had an immediate effect upon the affairs of the congregation. He had, however, some unpleasant situations to deal with, such as that described in the following letter written by the church to its senior deacon.[60]

Clinton, June 15th 1818

The Baptist Ch. in Clinton to Deacon Arthur Gray

Greeting:

Whereas you have signed an agreement to lend Elder John Upfold fifteen dollars to assist him in building his house:

And whereas you have since positively refused to do according to agreement, which conduct of yours is somewhat similar to that of Annanias as mentioned in the fifth chapt. of Acts, we therefore admonish you to repent of this your wickedness and settle this business within one month — and furthermore, should you neglect this admonition we will be under the necessity of excluding you from our fellowship.

Signed by order and in behalf of the ch.

JACOB BEAM, Ch. Clerk.

Deacon Gray was duly excluded from the church, and attempted to join another congregation in Canboro, but could not gain admittance when the members heard why he had been dismissed from Clinton. At length it was learned that through the failure of his son's business enterprise, he was in financial difficulties, and Mr. Upfold took the initiative in getting the church to agree that if definite evidence of this could be produced, its censure of Mr. Gray would be lifted. This was finally done in November 1821.

Mr. Upfold was regarded as a leader in the Baptist cause by all the churches in the province. He stimulated the move to form a conference of churches around Clinton in order to do away with the need for belonging to associations across the border. He pressed the claim of Baptist ministers for equal treatment with other denominations in the matter of solemnizing marriage, and kept the Lieutenant-Governor informed on Baptist affairs by sending him copies of the Clinton Conference minutes.[61]

His ministry at Clinton continued until 1825. That he was not without critics is seen by the fact that at the time of his departure the Clinton Church was communicating with the church in Oxford about "a complaint against Elder Upfold." What it was is not known, and probably does not matter. He returned to the United States and preached at Hannibal, New York, where he died in 1828. "His integrity as a man," said one of his contemporaries, "and his faithfulness as a minister secured him the friendship and Christian affection of many."

Joseph Winn

Joseph Winn, according to a petition addressed by him to Sir Peregrine Maitland in 1820, was born in Dutchess County, in New York State, in the year 1758.[62] He came of a very large family connection, and several of his relatives bore the same name as himself, so that records of the period contain references to more than one Joseph Winn. His own testimony, supported by affidavits from loyalist friends, shows that during the Revolution he supported the British side. In 1778 he gave shelter to John Meyers, a wounded British secret agent, who came seeking aid to the Winn home, which had been recommended to him as one of loyal subjects. Winn in 1780 guided another British agent, John Ferris, from a point on the Hudson to New York City, and saw him safely through to the British lines.[63] That same year, he enlisted in Colonel Delancey's corps, and served for some time under Captain Gilbert Totten of the Westchester Loyalists. Despite his record of service, his name was never entered on the United Empire List.

According to the sworn statement of John Platt, Winn was in Canada as a Baptist minister by 1796.[64] Between the close of the war and his coming to Canada, he resided at Coxsackie on the Hudson River, in what is now Green County, New York.[65] In 1797 he was granted a settler's lot in the township of Cramahe, but did not make his home there, and later sold it to a man named Ketchum. Most of his life in Canada was spent in Prince Edward County. The records of Baptist churches in other parts of the province show that he was a licensed preacher when he came to Canada, and that he returned to the United States to obtain ordination.

His first work in Canada was done in the township of Hallowell, on the shore of West Lake, and a large island in the lake still bears his name on government maps. At Hallowell in 1799 he presided over the ordination of Reuben Crandall. He was one of three ministers who founded the Thurlow Association in 1802, and in 1804 his church, according to the missionary, Joseph Cornell, was favoured with "a glorious revival of religion." In the year 1805 we find that he preached as far west as Townsend, where he baptized seven people, and in the month of August he assisted at the ordination of Elijah Bentley. One of the churches visited by him in 1809 was Philipsville (Steventown), to which he had been invited as preacher in the month of December. About this time he seems to have moved from West Lake to the Carrying Place, and there he formed the First Baptist Church of Ameliasburg, later called the Murray church.

During the War of 1812, Winn did his bit for the government by drawing supplies for the troops with his team, and after the war he continued his quiet work as a minister of the gospel around the Bay of Quinte. In January 1817, he held special services at Haldimand, where he baptized five people and helped to start the revival which led to the re-establishment of the local association. His request in 1820 to have his name inserted on the Upper Canada U.E. List was, as we have seen, not granted, the reason given being lack of sufficient evidence of his service. This same difficulty was experienced by many who had served with the Westchester Loyalists, which was not on the regular British establishment of army units and therefore lacked proper documentary records.

Joseph Winn's name is found again in various later source materials. In 1825, according to a record in the library at McMaster University, Hamilton, Ontario, the Ameliasburg church sent Joseph Winn, Deacon John Winn, and Brother William Beals as delegates to Haldimand to attend the ordination of Benjamin Farmer. In 1840, when he was eighty-two years of age, Mr. Winn wrote to the government for the last time, inquiring about the patent to the lot he had been granted over forty years before. Like many others who had employed Messrs. Danforth and Greeley as their agents in obtaining land grants, he had never received clear title to his lot, and had not been able to furnish a deed to it when he sold it to Mr. Ketchum. The Executive Council were sorry, but could do nothing about it.

From 1840 onwards Mr. Winn vanishes from sight, but the report of his little church in the village of Murray (formerly the Carrying Place) to the Association in 1845 stated that "during the year their former pastor, the aged and venerable Joseph Winn had been called away to his eternal rest, having preached the gospel in Canada for nearly fifty years."[66]

Mr. Winn's resting place is unknown, though it was probably in a small cemetery at the Carrying Place which has since disappeared from view. He is thus among those who "have no memorial" in a material sense, yet it cannot be said that he belongs to those who "have perished as though they had never been." The many faithful souls of this story have gone to rest from their labours, but their works follow them.

IX

The Baptists of Lower Canada

before 1820

WHEN NEW FRANCE fell into British hands after the capture of Quebec in 1759, the French population was settled almost exclusively on the land that lay along the River St. Lawrence. The rest of the country was a vast forest, uninhabited by white men. The region now known as the Eastern Townships received a few loyalists during the American Revolution but the real movement of settlers to that area did not take place until the last decade of the eighteenth century. In 1792 Lower Canada was divided into districts, counties, and townships and the great tract south of the St. Lawrence was thrown open to immigrants as the surveys were made. The legend persists, owing perhaps to a sentence in Lord Durham's report, that the majority of those who entered from the United States at that time were "loyalists," but this is not true.[1] For the most part, the Eastern Townships were settled by land seekers, many of whom had actually fought against the British during the War of Independence. The loyalists among them were few and far between, though there were some.

By 1793 there were settlements in the border counties of Brome, Stanstead, and Compton, in Shefford and Richmond, and in the old seigniories of St. Armand and Foucault. These two seigniories lay on either side of Missisquoi Bay at the north end of Lake Champlain. Foucault had been purchased by Sir John Caldwell and its name changed to Caldwell's Manor.[2] St. Armand, originally granted in 1748 to the ship builder René Levasseur, had been purchased by the Honourable Thomas Dunn, and part of it was included in the state of Vermont when the international border was finally settled. The names of the two old seigniories are perpetuated in the townships of Foucault and St. Armand in what is now Missisquoi County, between Brome County and the Richelieu River. These communities of the Eastern Townships made slow progress until around 1799, when the flow of immigration increased and growth became more rapid. By 1810, the French people from the older parts of the province had begun to move into the Eastern Townships alongside the English-speaking element, and this trend has continued steadily up to the present time.

The main period of development for Baptist work in the Townships was before the War of 1812, and missionaries from the United States were very active there between 1793 and 1811. Elsewhere in Quebec there was no organized Baptist church until 1831, when one was established in Montreal.

In the late summer of 1793 the Woodstock Baptist Association of Vermont sent two missionaries on a tour through the northern part of the state and into Lower Canada. Their names were John Hebbard and Ariel Kendrick. Mr. Hebbard was at that time pastor of the church in Royalton, Vermont. Mr. Kendrick came of the same well-known family as Clark and Nathaniel Kendrick, who toured Upper Canada a few years later.[3] After stopping in Fairfax, Vermont, where the Rev. Elisha Andrews was labouring as an evangelist, the two men crossed into Canada and visited Caldwell's Manor. There they found a community of immigrants from Connecticut. Preaching services were held, and quite a number professed conversion. The missionaries, however, did not find themselves able to baptize any converts and returned to the United States without organizing a church.

In January 1794, the people at Caldwell's Manor themselves sent out a request for a minister to visit them and administer the ordinance of baptism. Mr. Andrews responded to their request and in an account written by him and published more than forty years later, we have a description of his mission:

As I was the only Baptist minister in the region, except Elder Call, and he was an aged man, and ten miles further off, there could be no doubt with respect to the path of duty. A friend of mine volunteered to take me down in his sleigh. We started Monday morning and proceeded to Highgate, (Vt.); here we put up at the house of a German by the name of Wagoner. In the morning we followed his direction, crossed Missisque Bay and arrived at the Manor in season to appoint a meeting in the evening. We put up with Dr. Cune, a Baptist from Rhode Island. In the morning we crossed over to the west side of the Manor about eight miles, into the neighbourhood where the revival had been the most powerful. Soon after we arrived, the house was filled with people, and I preached to them; and again in the evening. The next day we met at 9 o'clock in the morning, and spent the whole day in examining candidates for baptism; we heard and received thirty of all ages from 10 to 50 years. . . . The next day we repaired to the Lake, cut a hole in the ice, and fifteen of those happy and devoted disciples were, in the name of the Father, Son and Holy Ghost, immersed agreeably to the command of the divine Saviour. The baptism of the remaining fifteen was deferred until the next Monday, it being their choice to have it performed in the vicinity where they resided.

After spending a full week in visitation, preaching, instructing, and baptizing, Mr. Andrews returned to Fairfax. Four weeks later he went again to Caldwell's Manor, accompanied by a delegation from the Fairfax church in order to form a council that might extend recognition to the new congregation in Canada. Several more converts were baptized, a church was formed, and the council recognized it as "The Baptist Church of Christ in Caldwell's Manor."

Though Elisha Andrews seems to have paid only two brief visits to Lower Canada, his career is not without interest to Canadian Baptists. According to a biographical sketch written by his son, the Rev. Erastus Andrews of Suffield, Connecticut, Mr. Andrews was born on September 29, 1768, in Middletown, Conn.[4] His father, Isaac Andrews, had been a sailor, but was also a school teacher and indeed his proficiency in mathematics qualified him as a land surveyor as well. Elisha was educated at home and taught school when he was sixteen years of age. He was baptized by Joseph Cornell while staying with an aunt in Galway where Cornell was minister. Though he was anxious to preach, the church where he was baptized did not feel that he had the gift, and refused to grant him a licence. However, on his way to Vermont he preached for the church in Granville, and they granted him what Galway had refused.

In 1793 Mr. Andrews took charge of the work in Fairfax, Vermont, and was quite successful, but the opinion that he might not be fitted for the pastorate still pursued him and instead of being ordained as minister of the church he was ordained as an evangelist. This ceremony took place at an open air service during his first year in Fairfax. He remained with the community until 1796, and was married during this time to Miss Wealthy Ann Lathrop. He subsequently held pastorates in Hopkinton, N.H., Hudson, N.H., and Templeton, Mass. He was very studious, reading Greek and Latin by himself and Hebrew under Rev. Dr. Murdock, a Congregationalist minister in Princeton. When war broke out in 1812 he strongly opposed the American part and as a result had to resign his church at Templeton in 1813, but he was reconciled with his congregation after the war. In 1816 he went to Hinsdale, N.H., and there died in 1840. There were eight children in his family, one of whom, Elisha Andrews Jr., survived his graduation from Brown University in 1821 only six years. Another son, Erastus, was ordained to the ministry.

Mr. Andrew's scholarly attainments were recognized by Brown University in 1803 when he was granted the honorary degree of Master of Arts. He published a book entitled *Moral Tendencies of Univer-salism,* printed in Boston, and also "A Brief Reply to James Bicker-staff's *Short Epistle to Baptists.*" Under the pseudonym "Gimel" he contributed articles on the Unitarian controversy to *The Christian Watchman* and it was this magazine which first published his account of how he helped to found the church at Caldwell's Manor. (In 1836 the story was reprinted in I. M. Allen's *Triennial Baptist Register.*) Writing about Mr. Andrews some years after his death, Rev. John Graves of Boston noted that "His purpose in preaching was not so much to excite as to instruct. He thought it much more important to sow the good seed of the Kingdom in good soil than to sway with his breath the stocks and plants before him."

Not long after Elisha Andrews' departure from Caldwell's Manor in the winter of 1794, the church gave a licence to preach to one of its members, William Marsh, Jr., who was born in Shaftsbury, Vermont, on July 4, 1757. His father was a magistrate who took the loyalist side in the American Revolution and was killed while serving in General Burgoyne's army. The family suffered a great deal during the rest of the war and moved up to Canada about 1783. Though they did not receive subsistence from the government as many loyalists did, they took up land and established themselves as settlers. William married Elizabeth, the daughter of Simon Huntingdon, also a loyalist who had fled to Canada. He became interested in religion when he was asked to read sermons at gatherings of friends and neighbours, and was con-verted by a printed sermon by Whitefield on "The Lord Our Righte-ousness" (Jer. 33:16).[5] His son gives the date of his baptism as 1793, which indicates that Elisha Andrews' visit in 1794 was not the first occasion on which the ordinance had been administered in Lower Canada.

In 1796 the church at Caldwell's Manor summoned a council to consider Mr. Marsh's ordination. The churches at Fairfax and Cam-bridge responded, and the minutes[6] kept on that occasion give us a description of this important step for a pioneer community:

Caldwells Manor
March 2nd 1796

In pursuance of a request from the Baptist Church of Christ in this place to a number of sister churches of ye same faith and order for an Advisory Council to advise with and assist them in examining and setting apart B[r] William Marsh, Junr. to the work of the ministry by solemn ordination, the following Eld[rs] and brethren were present

Churches	*Messengers*
Fairfax	Eld^r Joseph Call
	D^n Peter Thurston
	B^r Ichabod Orton
	B^r Leicester Grovener
	B^r Saml Cressy
Cambridge	Elder Ezra Willmarth
	D^n Robert Cochran

After having formed into a Council, been Rec^d by the Church, and addressed the throne of grace

1st Chose Eld^r Call moderator

2nd Chose Eld^r Willmarth clerk

3rd Read and examined the church's articles of faith and records of practice.

4th Enquired whether the chh. were satisfied with the candidate's ministerial qualifications.

5th Examined the candidate respecting 1st his adoption, 2nd his internal call to preach the gospel, 3rd his doctrinal knowledge.

6th The Council withdrew.

1st Voted that we are satisfied with the standing of the church.

2nd Voted that we are satisfied with the adoption of Brother Mash [*sic*]

3rd Voted that we are satisfied that he is called to the work of the ministry.

4th Voted that we are satisfied with his doctrinal knowledge and that he is ripe for ordination.

5th Voted that we will assist the church in ordaining B^r William Marsh J^r to the work of the ministry by solemn prayer and imposition of hands to-morrow at ten o'clock, A.M.

6th Voted that the following be the order in which we proceed on the morrow in the performance of the ordination (viz.)

Eld^r Call is to preach the ordination sermon

Eld^r Willmarth to make the ordination prayer

Eld^r Call to give the charge

Eld^r Willmarth to give the right hand of fellowship

B^r Orton to make the concluding prayer.

7th Adjourned till to-morrow at ten o'clock to meet at this place.

March 3rd 1796

Agreeable to yesterday's determination, Bro. William Mash Junr was set apart to the work of the ministry by solemn ordination.

Attest

JOSEPH CALL, Mod^r

EZRA WILLMARTH, Clerk

William
  Marsh

Soon after Mr. Marsh's ordination, the Baptist congregation in Caldwell's Manor moved in a body to Eaton Township (to the northeast in Compton County), where the Sawyerville church was later formed by the same people.[7] Mr. Marsh founded churches at Sutton Flats, Stanstead, and Hatley, making his home at the latter place. For a time he returned to Sutton and went in 1810 or 1811 to Stanbridge, preaching in Stanbridge, Dunham, and Brome, and supplementing his income by making shoes. In 1813 he moved to Dunham, where he lived till 1825. After these many years of activity in the Townships, Mr. Marsh now went to Whitby, Upper Canada and served churches in Whitby, Darlington, Markham and Reach townships. Apart from Elisha Andrews' account of Caldwell's Manor, and the record of the ordination kept by Ezra Willmarth, we have little information about his work: the missionaries who toured Lower Canada do not mention Mr. Marsh's work in their reports. Most of the facts outlined above were obtained from a tribute written at the time of his death in 1843 by his son, the Rev. Israel Marsh, who was his ministerial colleague in Whitby Township after his removal to Upper Canada.

In 1797, the Rev. Jedediah Hibbard, who had been in turn a soldier, land surveyor, and preacher, settled in the township of St. Armand, at a place called Abbott's Corner (Dr. Jonas Abbott settled there at about the same time).[8] Unlike William Marsh, Mr. Hibbard was no loyalist, but was ardently pro-American all his life. Born in Canterbury, Conn., on October 4, 1740, he was the son of John and Sarah (Durkee) Hibbard. His wife, who also was from Canterbury, was Mary Porter, and came of a well-to-do family of Congregationalists. They were married in 1762, but Mrs. Hibbard never joined her husband's church, remaining a staunch Congregationalist till her death in 1813.[9]

Soon after his marriage, Hibbard moved to Lebanon, N.H., with his father-in-law, Colonel Porter. He was well established there by 1766, when he was elected "tything man" and he also served as a public land surveyor. In addition to his municipal duties and his farming, he preached a good deal. In June and July 1777 he served under Colonel Chase in the American forces at Ticonderoga, and he took part in the battle of Saratoga in October of that year when the British general, Burgoyne, surrendered to the Americans led by General Gates. After the war he resumed his preaching, and was ordained to the ministry at Lebanon in 1784. He went on many missionary journeys, some of which, it is said, took him into Canada, though there is no official record of these before he settled there in 1797.

By 1799 Mr. Hibbard had organized a church at Abbott's Corner, and he continued to serve as its minister until his death in 1809. Mr. Hibbard's immediate successor after his death was the Rev. William Galusha. For a number of years the church at Abbott's Corner belonged to the Richmond (later Fairfield) Association in Vermont, until the War of 1812 interfered with the arrangement. After the war it continued its relationship with churches on the American side of the border, belonging at various times to the Danville and Lemoille Associations. Ultimately it joined the Eastern Association of the Baptist Convention of Ontario and Quebec, and a largely attended centenary celebration was held in 1899. In recent years it has formed part of the same Home Mission field as Sutton, Quebec.

In the same year that he organized the Abbott's Corner church in St. Armand Township, Jedediah Hibbard co-operated with William Marsh in establishing the church in Hatley and Stanstead. Mr. Marsh himself shepherded this congregation until 1811, when one of the members, Hervey Clarke, was ordained as pastor during a visit by the missionary, Barnabas Perkins. Mr. Clarke, in turn, was succeeded at Hatley and Stanstead by the Rev. Edward Mitchell, who wrote an interesting account of the church's history for the *Canada Baptist Missionary Register* on the occasion of its fiftieth anniversary.[10]

The years 1806 and 1807 each saw a visit to Lower Canada by an American Baptist missionary, the first, as far as we know, in nearly seven years. The visitor in 1806 was the Rev. Barnabas Perkins, of Hanover, New Hampshire. On October 8 he crossed into the province from Vermont and spent about three weeks visiting Eaton, Newport, Ascot, Brompton, Compton, and Hereford.[11] Mr. Perkins reported having to travel through a dreary wilderness and over a dreadful road. In one part of his journey he rode seventeen miles without seeing a single house. The people, however, received him "with much affection" and at the places where he preached his meetings were well attended. We might say also that he seems to have been somewhat in doubt as to the spelling of their names! In 1807 the missionary to Lower Canada was the Rev. Phinehas Pillsbury, of Maine, who represented the Massachusetts Baptist Missionary Society. The goal of his journey was really Upper Canada, but he touched at several places in the lower province as he travelled. On March 15, he was at Stanbridge in Missisquoi County, and later visited a church at Ellis's seigniory, which he reported to be a branch of the church in Champlain, N.Y.[12]

Mr. Perkins again "laboured in the northerly parts of New Hampshire, Vermont, and Lower Canada" in 1808, but he was in poor health that year and unable to complete his full term of service with the Massachusetts Society.[13] His report was not as detailed as usual and as a result we do not know what places he visited. Two representatives of the Shaftsbury Association, Elders Calvin Chamberlain and Jonathan Finch, were also in the province in 1808, but again no details of their trip are given. The report of the Association's missionary committee implies that Finch had also visited Lower Canada in 1807 and that he did so again in 1809.[14]

A more extended visit was made to the Eastern Townships in 1809 by the Rev. Samuel Ambrose, of Sutton, New Hampshire, who was sent by the Massachusetts Baptist Missionary Society. He went to Hatley, Compton, Ascot, Barnston, and Stanstead.[15] We know some of the homes that were opened to him: in Ascot he preached at the home of Noah Worcester (eldest son of the Rev. Noah Worcester of Thornton), and at Felix Ward's; in Barnston he preached at Mr. Rosewell Smith's and in Stanstead at Mr. Shurtleff's.

Four missionaries spent some time in Lower Canada in 1810 — Samuel Ambrose, Barnabas Perkins, Cyrus Andrews, and Samuel Churchill. Mr. Ambrose came in January and preached at the homes of Mr. Gould and Mr. Bernard in Barnston. At Hatley he preached at Mr. Little's and in Ascot at Mr. Elliot's. Visits were also made to Shipton, Brompton, and the home of Mr. Key, "five miles up the river from Brompton." He was entertained at Stanstead by Dr. Whittier.[16]

Elder Perkins reported concerning his 1810 mission that he had "met with some opposition from the enemies of Christianity," but he had been able to see some "happy fruits of his labours."[17] Rev. Cyrus Andrews was conservative in his estimate of the results of his visit, but his report to the Shaftsbury Association was favourable.[18] As for the Rev. Samuel Churchill, of Littleton, N.H., make of his reports what you can! He went, he said, at the request of Deacon Griswold, to "Barnstead," Lower Canada. Did he mean Barnston or Stanstead? The editor who published his reports was not too sure what Elder Churchill meant, for he said, cryptically, in a footnote, "We spell these names as we find them, unless we know them to be wrong." Whatever the place was, Mr. Churchill reported that there had been an epidemic there recently and that one hundred people had died. He also reported that a Baptist elder, R. Smith, lived there, but was unable to preach because of advanced age and failing health. Mr. Smith, however, despite his age and infirmity, expressed the thanks of the community to Mr. Churchill for his visit and to the Missionary Society for sending him.[19]

The year 1811 marked the last missionary visit from the United States to Lower Canada. In July that year the Rev. Barnabas Perkins attended an ordination council in Hatley for the purpose of setting apart "Brother" Clarke to the work of the ministry. Mr. Perkins was impressed with what he saw. "The assembly was large and respectable, for so new a place, and during the exercises the people were very solemn. On the whole, the prospect here appears quite flattering."[20] So ended the first era of Baptist expansion in Lower Canada. The coming of the Swiss Baptist missionaries to the country between the Richelieu and St. Lawrence rivers, which led to the founding of the Grande Ligne Mission, and the planting of Baptist churches in the cities of Montreal and Quebec are events belonging to a later period of history.

Missionary Tours into Lower Canada

Year	Missionary	Sponsor	Places visited
1793	John Hebbard	Woodstock (Vt.) Assoc.	Caldwell's Manor
	Ariel Kendrick	Woodstock (Vt.) Assoc.	Caldwell's Manor
1794	Elisha Andrews	Two personal visits	Caldwell's Manor
1796	Ezra Willmarth	Council to ordain	Caldwell's Manor
	Joseph Call	William Marsh	
1797	Jedediah Hibbard		Abbott's Corner
1806	Barnabas Perkins	Mass. B.M.S.	Eaton, Newport, Ascot, Brompton, Compton and Hereford
1807	Phinehas Pillsbury	Mass. B.M.S.	Stanstead and Ellis's Seigniory
1808	Barnabas Perkins	Mass. B.M.S.	Not stated
	Calvin Chamberlain	Shaftsbury Assoc.	Not stated
	Jonathan Finch	Shaftsbury Assoc.	Not stated
1809	Jonathan Finch	Shaftsbury Assoc.	Not stated
	Samuel Ambrose	Mass. B.M.S.	Hatley, Compton, Ascot, Barnston and Stanstead
1810	Samuel Ambrose	Mass. B.M.S.	Barnston, Hatley, Ascot, Shipton, Brompton and Stanstead
	Barnabas Perkins	Mass. B.M.S.	Not stated
	Cyrus Andrews	Shaftsbury Assoc.	
	Samuel Churchill	Mass. B.M.S.	Barnston or Stanstead
1811	Barnabas Perkins	Council to ordain Brother Clarke	Hatley

X

Associations and Conferences

THE BAPTISTS OF THE UNITED STATES had developed at the beginning of the nineteenth century a threefold form of organization, and this pattern prevailed in Upper and Lower Canada. Their work was done through local churches, associations of churches, and voluntary societies of individuals formed for specific missionary, charitable, or educational enterprises. The local church, led by its minister, was, nevertheless, the keystone of the Baptist arch. All other forms of organization were adapted to the autonomy of this unit. Its right to self-government was unquestioned, and its power could not be delegated to any other body. Even when units larger than associations became necessary, they were still composed of representatives from individual churches. Anything resembling a chain of authority from smaller units of organization to larger, or from larger to smaller, was instinctively avoided. The system has often proved to be unwieldy in more recent times, but in pioneer days its flexibility was a distinct advantage.

Though autonomy was so much prized, there were found to be many rewards in wider organization. The British Baptist historian, W. T. Whitley, has stated that "Baptists from the beginning sought to maintain sisterly intercourse between local churches; they never thought that one church was independent of others."[1] The same authority contrasts the tendency of Baptist churches to "associate" with that of the British Independents to follow an isolationist course. From the very first, Baptist churches in Ontario and Quebec showed a strong desire to achieve full fellowship with sister churches through some form of local grouping. It was not an easy task, for congregational autonomy had to be reconciled with joint responsibility, but true Baptists have never been content to have the one without the other. Before 1820, there was no such thing in Upper or Lower Canada as an "unassociated" Baptist church. It was not until later that this type of schismatic heresy invaded the Baptist body. It probably reached its peak around 1880 when it was reported that at least twenty-four churches in the two provinces were unassociated, yet called themselves Baptist.

In the early days of Baptist work in this part of Canada every church was connected with some association, however distant, from the time of its organization, or as soon afterwards as possible. The churches in the Bay of Quinte region, only three in number at the time, in 1802 formed the Thurlow Baptist Association to which frequent reference has been made in these pages. It was named after the church where it first met, Thurlow, the other two members of the Association being Hallowell and Cramahe-Haldimand. The ministers who co-operated in this effort were Asa Turner of Thurlow, Joseph Winn of Hallowell, and Reuben Crandall of Cramahe-Haldimand. No written record of the first two meetings of the Thurlow Association has come to light, but fortunately the third meeting, held at Haldimand in 1804, on February 16 and 17, was attended by Joseph Cornell and Peter Roots of the Massachusetts Baptist Missionary Society, and extracts from the minutes of the sessions were later published in the *Massachusetts Baptist Missionary Magazine*.[2] A letter addressed to the Society by the Association read in part:

Two years since, our three churches in this quarter, agreed to form into an association for our mutual improvement, and assistance in promoting the cause of truth: but last year some things took place which interrupted, and we were afraid would continue to interrupt, if not destroy, the union and sweet friendship, which we had before felt: but according to our prayers, and by the blessing of God attending the labours of our brethren, who came from the States to visit us, our harmony in gospel bonds is all restored, and much increased. We have received one church this year. . . .

P.S. Our next Association is to be holden at Thurlow, the second Friday in Feb. 1805, at 10 o'clock, A.M.

From the above record, and from references found in missionary reports over the next few years, it has been ascertained that the Thurlow Association met at Thurlow in 1802, at Hallowell (most likely) in 1803, at Haldimand in 1804, again at Thurlow in 1805, at Percy in 1806, at Markham in 1808, and at Cramahe in 1809. By 1810 it employed a travelling representative, Elder Elijah Bentley, of Markham, and several other churches, including Steventown and Townsend, had been brought into its fellowship. Townsend was also a member of the Shaftsbury Association in the United States at that time.

The War of 1812 disrupted the work of the Association and prevented its holding regular meetings, but after the war it was revived. In 1819 it was re-organized and called the Haldimand Association. The churches east of Kingston withdrew to form the Johnstown Association, leaving the Haldimand group with only six: Ameliasburg,

Cramahe, Haldimand, Rawdon, Sidney, and Thurlow. Gradually its numbers increased, with the addition of churches in Whitby, Toronto, Hamilton, and other points west and north. In 1871 it changed its name to the Eastern Ontario Association. It dismissed nineteen of its forty churches in 1874 so that the Toronto Association might be formed. Starting afresh with twenty-one churches, it increased to thirty-four, and in 1887 it dismissed seventeen of these to form the Whitby-Lindsay Association. The following year, 1888, it changed its name to the Peterborough Association, and so remained till 1954. That year, the processes of history were reversed, when the Whitby-Lindsay and Peterborough Associations re-united, adopting the name of the Trent Valley Association. For the humble beginnings at Thurlow in 1802, and the formation of the powerful associations of later years, one impulse was responsible, and that was the conviction that no congregation formed on the New Testament pattern could live unto itself.

In the Niagara Peninsula, on Lake Erie, and along the River Thames, the early Baptist churches were content at first to be members of associations in the United States. Charlotteville, Townsend, Clinton, Oxford, and Malahide (Talbot Street), all belonged to the Shaftsbury Association of Vermont, New York, and Massachusetts. Queenston (Niagara), because of its minister's former connection with the New York Association, belonged to that body. It was soon evident, however, that membership in such far away associations did not provide the Canadian churches with the fellowship that they needed. Most of them reported faithfully by letter to the annual assemblies, but delegates were not sent to the meetings. Personal contact between the associations and the churches depended upon the visits made by missionaries sent for the purpose, and these were all too few and far between. During the War of 1812-14 they ceased entirely.

From the very beginning of Baptist work in that area, however, a feature of it had been the habit of meeting together for informal conference. Before churches were established we have evidence of "conferences" being held by individual Baptists, sometimes with a missionary present. As churches were formed the habit continued, and Clinton became a centre for such gatherings. As early as 1810, before the war had cut off communication with the United States, the so-called Clinton Conference had become a regular feature of the work carried on by Baptist churches in the area. On September 22, 1810, and again on October 4, 1811, the Townsend church "voted to attend conference at Clinton." Such references prepare us for the development after 1815, when the Clinton Conference had become a well-established body. In 1816 it met at Townsend on the fourth Wednesday in August, and the minutes of the Clinton church state that Jonathan Wolverton, Samuel Corwin, and Jacob Beam were appointed to attend. Mr. Beam was instructed by the church to "write a letter to lay before the Conference." The sessions occupied three days, and one of the results was the formation of "The Upper Canada Domestic Missionary Society for the sending of the Gospel among the destitute of this Province and parts adjacent."[3]

In 1819 the Shaftsbury Association formally dismissed its five Canadian churches to the Clinton Conference, and the church at Queenston also joined the Conference officially about that time. For a number of years it continued to function with all the powers of an association. John Upfold, in his letter to the Lieutenant-Governor in 1821, enclosed for His Excellency's information a copy of the minutes of the previous session of the Conference, but unfortunately they did not find their way to the Public Archives with the letter itself. The churches of the Clinton Conference gradually re-grouped to form the Eastern, Western, and Grand River Associations, and further subdivisions followed as the churches increased in number.

In the period prior to 1820 the Baptist churches of Lower Canada, all of which were in the Eastern Townships, maintained a connection with the associations in Vermont which had sponsored missionary tours into the area. This relationship ceased during the War of 1812-14 with the termination of missionary activity, but it was later reestablished. The Fairfax Association, of Franklin County, the Lamoille Association, of Lamoille County, and the Danville Association, of Caledonia County, all had churches in Lower Canada in their membership at times. The last named, Danville, as late as 1880, included nine Canadian churches; at the same date, the Lamoille Association included one, Abbott's Corners. The gradual evolution of the Eastern Association, which sprang from the Ottawa (1835) and Montreal (1845) Associations, made it possible for most of the English-speaking churches in the province of Quebec to unite in one body. The few that are not in the Eastern Association, due to their location, are members of the Ottawa Association.

The history of the pioneer Baptists of Upper and Lower Canada reveals that in their churches, despite the faults and limitations imposed by primitive conditions, there was always present a sense of belonging to what the greatest of Baptist confessions described as "the Catholick or universal Church." Their constant endeavour, despite their emphasis on congregational autonomy, to combine in associations, was, in a very true sense, an expression of what they conceived the visible church, in its larger aspect, to be. They were convinced, as all who bear the name of Baptist should be, that, "As each Church, and all the Members of it, are bound to pray continually for the good and prosperity of all the Churches of Christ, in all places; and upon all occasions to further it (every one within the bounds of their places and callings, in the Exercise of their Gifts and Graces) so the Churches (when planted by the providence of God so as they may enjoy opportunity and advantage for it) ought to hold Communion amongst themselves for their peace, increase of love, and mutual edification."[4]

NOTES

CHAPTER I

1. Joseph Hall, *Common Apologie*, sec. 11, quoted by W. I. Whitley, ed., *The Works of John Smyth* (Cambridge, 1915), I, xcvii.
2. Henry C. Vedder, *A Short History of the Baptists* (Philadelphia: American Baptist Publication Society, 1891), 174.
3. *Ibid.*, 158.
4. Cf. A. H. Newman, "Sketch of the Baptists of Ontario and Quebec to 1851" in the *Baptist Year Book for Ontario and Quebec, Manitoba and the Northwest Territories and British Columbia* (1900), 73.
5. Vedder, *Short History of the Baptists*, 174.
6. John Rippon, ed., *The Baptist Annual Register* (1794), 196.
7. Stephen Wright, *History of the Shaftsbury Baptist Association from 1781 to 1853* (Troy, N.Y.: A. G. Johnson, 1853); also "Vermont Baptists" in William Cathcart, ed., *The Baptist Encyclopaedia* (Philadelphia, 1891), II, 1193; David Benedict, *A General History of the Baptist Denomination in America and Other Parts of the World* (2nd ed., New York, 1848), 486; and Mrs. D. C. Brown, *Memoir of Lemuel Covell* (Boston, 1835), *passim*, especially p. 26.
8. Stephen Wright, *The Old Shaftsbury Association* (1885, pamphlet, 12 pp.).
9. W. N. Eaton, *Historical Sketch of the Massachusetts Baptist Missionary Society and Convention, 1802-1902* (Boston, 1903).
10. *Massachusetts Baptist Missionary Magazine*, II, 115.
11. *Ibid.*, I, 8.
12. *Ibid.*, I, 45; II, 150.
13. John Peck and John Lawton, *An Historical Sketch of the Baptist Missionary Convention of the State of New York* (1837).
14. Minutes of the Beamsville Baptist Church, entry dated September 9, 1815; also J. T. Dowling, "Historic Review of the Peterborough Association" in the Association *Minutes* (1889).
15. See Peck and Lawton, *Baptist Missionary Convention of New York*, for sketches of missionaries' careers.
16. *Baptist Encyclopaedia*, II, 848.
17. *Baptist Annual Register* (1794), 195.
18. *Massachusetts Baptist Missionary Magazine*, II, 329.
19. *Buffalo Historical Society Publications*, VI, 125 ff.
20. *Ibid.*, 187, 188.
21. William L. Stone, *Life of Joseph Brant*, 2 vols. (New York, 1838), II, 439.
22. *Massachusetts Baptist Missionary Magazine*, II, 329, 330.
23. *Ibid.*, 93.
24. *Ibid.*, 174 ff.
25. David Benedict, *General History*, 562, 563.
26. Peck and Lawton, *Baptist Missionary Convention of New York*, 195.
27. Cathcart, *Baptist Encyclopaedia*, Appendix.

CHAPTER II

1. A. C. Casselman, "Pioneer Settlements," in Shortt and Doughty, eds., *Canada and Its Provinces: A History of the Canadian People and their Institutions* (Toronto: Glasgow, Brook & Company, 1914), XVII, 23.
2. Ontario Bureau of Archives, *Report* (1905), lxii.

3. *Ibid.*, liv.
4. Norman Macdonald, *Canada, 1763-1841, Immigration and Settlement: The Administration of the Imperial Land Regulations* (London, New York and Toronto: Longmans, Green and Co., 1939), 45, 46.
5. Deputy Surveyor Collins to surveyor Patrick McNiff, Cataraqui, June 18, 1785, in Ontario Bureau of Archives, *Report* (1905), 372.
6. Norman Macdonald, *Immigration and Settlement*, 48.
7. Public Archives of Canada, Series B (Haldimand Papers), vol. 168, p. 42.
8. A. C. Casselman, "Pioneer Settlements," 26.
9. Collins to MacDonnell, Quebec, June 30, 1788, in Ontario Bureau of Archives, *Report* (1905), 382.
10. Report of Rev. Joseph Cornell and Rev. Phinehas Pillsbury, *Massachusetts Baptist Missionary Magazine*, I, 68, 355.
11. Lord Dorchester to Hon. John Collins, Quebec, July 19, 1787, in Ontario Bureau of Archives, *Report* (1905), 453.
12. Dorchester to Samuel Holland, February 14, 1791, *ibid.*, 389.
13. Public Archives of Canada, Series M (Berczy Papers), *passim;* also Upper Canada Sundries, Berczy to Hillier, October 20, 1818.
14. E. A. Cruikshank, *Ten Years of the Colony of Niagara* (Welland: Niagara Historical Society Publication no. 17, 1908), 3, 4.
15. Public Archives of Canada, Series B, vol. 114, pp. 175, 176.
16. *Ibid.*, vol. 169, p. 1.
17. *Ibid.*, vol. 103 (Letters from Officers Commanding at Niagara).
18. Ontario Bureau of Archives, *Report* (1905), 489.
19. *Ibid.*, 486-88.
20. Public Archives of Canada, Series B, vol. 168, p. 38.
21. *Ibid.*, vol. 162, p. 333.
22. "The Silver of the Mohawks," *Saturday Night*, September 6, 1949.
23. Ontario Bureau of Archives, *Report* (1905), 308, 316.
24. *Ibid.*, 336.
25. E. A. Cruikshank, *Colony of Niagara*, 23.
26. Ontario Bureau of Archives, *Report* (1905), 313.
27. Jones to Ridout, 1825, in Willis Chipman, *Report of Ontario Land Surveyors' Association* (1923).
28. Ontario Bureau of Archives, *Report* (1904), 955, 991.
29. *Ibid.*, 972.
30. Public Archives of Canada, Upper Canada Land Book D, 305.
31. Ontario Bureau of Archives, *Report* (1905), 28, 29, 85, 123.
32. *Ibid.*, 70.
33. E. A. Cruikshank, ed., *The Correspondence of Lieut. Governor John Graves Simcoe, with Allied Documents relating to his Administration of the Government of Upper Canada*, 5 vols. (Toronto: Ontario Historical Society, 1923-26), known as *Simcoe Papers*. See references to Long Point.
34. *Ibid.*, II, 284; III, 255.
35. E. A. Cruikshank, "Petitions for Grants of Land, 1792-1796" in *Ontario Historical Society, Papers and Records*, XXIV (Toronto; 1927), 142, 143.
36. Dundas to Simcoe, March 16, 1794, in *Simcoe Papers*, II, 185.
37. Simcoe to Dundas, September 20, 1793, *ibid.*, II, 56.
38. *Handbook of the Indians of Canada*, published as sessional paper No. 21a (Ottawa: King's Printer, 1912), 315.
39. *Simcoe Papers*, I, 293.
40. Rev. Asahel Morse, "Journal of a Mission," in *Massachusetts Baptist Missionary Magazine*, II, 152.
41. Minute book of the Townsend church, entry dated February 16, 1811.

42. *Historical Sketches of the County of Elgin* (St. Thomas: Elgin Historical and Scientific Institute, 1895), 16.
43. G. W. Spragge, "The Districts of Upper Canada, 1788-1849," in *Ontario Historical Society, Papers and Records*, XXXIX (Toronto; 1947), 91.

CHAPTER III

1. Lemuel Covell, *A Narrative of a Missionary Tour through the Western Settlements of the State of New York and into the south-western parts of the Province of Upper Canada, performed by Lemuel Covell of Pittstown, in company with Elder Obed Warren of Salem, in the Fall of 1803: with an appendix containing several speeches to and from the Indians* (Pittstown, July 1804). Reprinted in Mrs. D. C. Brown, *Memoir of Lemuel Covell* (Boston, 1835), and partly reprinted in *Buffalo Historical Society Publications*, VI, 215 ff.
2. *Massachusetts Baptist Missionary Magazine*, II, 174-78.
3. *Ibid.*, I, 45.
4. Shaftsbury Baptist Association, *Minutes* (1803).
5. W. N. Eaton, *Historical Sketch of the Massachusetts Baptist Missionary Society and Convention, 1802-1902* (Boston, 1903), 13.
6. *Massachusetts Baptist Missionary Magazine*, I, 13 ff.
7. Shaftsbury Baptist Association, *Minutes* (1803).
8. *Massachusetts Baptist Missionary Magazine*, I, 48 ff.
9. Mrs. D. C. Brown, *Lemuel Covell*, 61.
10. Shaftsbury Baptist Association, *Minutes*, (1804).
11. For the chronological and other details of this tour, including the passages quoted from Covell's diary, see his *Narrative*, cited above in note 1.
12. On Thomson, see Ernest Green, "Township No. 2—Mount Dorchester-Stamford," in *Ontario Historical Society, Papers and Records*, XXV (Toronto, 1928), 325.
13. On Swayze, see E. A. Cruikshank, ed., *Correspondence of Lieut. Governor John Graves Simcoe* (i.e., *Simcoe Papers*), III, 342.
14. It was customary to refer to preaching, especially by laymen, as "improving one's gifts in public."
15. Mrs. D. C. Brown, *Lemuel Covell*, 61.
16. *Massachusetts Baptist Missionary Magazine*, I, 71.
17. *Ibid.*, 67, 76.
18. Stephen Wright, *History of the Shaftsbury Baptist Association from 1781 to 1853* (Troy, N.Y.: A. G. Johnson, 1853), 362.
19. *Ibid.*, 101.
20. *Massachusetts Baptist Missionary Magazine*, I, 152.
21. *Ibid.*, 203.
22. *Ibid.*, 259.
23. Report of Rev. Roswell Burrows to Groton Union Conference, January 2, 1807; in *Buffalo Historical Society Publications* VI, 236.
24. *Massachusetts Baptist Missionary Magazine*, I, 354, 355.
25. *Ibid.*, II, 52, 91.
26. *Ibid.*, 149.
27. J. Babcock, J. O. Choules and John M. Peck, eds., *The Baptist Memorial and Monthly Record* (New York: John R. Bigelow, 1844), *passim*.
28. *Massachusetts Baptist Missionary Magazine*, II, 196.
29. *Ibid.*, 173.
30. Shaftsbury Baptist Association, *Minutes* (1809), p. 11.

31. Minutes of the First Baptist Church of Oxford, quoted by Zella M. Hotson, *Pioneer Baptist Work in Oxford County* (Woodstock, Ont., no date), 14.
32. S. W. Adams, ed., *Memoirs of Nathaniel Kendrick* (Philadelphia: American Baptist Publication Society, 1860).
33. Beamsville Baptist Church, Minutes, April 9, 1809.
34. S. W. Adams, *Nathaniel Kendrick*.
35. Beamsville Baptist Church, Minutes, November 6, 1809.
36. Stephen Wright, *Shaftsbury Baptist Association*, 129, 369.

CHAPTER IV

1. David Benedict, *A General History of the Baptist Denomination in America and Other Parts of the World* (Boston, 1813), 560.
2. Shaftsbury Baptist Association, *Minutes* (1812).
3. *Massachusetts Baptist Missionary Magazine*, IV, 124.
4. *Ibid.*, III, 44.
5. Shaftsbury Baptist Association, *Minutes* (1816), entries dated June 5 and 6.
6. Cf. E. T. Newton, "Jepson Street Baptist Church, Niagara Falls," in the *Canadian Baptist*, September 30, 1937, pp. 6, 7, and 11.
7. Beamsville Baptist Church, Minutes, September 9, 1815.
8. John Peck and John Lawton, *An Historical Sketch of the Baptist Missionary Convention of the State of New York* (1837), 232; also Shaftsbury Baptist Association, *Minutes*, for the period 1817-26.
9. J. T. Dowling, "Historic Review Prepared on Request of the Peterborough Association of Baptist Churches," in the Association *Minutes* (1889).
10. John Peck and John Lawton, *Baptist Missionary Convention of New York*, 61.
11. First Baptist Church, Oxford, Minutes, quoted by Zella M. Hotson, *Pioneer Baptist Work in Oxford County* (Woodstock, Ont., no date), 17.
12. Townsend church Minutes; see especially entries dated September 22, 1810, and October 4, 1811, where the church "voted to attend conference at Clinton."
13. A. H. Newman, "Sketch of the Baptists of Ontario and Quebec to 1851," in the *Baptist Year Book for Ontario and Quebec, etc.* (1900), 74.
14. Stephen Wright, *History of the Shaftsbury Baptist Association from 1781 to 1853* (Troy, N.Y.: A. G. Johnson, 1853), 159; also Shaftsbury Baptist Association, *Minutes* (1819)

CHAPTER V

1. See Shaftsbury Baptist Association *Minutes* covering the period of Caleb Blood's activities with that body.
2. Nathaniel Kendrick in the *Massachusetts Baptist Missionary Magazine*, II, 174.
3. *Catalogue of the Officers of Government and Instruction, the Alumni and Other Graduates of the University of Vermont and State Agricultural College, Burlington, Vermont, 1791-1890* (Burlington: Free Press Association, 1890).
4. *Journal of the General Assembly of the State of Vermont*, October 26, 1791.
5. Quoted in Isaac Backus, *A History of New England with particular reference to the Denomination of Christians Called Baptists*, 2 vols. (Newton, Mass.: Backus Historical Society, 1871), II, 457, 546.

6. Caleb Blood, A Discourse delivered July 11, 11, at the Opening of the New Meeting House Belonging to the First Baptist Church and Society in Portland (Portland: J. McKown, Printer, 1811).
7. Caleb Blood, A Concise View of the Principal Points of Difference between the Baptists and Pedo-Baptists, to which are added Remarks on the Atonement, on Abraham's Covenant, the Olive-Tree etc. (Boston: Lincoln & Elmands, 1815).
8. David Benedict, A General History of the Baptist Denomination (2nd ed., New York, 1848), 489.
9. Information given by Peck and Lawton, An Historical Sketch of the Baptist Missionary Convention of the State of New York (1837), on some of the details of Cornell's career conflicts with that furnished by David Benedict and others.
10. Daniel Hascall, The Meaning of the Greek, Baptizo (Hamilton, N.Y., 1819), 19 pp.
11. Shaftsbury Baptist Association, Minutes (1817, 1818).
12. H.S.T. Griswold in Minutes of the 12th session, Harmony Baptist Association, 1850.
13. See Minute Book of the Beamsville Baptist Church in the Baptist Historical Collection at McMaster University, Hamilton, Canada.
14. See "Extracts from American Letters" in the Baptist Annual Register (1792), ed. John Rippon.
15. Mr. Roots' book is said by David Benedict to have been published at Hartford in 1794.
16. Colgate-Rochester Divinity School Bulletin, XV, no. 2, 86-88.
17. The First Half Century of Madison University (1819-1869); or, The Jubilee Volume (New York, Boston and Philadelphia, 1872), 37, 38.
18. Ibid., 408-9.

CHAPTER VI

1. Massachusetts Baptist Missionary Magazine, I, 67.
2. Ibid., 71.
3. William Canniff, The Settlement of Upper Canada (1869), 491.
4. Massachusetts Baptist Missionary Magazine, I, 72, 153.
5. The minute book of the Haldimand church is in the library of McMaster University, Hamilton, Ontario.
6. Public Archives of Canada, Upper Canada Land Petitions, 1819-24, vol. C, part II, no. 184.
7. Ibid., vol. E, no. 4, dated March 24, 1819, and no. 14, dated 1824.
8. Massachusetts Baptist Missionary Magazine, I, 67.
9. Public Archives of Canada, Upper Canada Land Petitions, 1789.
10. E. A. Cruikshank, ed., Correspondence of Lieut. Governor John Graves Simcoe, (i.e., Simcoe Papers), IV, 261.
11. Massachusetts Baptist Missionary Magazine, I, 13.
12. Daniel Derbyshire's will was dated April 15, 1808. His widow married Jedediah Wing and registered a memorial of the will at the Leeds County registry office, on March 17, 1827.
13. Public Archives of Canada, Upper Canada Land Book D, 1797-1802, p. 617, and extracts from the diary of Samuel Day, in the Baptist Historical Collection, Hamilton, Ontario.
14. The First Half Century of Madison University (1819-1869); or, The Jubilee Volume (New York, Boston and Philadelphia, 1872), 145, 229.

15. M. L. Orchard and K. S. McLaurin, *The Enterprise* (Toronto: Canadian Baptist Foreign Mission Board, 1924), p. 135.
16. *Massachusetts Baptist Missionary Magazine*, I, 153.
17. Sidney Township Record Book, 1790-1849.
18. *Massachusetts Baptist Missionary Magazine*, II, 174.
19. J. T. Dowling, in Peterborough Association, *Minutes* (1889).
20. J. G. Harkness, *Stormont, Dundas and Glengarry, a History* (Oshawa, 1946).
21. Daniel McPhail, "History of the Churches Composing the Ottawa Association" in the *Minutes of the Ottawa Baptist Association* (1865), 13.
22. Alexander Haldane, *The Lives of Robert Haldane of Airthrey, and of his Brother, James Alexander Haldane* (London: Hamilton Adams and Co., 1853), p. 320.
23. Zella Hotson, *Pioneer Baptist Work in Oxford County*, 16.
24. James Edwards, ed., *Correspondence and Papers on Various Subjects by the Late William Edwards of Clarence, Ont.* (Peterborough: J. R. Stratton, 1882), pp. 1-16.
25. *Massachusetts Baptist Missionary Magazine*, I, 355.
26. J. E. Wells, *Life and Labours of Robert Alex. Fyfe, D.D.* (Toronto: W. J. Gage & Company), 434.
27. *Baptist Year Book for Ontario, Quebec and Manitoba* (1879), 66.

CHAPTER VII

1. George Edward Levy, *The Baptists of the Maritime Provinces, 1753-1946* Saint John, N.B.: Barnes-Hopkins Ltd., 1946), p. 60.
2. Ontario Archives, *Report* (1933), p. 98.
3. *History of Toronto and County of York* (Toronto: C. Blackett Robinson, 1885), I, 118.
4. Minutes of the Court of Quarter Sessions, Home District, 1805-6, *passim*, in Ontario Archives, *Report* (1932).
5. *Massachusetts Baptist Missionary Magazine*, II, 150.
6. See Ken Ford, "Believe Congregation Established in 1782 by United Empire Loyalists," in *Globe and Mail* (Toronto), October 18, 1947.
7. Public Archives of Canada, Upper Canada Land Book A, 1792-96, 139, 203.
8. Public Archives of Canada, Upper Canada Land Petitions, 1835-36, part I, no. 30.
9. Public Archives of Canada, Upper Canada Land Book K, 1819-20, 56.
10. *Massachusetts Baptist Missionary Magazine*, II, 175.
11. Zella M. Hotson, *Pioneer Baptist Work in Oxford County* (Woodstock, Ont., n.d.), 6.
12. *Ibid.*, 14.
13. J. Cooper, ed., *Memoir of the Late Elder Baker of Malahide* (Aylmer: Express Steam Printing Works, 1881).
14. Edith Loucks and J. H. Curtis, "Historical Sketch of Port Burwell Baptist Church" (MS. copy in Baptist Historical Collection, Hamilton, Ont.).
15. Public Archives of Canada, Upper Canada Land Petitions, 1817, vol. M, no. 183; London District Marriage Register, 1784-1833, pp. 178, 179; obituary in the *Montreal Register*, May 25, 1843.
16. Public Archives of Canada, Upper Canada Land Petitions, 1811, vol. E, no. 15.
17. *Ibid.*, no. 14.
18. See Muster Rolls of the 1st Regiment, Middlesex Militia, in the Public Archives of Canada (not indexed)

19. Charles Lindsey, *Life and Times of Wm. Lyon Mackenzie* (Toronto: P. R. Randall, 1862), I, 399.
20. Minutes of the Court of Quarter Sessions, London District, in Ontario Archives, *Report* (1933), 162, 165, 182.

CHAPTER VIII

1. William Cathcart, ed., *The Baptist Encyclopaedia* (Philadelphia: Louis H. Everts, 1881), II, 1311 ff.
2. *Minutes of the Warren Association, held at the Baptist Meeting-House in Warren, September 10 and 11, 1805* (Boston: Manning and Loring, 1805), 7.
3. A. M. Caverly, *History of the Town of Pittsford, Vermont, with Biographical Sketches and Family Records* (Rutland: Tuttle and Co., 1872), 629-30.
4. W. Gregg, *The History of the Presbyterian Church in Canada* (Toronto, 1885), 211.
5. Public Archives of Canada, Series S, January 16, 1821.
6. William Cathcart, *Baptist Encyclopaedia*, I, 96.
7. *History of Toronto and County of York* (Toronto: C. Blackett Robinson, 1885), I, 118.
8. Ontario Archives, *Report* (1932).
9. Reuben Butchart, *The Disciples of Christ in Canada since 1830* (Toronto: Canadian Headquarters' Publications, Churches of Christ (Disciples), 1949), 74.
10. John Cortland Crandall, *Elder John Crandall of Rhode Island and His Descendants* (New Woodstock, New York, 1949), p. 735.
11. J. T. Dowling, in *Peterborough Association Minutes* (1889).
12. John Cortland Crandall, *Elder John Crandall*, 38, 105, also David Benedict, *General History of the Baptist Denomination* (1855 ed.), 899.
13. See Certificate to Reuben Crandall, in Canadian Baptist Miscellany, Baptist Historical Collection, McMaster University Library, Hamilton, Ontario.
14. Public Archives of Canada, Upper Canada Sundries, September 1820.
15. I. M. Allen, ed., *Annual Baptist Register* (1833), 31 and the *Triennial Baptist Register* (1836), 288.
16. Cf. Fred Landon, *Western Ontario and the American Frontier* (Toronto, New Haven, London, 1941), 101; here it is stated that Fairchild was a native of New Jersey.
17. E. A. Owen, *Pioneer Sketches of the Long Point Settlement* (Toronto: William Briggs, 1898).
18. A. H. Newman in *The Baptist Year Book for Ontario, Quebec, Manitoba and the Northwest Territories and British Columbia* (1900), 76.
19. E. R. Fitch, *The Baptists of Canada* (Toronto: Standard Publishing Co., 1911), 107.
20. Petition by Titus Finch and others, dated May 12, 1806.
21. Public Archives of Canada, Series C, documents of the Prince of Wales' American Regiment, from 1777 to 1783.
22. York County (N.B.) Records, Memorial No. 348, in the Crown Land Office, Fredericton, N.B.
23. Lieutenant-General Drummond to Sir George Prevost, May 31, 1814 in E. A. Cruikshank, ed. *Documentary History of the Campaign on the Niagara Frontier in 1814* (Welland: Tribune Office, 1896), I, 16; also L. H. Tasker in *Ontario Historical Society, Papers and Records*, II, 96 ff.
24. Ontario Bureau of Archives, *Report* (1933), 97.
25. F. T. Rosser, "First London Welsh Baptist Church (Denfield)" in *Ontario Historical Society, Papers and Records*, XXXIII, 107.

26. I. M. Allen, ed., *Annual Baptist Register* (1833), 31.
27. William Parkinson, *The Funeral Sermon of Elder Elkanah Holmes* (New York, 1832).
28. *Ibid.*
29. New York Baptist Association, *Minutes* from 1791 onward, also John Rippon, ed., *Baptist Annual Register* (1792-94).
30. New York Baptist Association, *Minutes,* record of proceedings of Wednesday, October 19, 1791.
31. Elkanah Holmes, *A Church Covenant Including a Summary of the Fundamental Doctrines of the Gospel* (New York: John Tiebouts, 1797).
32. "Letters of Rev. Elkanah Holmes from Fort Niagara, 1800" in *Buffalo Historical Society Publications,* VI (1903).
33. Robert W. Bingham, *Cradle of the Queen City: A History of Buffalo* (Buffalo, N.Y., 1931), 169.
34. William L. Stone, *Life of Joseph Brant,* 2 vols. (New York, 1838), II, 440.
35. *Buffalo Historical Society Publications,* VI, 125 ff.
36. William L. Stone, *Joseph Brant,* II, 439.
37. *Buffalo Historical Society Publications,* VII, 362-3.
38. Aaron Perkins, Moderator of the New York Baptist Association, in the Association's *Minutes* (1840), p. 22.
39. Rev. William Parkinson, *Funeral Sermon of Elder Holmes;* also William Ketchum, *History of Buffalo* (Buffalo, N.Y., 1865), II, 405, and John Armstrong, *Notices of the War of 1812* (New York, 1836), I, appendix no. 24.
40. William Canniff, *History of the Settlement of Upper Canada* (Toronto, 1869), 270.
41. "Peter Teeple, Pioneer and Loyalist" in *Ontario Historical Society, Papers and Records,* I (1899).
42. Zella M. Hotson, *Pioneer Baptist Work in Oxford County* (Woodstock, Ont., n.d.), p. 12.
43. Rev. William Rees in the *Montreal Register,* May 25, 1843.
44. Ontario Bureau of Archives, *Report* (1933), *passim.*
45. A. M. Caverly, *History of the Town of Pittsford, Vermont,* 726.
46. E. A. Cruikshank, "Adventures of Roger Stevens," in *Ontario Historical Society, Papers and Records,* XXXIII, 11.
47. A. M. Caverly, *Pittsford,* 686-7.
48. *Ibid.,* 182-3.
49. Public Archives of Canada, Upper Canada Land Petitions, S. 131, (not dated).
50. *Ibid.,* Petition S. 64, June 21, 1793.
51. Public Archives of Canada, Upper Canada Land Book A, 1792-96, p. 279.
52. E. A. Cruikshank. "The Activities of Abel Stevens as a Pioneer," in *Ontario Historical Society, Papers and Records,* XXXI, 56.
53. Public Archives of Canada, Upper Canada Land Book A, p. 359.
54. Public Archives of Canada, Upper Canada Land Book G, 1806-8, p. 182, also Upper Canada Land Petition S. 58, December 1, 1806.
55. E. A. Cruikshank, "Abel Stevens."
56. J. George Hodgins, ed., *Documentary History of Education in Upper Canada from the Passing of the Constitutional Act of 1791 to the Close of Rev. Dr. Ryerson's Administration of the Education Department in 1876* (Toronto: Warwick Bros. and Rutter, 1894); vol. I, *1790-1830.*
57. A photostatic copy is on file in the Public Archives of Canada at Ottawa.
58. John Peck and John Lawton, *An Historical Sketch of the Baptist Missionary Convention of the State of New York* (1837), 232.
59. Public Archives of Canada, Upper Canada Sundries.
60. Beamsville Church Minutes.

61. Public Archives of Canada, Upper Canada Sundries, letter from Upfold to Sir Peregrine Maitland, January 16, 1821. The minutes of the Conference unfortunately are not filed with the letter.
62. Public Archives of Canada, Upper Canada Land Petitions, Petition W. 12, August 30, 1820.
63. *Ibid.* The affidavits of Ferris and Meyers, along with those of five other friends, are attached to his petition of August 30, 1820.
64. *Ibid.*
65. United States census for Coxsackie, 1790.
66. *Minutes* of the Peterborough Baptist Association, 1845.

CHAPTER IX

1. Shortt and Doughty, eds., *Canada and Its Provinces, a History of the Canadian People and their Institutions* (Toronto: Glasgow, Brook & Company, 1914), XVI, 456.
2. Geographic Board of Canada, *Ninth Report* (Sessional Paper No. 21a, 1910), Part II, 166.
3. I. M. Allen, *Triennial Baptist Register* (1836), no. 2, 289.
4. William B. Sprague, ed., *Annals of the American Pulpit*, 9 vols. (New York: Robert Carter and Bros., 1857-69), VI.
5. Israel Marsh, "Memoir of Wm. Marsh," in *Montreal Register*, July 27, 1843.
6. Documents on William Marsh in Canadian Baptist Miscellany, McMaster University Library, Hamilton, Ontario.
7. I. M. Allen, *Triennial Baptist Register* (1836), no. 2, 291 and E. R. Fitch, *The Baptists of Canada* (Toronto, 1911), 103.
8. C. L. Thomas, *Contributions to the History of the Eastern Townships* (Montreal: John Lovell, 1866).
9. Isaac Backus, *A History of New England with Particular Reference to the Denomination of Christians called Baptists* (Newton, Mass.: Backus Historical Society, 1871) II, 540, and L. B. Hibbard, in an address given at the centenary of the Abbott's Corner Church, 1899.
10. Edward Mitchell, "The Rise and Progress of the Church in Hatley and Stanstead, L.C.," in the *Canadian Baptist Missionary Register*, March 1, 1841.
11. *Massachusetts Baptist Missionary Magazine*, II, 28.
12. *Ibid.*, I, 354 ff.
13. *Ibid.*, II, 313.
14. Shaftsbury Baptist Association, *Minutes* (1808-10).
15. *Massachusetts Baptist Missionary Magazine*, III, 12ff.
16. *Ibid.*, III, 49, 50.
17. *Ibid.*, III, 91.
18. Shaftsbury Baptist Association, *Minutes* (1811); also Stephen Wright, *History of the Shaftsbury Baptist Association from 1781 to 1853* (Troy, N.Y.: A. G. Johnson, 1853), 129, 369.
19. *Massachusetts Baptist Missionary Magazine*, III, 117.
20. *Ibid.*, III, 119.

CHAPTER X

1. W. T. Whitley, *A History of British Baptists* (London: Kingsgate Press, 1932), 86.

2. *Massachusetts Baptist Missionary Magazine,* I, 71.
3. Cf. A. H. Newman, "Sketch of the Baptists of Ontario and Quebec" in the *Baptist Year Book: Historical Number* (1900), 74.
4. *The Particular Baptist Confession of 1677,* chap. XXVI, sec. 14, as in E. A. Payne, *The Fellowship of Believers* (London: Kingsgate Press, 1944), 95.

INDEX

(Information relating to the denominational organization is brought together under the main heading Baptist ———, or Baptists, with appropriate sub-headings.)

A

ABERDEEN (Scotland), 95
Abbott, Jonas, 160
Abbott's Corner, P.Q., 160, 163
Addington Co., 33
Adolphustown Twp., 18, 20
Aldborough Twp., 31, 126
Allen, I. M., *Annual Baptist Register, Triennial Baptist Register*. See Baptist publications
Allen, William, 6
Alnwick Twp., 86
Alward, Elder, 105, 119
Ambrose, Samuel, 162, 163
Ameliasburg Twp., 20, 21, 56, 83
American Revolution, 3, 8, 9, 24, 29, 30, 41, 52, 107, 108, 119, 135, 138, 142, 145, 147, 153, 155, 158
Amherst Island, Ont., 32
Amherstburg, Ont., 3, 27, 30, 32
Amsterdam (Holland), 4
Anabaptist, 4, 125, 130, 132
Ancaster Twp., 104
Andrews, Cyrus, 58, 61, 112, 162
Andrews, Elisha, 156, 157, 158, 160, 163; *Moral Tendencies of Universalism*, 158
Andrews, Elisha, Jr., 157
Andrews, Erastus, 157
Andrews, Isaac, 157
Anglican Church, 4, 5, 23, 149
Anne, Queen, 24
Appleton, Thomas, 148, 149
Arminian creed, 5, 15, 47, 51, 77, 78, 106, 108, 109, 128
Ascott, P.Q., 161, 162, 163
Athol Twp., 20
Augusta Twp., 18, 20, 21, 50, 90, 95, 96, 128
Aurelius, N.Y., 48
Aylmer, Ont., 60, 118, 132

B

BABCOCK, Rufus, 77
Baker family, eastern Ont., 97

Baker, Nathan, 12, 58, 61, 112
Baker, Samuel, 117, 118
Baldwin, Thomas, 10, 11, 74, 150
Baptist Academical Institution, 57
Baptist Associations, 3, 8, 81, 82, 84, 164, 168
Lower Canada
Eastern, 161, 167
Montreal, 167
United States
Black River, 9, 14, 15, 87, 127
Danville, 161, 167
Fairfax, 167
Fairfield, 161
Groton Union Conference, 140
Hudson River, 12
Lamoille, 161, 167
New York, 8, 13, 76, 113, 114, 138, 139, 140, 141, 166
Otsego, 52
Philadelphia, 13, 15
Richmond, 161
Shaftsbury, 9, 10, 11, 12, 34, 35, 36, 37, 40, 41, 43, 44, 46, 48, 51, 52, 53, 54, 55, 57, 58, 60, 61, 62, 63, 65, 68, 69, 70, 73, 74, 75, 77, 80, 98, 99, 100, 103, 104, 105, 109, 110, 112, 115, 116, 118, 125, 134, 136, 140, 141, 161, 162, 163, 165, 166, 167
Vermont, 66
Warren, Massachusetts and Rhode Island, 69, 121
Woodstock, 156, 163
Upper Canada
Clinton Conference, 62, 63, 75, 100, 104, 105, 116, 152, 166, 167
Eastern, 167
Eastern Ontario, 166
Fellowship of Independent Baptist Churches of Canada, 105
Grand River, 167
Haldimand, 61, 62, 63, 85, 86, 91, 92, 93, 142, 154, 165